Religion and Atheism

Arguments between those who hold religious beliefs and those who do not have been at fever pitch. They have also reached an impasse, with equally entrenched views held by believer and atheist – and even agnostic – alike. This collection is one of the first books to move beyond this deadlock. Specially commissioned chapters address major areas that cut across the debate between the two sides: the origin of knowledge, objectivity and meaning; moral values and the nature of the human person and the good life; and the challenge of how to promote honest and fruitful dialogue in the light of the wide diversity of beliefs, religious and otherwise. Under these broad headings leading figures in the field examine and reflect upon:

- secular and religious humanism
- the idea of the sacred
- the vexed issue of science in both religious and secular accounts of knowledge
- spirituality for the godless
- non-Western perspectives on the atheism/theism debate.

A key feature of the collection is a dialogue between Raymond Tallis and Rowan Williams, former Archbishop of Canterbury. *Religion and Atheism: Beyond the Divide* will interest anyone who is concerned about the clash between the religious and the secular and how to move beyond it, as well as students of ethics, philosophy of religion and religious studies.

Contributors: Ruth Abbey, Julian Baggini, Ankur Barua, Anthony Carroll, Andrew Copson, John Cottingham, Fiona Ellis, Fern Elsdon-Baker, Robin Gill, Simon Glendinning, Angie Hobbs, Dilwar Hussain, Stephen Law, Lois Lee, Michael McGhee, Richard Norman, Brian Pearce, Jonathan Rée, Nick Spencer, Anna Strhan, Raymond Tallis and Rowan Williams.

Anthony Carroll is Senior Lecturer in Philosophy and Theology at Heythrop College, University of London, UK. His publications include *Protestant Modernity: Weber, Secularization, and Protestantism* (2007), and he is an Anglican priest.

Richard Norman is Emeritus Professor of Moral Philosophy at the University of Kent, UK. His publications include *On Humanism* (2nd edition 2012), and he is a founder-member of the Humanist Philosophers' Group, and a Patron of the British Humanist Association.

Religion and Atheism
Beyond the divide

Edited by
**Anthony Carroll
and Richard Norman**

Routledge
Taylor & Francis Group

LONDON AND NEW YORK

Best wishes Richard Norman
30 Nov 2016

First published 2017
by Routledge
2 Park Square, Milton Park, Abingdon, Oxon OX14 4RN

Simultaneously published in the USA and Canada
by Routledge
711 Third Avenue, New York City, NY 10017

Routledge is an imprint of the Taylor & Francis Group, an informa business

British Library Cataloguing in Publication Data
A catalogue record for this book is available from the British Library

Library of Congress Cataloging in Publication Data
Names: Carroll, Anthony J., 1965– author.
Title: Religion and atheism : beyond the divide / edited by Anthony
Carroll and Richard Norman.
Description: 1 [edition]. | New York : Routledge, 2016. | Includes
bibliographical references and index.
Identifiers: LCCN 2016010440| ISBN 9781138891890 (hardback :
alk. paper) | ISBN 9781138891913 (pbk. : alk. paper) |
ISBN 9781315521497 (e-book)
Subjects: LCSH: Religion—Philosophy. | Philosophy. | Ethics. | Atheism.
Classification: LCC BL51 .R3459 2016 | DDC 201/.51—dc23
LC record available at https://lccn.loc.gov/2016010440

ISBN13: 978-1-138-89189-0 (hbk)
ISBN13: 978-1-138-89191-3 (pbk)
ISBN13: 978-1-315-52149-7 (ebk)

Typeset in Sabon
by Book Now Ltd, London

Printed and bound by CPI Group (UK) Ltd, Croydon, CR0 4YY

Contents

Contributors

Ruth Abbey is the author of *Nietzsche's Middle Period* (Oxford), *Philosophy Now: Charles Taylor* (Princeton) and *The Return of Feminist Liberalism* (McGill-Queens). She is the editor of *Contemporary Philosophy in Focus: Charles Taylor* (Cambridge) and *Feminist Interpretations of Rawls* (Penn State). She is currently the Book Review Editor for *The Review of Politics* and is serving as the Interim Director for the Kroc Institute for International Peace Studies.

Julian Baggini is the founding editor of *The Philosophers' Magazine*. He is the author, co-author or editor of over twenty books including *The Virtues of the Table*, *The Ego Trick*, *Welcome to Everytown* and, most recently, *Freedom Regained* (all Granta). He has written for numerous newspapers and magazines, as well as for think tanks including the Institute of Public Policy Research, Demos and Counterpoint.

Ankur Barua is Lecturer in Hindu Studies, University of Cambridge. His research interests include classical and modern Vedantic Hindu thought, Indian Christianity, and comparative philosophy of religion.

Anthony Carroll is an Anglican priest and Senior Lecturer in Philosophy and Theology at Heythrop College, University of London, and Robert Bellah Distinguished Fellow at the Max Weber Kolleg. He is co-author of *On the Way to Life* (2005), author of *Protestant Modernity: Weber, Secularization, and Protestantism* (2007), and has edited *Towards a Kenotic Vision of Authority in the Catholic Church* (2015) and *Spiritual Foundations and Chinese Culture: A Philosophical Approach* (forthcoming).

Andrew Copson is the Chief Executive of the British Humanist Association and President of the International Humanist and Ethical Union. He has debated, cooperated, agreed and disagreed with religious believers on a range of boards and panels from the Religious Education Council, to the Commission on Religion and Belief, to the National Council of Faiths and Beliefs in Further Education.

John Cottingham is Professor Emeritus of Philosophy at Reading University, Professorial Research Fellow at Heythrop College, London, and an Honorary

Fellow of St John's College Oxford. His many books include *Philosophy and the Good Life* (1998), *The Spiritual Dimension* (2015), *Cartesian Reflections* (2008), *Philosophy of Religion: Towards a More Humane Approach* (2014) and, most recently, *How to Believe* (2015).

Fiona Ellis is Reader in Philosophy at Heythrop College, University of London. Her book *God, Value, and Nature* was published by Oxford University Press in 2014, and some of the themes of this work were taken up in the Templeton-funded project New Models of Religious Understanding, for which she was principal investigator. The other strand of her research involves the philosophy of love and desire, and she is currently working on the question of the relation between desire and the spiritual life with reference to Levinas, Schopenhauer and Nietzsche.

Fern Elsdon-Baker is the Director for the Centre for Science, Knowledge and Belief in Society, at Newman University, Birmingham. She is currently the principal investigator on the Science and Religion: Exploring the Spectrum project, examining the social and cultural contexts of public perceptions of the relationship between science and religion across all faiths and none. She briefly left academia from 2008 to 2012 to work for the British Council, where she was Head of the Darwin Now project and then Director of the Belief in Dialogue programme.

Robin Gill held the Michael Ramsey Chair of Modern Theology in the University of Kent, Canterbury, for twenty years and now is Emeritus Professor of Applied Theology there. He is an Honorary Provincial Canon of Canterbury Cathedral and Canon Theologian at Gibraltar Anglican Cathedral. He is editor of the journal *Theology* and the Cambridge University Press monograph series, New Studies in Christian Ethics, and author or editor of some forty books, including *Health Care and Christian Ethics* (Cambridge, 2007) and *A Textbook of Christian Ethics* (4th edition, T&T Clark, 2014).

Simon Glendinning is Professor of European Philosophy in the European Institute at the London School of Economics and Political Science. His recent work explores themes in the philosophy of Europe, including European identity, Europe's modernity and the philosophical foundations of European union. He is the author of *Derrida: A Very Short Introduction* (Oxford, 2011), as well as many books and articles on European traditions of philosophy.

Angie Hobbs was, in 2012, appointed Professor of the Public Understanding of Philosophy at the University of Sheffield, the first position of its kind. Her chief interests are in ancient philosophy, ethics and political theory, and her publications include *Plato and the Hero* (Cambridge, 2000). She contributes regularly to radio and TV programmes, newspaper articles and philosophy websites, and gives public and invited lectures and talks around the world.

Dilwar Hussain is founding Chair of New Horizons in British Islam, a charity that works for reform in Muslim thought and practice. He is also a

Senior Programme Advisor to the Institute for Strategic Dialogue, a Research Fellow at the Lokahi Foundation, an Associate of the Centre for Islamic Studies, University of Cambridge, and a Research Fellow at the Centre for Trust, Peace and Social Relations, Coventry University.

Stephen Law is Provost of Centre for Inquiry UK, and Senior Lecturer in Philosophy at Heythrop College, University of London. He is the author of a number of books on religious belief including *Humanism: A Very Short Introduction* (Oxford, 2011) and *The Evil God Challenge* (Oxford, forthcoming).

Lois Lee is author of *Recognizing the Non-religious: Reimagining the Secular* (Oxford, 2015) and co-editor of *Negotiating Religion: Cross-disciplinary Approaches* (Ashgate, forthcoming) and *Secularity and Non-religion* (Routledge, 2013). She has published many articles and chapters on non-religion, atheism, secularism and religion, and is director of the Nonreligion and Secularity Research Network. She is a research associate at the Institute of Advanced Studies, University College London.

Michael McGhee taught Philosophy at the University of Liverpool before he retired. He has been a practising Buddhist since the late seventies and is interested in the contribution that this tradition can make to the dialogue between religion and secularism, a dialogue usually conceived in terms of the Abrahamic traditions. He is the author of *Transformations of Mind* (Cambridge, 2000).

Richard Norman is Emeritus Professor of Moral Philosophy at the University of Kent, where he taught from 1970 until 2006. His published books include *On Humanism* (Routledge, 2004, 2nd edition 2012), and he is a Patron of the British Humanist Association.

Brian Pearce OBE, after working for twenty-five years in the Civil Service, was engaged for two years in a consultation on the development of inter-faith work in this country. This led to his becoming the first Director of the Inter Faith Network for the UK when it was established in 1987. He served in that post until 2007, and as its part-time Adviser on Faith and Public Life from 2007 to 2012. In his belated retirement, he spends some of his time working to promote 'religious/non-religious' dialogue in various ways.

Jonathan Rée is a philosopher and historian who taught philosophy at Middlesex University before escaping to a more interesting life as a musing freelancer. His books include *Philosophical Tales* (Routledge, 1987) and *I See a Voice* (HarperCollins, 1999).

Nick Spencer is Research Director at Theos, the religion and society think tank. He is the author of a number of books, including *Darwin and God* (SPCK, 2009) and *Atheists: The Origin of the Species* (Bloomsbury, 2013)

Anna Strhan is a Lecturer in Religious Studies at the University of Kent. She is the author of *Aliens and Strangers? The Struggle for Coherence in the Everyday*

Lives of Evangelicals (Oxford, 2015) and *Levinas, Subjectivity, Education: Towards an Ethics of Radical Responsibility* (Wiley-Blackwell, 2012).

Raymond Tallis is a philosopher, poet, novelist and cultural critic, and a retired physician and clinical neuroscientist. He is a Fellow of the Academy of Medical Sciences. The author of over thirty books, he has honorary degrees of DLitt and LittD for contributions to the humanities and DSc for contributions to medicine.

Rowan Williams (Lord Williams of Oystermouth) was Archbishop of Canterbury from 2002 to 2012, having previously been Bishop of Monmouth and Archbishop of Wales. He is now Master of Magdalene College Cambridge. His published writings include poetry and many works on religion, theology, philosophy and literature.

Acknowledgements

We owe to Brian Pearce the idea for this collection. In his Foreword he outlines the origins of the project. What he does not mention is the enormous amount of work which he himself has done to recruit contributors, to encourage them and communicate with them, and to discuss with us the organisation and content of the book. We are hugely grateful to him.

Thanks are due also to Adam Johnson and Tony Bruce at Routledge for their encouragement and support, and for guiding us through the process of working with the contributors and preparing the material for publication.

We are very grateful to Raymond Tallis and Rowan Williams for agreeing to meet and hold the conversation which forms the first chapter of the book, and for allowing us to record it. Special thanks must go to Jo Hornsby, the Master's Secretary at Magdalene College Cambridge, for making the practical arrangements which enabled that event to go smoothly.

Finally, we wish to thank all the contributors to the collection. They all, without exception, lead very busy lives, and we are very grateful to them for finding the time not only to write for us but also to respond patiently to our comments and queries. We did not set them any precise agenda other than to write about dialogue between the religious and the non-religious. We did not ask them to take any particular line, and we are delighted with the variety of perspectives which they have adopted. We left open the question of whether their contributions might point the way to any meeting of minds between the religious and the non-religious, or to any establishing of common ground. Some of them are more combative than others, some are more reconciliationist than others, and that is as we would wish, for it testifies to the landscape of diversity in religion and belief. The idea of a simple division between a uniform camp of religion and a uniform camp of atheism is more misleading than ever in the contemporary world, and we are grateful to all our contributors for pointing the way beyond the divide.

Foreword

Brian Pearce

The genesis of this book lies in an event in November 2009. To mark the launch of the first Inter Faith Week in England and Wales, the Inter Faith Network for the UK and the British Humanist Association brought together a number of invited guests from a range of religious traditions and from a Humanist background. As its Adviser on Faith and Public Life at the time, I helped to organise this on behalf of the Network. The aim of the event was not to focus on current issues relating to the place of religion in the 'public square', such as faith schools and religious representation in the House of Lords, but rather to have a dialogue on the substance of one another's beliefs. Not surprisingly perhaps, the common ground which, encouragingly, emerged from the discussion related primarily to ethical principles and attitudes rather than questions of a more metaphysical kind.[1]

Two philosophers, Professor John Cottingham and Professor Richard Norman, from a Christian and Humanist perspective respectively, made introductory presentations. In subsequent conversations from time to time with Richard and others, I suggested bringing together a collection of essays from a variety of perspectives with a view to taking forward more widely the dialogue between the religious and the non-religious. This book, several years later, is the result, Richard having kindly agreed to become one of its co-editors. He is joined in that role by Dr Anthony Carroll, a Christian philosopher and theologian.

In the years post-Second World War there were a number of significant and thoughtful dialogues between Christians and Humanists. However, some of the energy behind these subsequently became channelled more specifically into exploring the narrower field of the relationship between religion and science, and also, as Britain's landscape became more religiously diverse, into a variety of interfaith dialogues, in which the non-religious did not participate. Perhaps as a consequence of these shifts, engagement between Christians (and other faith groups) and Humanists came to focus predominantly on public-square issues, arguably bringing with this a greater degree of polarisation.

Humanists pressed for recognition of their legitimate interests in various areas and particularly in the field of education. They were opposed to what they saw as instances of unjustified religious privilege in what was becoming an increasingly secular society, a process which they welcomed. Some Christians and other religious people, who understood their faith as an integral part of their social as well as their personal identity, were concerned at what they perceived as pressure for greater 'privatisation' of religious expression. They did not think that a strongly secularised society would be a 'neutral' one in this respect and feared that it would bring with it undue restrictions being placed on the freedom of religious groups to conduct their activities in the public realm.

There are, of course, significantly different interpretations of what secularism involves. One form of it simply seeks to achieve through negotiation between interested parties a level playing field as a basis for a truly inclusive society. This contrasts with a more aggressive secularism, which wants, as far as possible, to eliminate religion from public life. In this country, by contrast with France for example, it is the former approach which has in practice commanded broad support, even if there are continuing arguments over what concrete steps it should entail.[2]

Arguments about public-square issues are, of course, important and need to be taken forward with mutual respect and in shared conversation. But the extent to which they have dominated the dialogue between the religious and the non-religious in recent years has tended to sideline the exploration together of different beliefs, values and worldviews, paralleling such dialogue between people of different religious faiths, which has expanded so significantly in recent years. Even though there remains a need for specifically interfaith engagement and dialogue, both bilateral and multilateral (and for interfaith organisations dedicated to this work), it is increasingly important to develop fresh contexts for the promotion of a wider dialogue on a more structured basis and on its own terms.

Today's context for this dialogue here in the UK is very different from that in which it took place some decades ago, with a much greater diversity of belief and personal practice. There is more public awareness of the variety of different religious traditions and distinctive strands within them. Recent sociological research, reflected in this book, has shown that there is also considerable variety among those who could be categorised in broad terms as Humanist, agnostic or atheist. There has also been a significant growth in the number of people who declare themselves to be 'spiritual, but not religious', having left, or never having been involved in, institutional religion. The notion of there being two coherent and unified categories of the 'religious' and the 'non-religious', separated by a deep ditch, is difficult to sustain in such complex terrain. Moreover, an individual Christian may find more in common with an individual Humanist than with some other religious people, just as an individual Christian may find more common ground with, for example, an individual Buddhist than with some of their fellow Christians.

There have also been notable shifts in how people understand the world and, in consequence, in their beliefs. The writings of the so-called 'new atheists' during the last two decades initially encouraged a somewhat combative public argument, with some religious protagonists responding in kind. However, more recently the controversy stirred up by this has led to an increase in thoughtful and open engagement in a variety of ways. Importantly, this has underlined the need for us to be alert to issues of language and to be aware that we might use the same terms but with different understanding of their meanings – the word 'God' being a notable example in the present context!

Both the religious and the non-religious find that the more that science reveals of the extraordinary intricacy, variety and interconnectedness of the beautiful and ordered world we inhabit, the more this induces a sense of awe and wonder. This is so for many scientists. It raises questions about whether the physicalism and reductionism which are sometimes seen as the implications of a scientific worldview can do justice to that kind of shared human experience.

That is one example of the questions which require exploration. Others which are addressed in the essays in this book include:

- How far are science and religion compatible – and faith and reason?
- To what extent are disagreements between religious believers and atheists rooted in different understandings of religious language and of the role of analogy, metaphor and story?
- What are the implications for our understanding of the human person of our possessing attributes of consciousness and the capacity for free choice?
- Do we need to reassess the boundaries of the 'natural'?
- Will a renewed engagement between philosophy and theology help to develop more fruitful perspectives for both of them?
- Can the non-religious make use, with integrity, of concepts of 'transcendence' and a 'spiritual' dimension of human existence – or are these terms too slippery to be helpful?
- What is the basis for the values we espouse, both individually and as a society?

In dialogue on questions such as these, we can learn from others of their experiences and their interpretations of these, reflecting together on their relevance for our understanding of the universe and of ourselves. In encounter at its best we can find our own horizons are expanded, with mutual enrichment. In an increasingly plural society we can only gain from having a better understanding of one another, including the beliefs and values which shape our attitudes and hopes. We need to think together, as well as work together, to achieve this.

Good dialogue requires us to show respect to our dialogue partners and to take seriously all those who themselves take life seriously. This involves being prepared to listen with an open mind and heart and being willing to change our views in the light of what we learn. But dialogue does not presuppose that agreement will be reached, rather that understanding will be deepened in creative ways. The premise on which this book is based is that we can indeed gain much from this engagement.

I am grateful to its co-editors for their kind invitation to offer this foreword to it. Let us hope that there will be further volumes of this kind to stimulate taking the dialogue forward in fruitful ways.

Notes

1 See note on Inter Faith Week 2009 event held by the Inter Faith Network for the UK in association with the British Humanist Association, at the Inter Faith Network website, <http://www.interfaith.org.uk/publications/all-publications/all-publications/6-note-on-inter-faith-week-event-2009/file>.
2 See José Casanova, 'The Secular, Secularizations, Secularisms', in Craig Calhoun, Mark Juergensmeyer and Jonathan VanAntwerpen (eds), *Rethinking Secularism* (Oxford: Oxford University Press, 2011), 54–74; and Humanist Philosophers' Group, *The Case for Secularism: A Neutral State in an Open Society* (London: British Humanist Association, 2007).

Part I
A dialogue

In a collection about dialogue between religious believers and non-believers, it is appropriate that the first contribution should be an actual dialogue. This conversation between Raymond Tallis and Rowan Williams was recorded at the Master's Lodge, Magdalene College, Cambridge, on 17 July 2015. A previous conversation between them had been hosted by the Faraday Institute in the University of Cambridge in December 2013, and is referred to by them in the course of the present dialogue.

1 Science, stories and the self
A conversation between Raymond Tallis and Rowan Williams

Raymond
Tallis (RT): Rowan, it's a really great privilege to talk to you today. What I'd like to do is to explore our different positions, particularly focusing on the unresolved business, as it were, that we both have. Perhaps I could state where I think I'm coming from as opposed to where you're coming from, in a very simplifying way. I imagine you're coming from somewhere definite – from a definite position in relation to your beliefs. I have the fantasy that I'm coming from nowhere, as it were, that I'm not committed to any set of beliefs. I am an atheist, and therefore reject religious explanations of the kinds of creatures we are, of how we should live, where we're going to and so on. But, unlike most atheists, I am equally opposed to a naturalistic account of what we are, particularly a scientistic naturalism that says we are essentially explicable as biological organisms. I find naturalism much more threatening, actually, than supernatural beliefs. So that's why I imagine I'm coming from nowhere, but of course what it means is that I'm bringing to the party all sorts of unacknowledged prejudices and assumptions that I am sure, and I hope, you will expose and explore.

Rowan
Williams
(RW): Well thank you. I've been looking forward to this very much indeed as a huge admirer of what you've written, and I guess where I'm coming from is certainly a commitment to the view that the universe exists because of some prior or independent agency which can, in certain circumstances, be called intelligent, which is God, and that that's the context within which I make sense of what goes on in my life and the life of the universe. And I guess that the challenge for me is how you articulate that without slipping in by the back door what a great deal of traditional philosophy and theology tries to keep out, which

is the idea that God is another thing in a list, another agent among agents, and can be drawn on as a sort of rabbit out of a hat to solve problems. And I guess that one of the things we may again find common ground with is that solving problems is not the most important thing or the only thing that humans do. It is an important thing, it is a significant thing, but there is something about – what shall I call it? – redrawing the boundaries of our map, exploring the implications, the depths, the resonances, of where we are, which doesn't necessarily solve problems, it won't always get you through exams, but it is one of the things we do as human beings.

RT: I couldn't agree with you more. It seems to me that philosophy is often criticised because its clear-up rate of problems is so low that if it were a police force it would be in special measures. And of course philosophy isn't about clearing up problems. It is about creating question-and-answer pairs. It's about waking up, and when you wake up, you haven't solved the problem, but you've become something rather different. And I think in many ways for you religion is a form of wakefulness, and for me the pursuit of philosophy and even scientific thought to some extent is a mode of wakefulness. One of the things that, I feel, you don't think separates us is a set of very clearly defined beliefs which can be written down on a piece of paper, and amongst them the idea of God. The reason I'm an atheist and not an agnostic is that any account of the idea of God, to me, always seems to entrain contradictions; and if, as a thinker, I allow self-contradictory notions such as 'the square circle' into the list of things that I believe in or allow, then clearly I may as well give up on thought. But you have already anticipated one anxiety, which is, you set aside the notion of God as a 'thing' within the universe, as something offset from the universe, and you set aside the notion of God as an agent, a distinct agent. But that does seem to drain God of quite a lot of job description, and 'presence description' as it were, and I just wonder whether we can talk about that a bit more.

RW: Yes, sure. A couple of things. One is about contradiction. I think anybody who has got in their repertoire a concept like 'a square circle' can't be serious, because there are things you can't think, and that's one of them. There are, in most of our repertoires, though, areas where there are tensions, where there are unresolved relationships – freedom and determinism, that sort of area – which look very much like contradictions on the surface, but when you push them you see, 'oh, there's some give there, and some give there, but I don't quite see how it all comes together.' If I thought that belief in God, or indeed belief in the divinity of Christ, was a 'square circle' issue I would, I think, properly need to be caught up on my consistency. But I don't think they're that kind of thing. They are much more issues about your being prodded to say, 'well I think you got the definition of that end right, or that end right, but isn't there a lot more work to be done than that?' So, as for agency, I think the sort of thing you find in Augustine or Aquinas or, indeed, more modern writers on this, is not that agency is denied to God, but that whatever anyone says about God's act it can't just be one item in a list of actions, one point in a series, even if the first point in a series. And right at the heart of the classical theism of Thomas Aquinas, you have actually got some quite surprising clarity about that. To say that God causes things is not to say that God is the first item in a series of events in a causal chain, but that there is a causal chain because there is an active God. So that Aquinas is quite agnostic about whether the world has a beginning in time or not.

RT: That is extraordinarily interesting and I wish that some scientists would share that agnosticism. When science dates the beginning of the universe to 13.8 billion years ago, one feels that actually, first of all, it appears to be at odds with the Einsteinian notion that there is no global time and, secondly, it raises all sorts of questions about the notion of what was happening before the big bang and why you deny the notion of a 'before'. Stephen Hawking has famously said that asking what happened before the big bang is like asking what's north of the North Pole. Well, actually, that is not a valid analogy, simply because we're talking about a certain direction which can actually go beyond the North Pole indefinitely.

RW: Yes, I agree. I think there is a huge amount of unexamined mythology in what cosmologists come up with, the narrative structure they use. Because we love stories, we want to know when it all started, in a galaxy long ago, and we say, yes, that was the beginning, if we were there to watch it that's when it would have started, the curtain would go up. And you want to think, at every clause's end, really, wait a minute, wait a minute, the mythological and anthropomorphic assumptions are flooding in all through that. Again, it's an issue which is already being discussed in the early church, and St Augustine mentions the joke that was going around in the fifth century about this. The answer to the question, 'what was God doing before the universe was created?', was that he was creating the hell for people who asked silly questions!

RT: Yes. Richard Dawkins famously says that astrophysicists have now taken away the theologians' trump card, that they have an answer to why there is something rather than nothing, why there is a world rather than nothing. And it seems to me they haven't. It's very easy to be dazzled by all the precision that surrounds cosmology, ten to the minus this, and ten to the minus that, but actually, in their starter pack, it seems to me they have something just as difficult as the idea of God as first cause.

RW: The idea of an absolute beginning.

RT: Absolutely. They have the idea of an absolute beginning. They also have the idea of a vacuum that has a built-in restlessness, they have the laws of nature given free – thank you very much indeed – you take those off the shelf. They have all sorts of things that are delivered. So they don't actually begin with a genuine nothing.

RW: No, exactly. The table is littered with Get Out of Jail Free cards, I think. I don't want to be critical of cosmologists – God (or something!) forbid – because it seems the elegance, the precision, the depth of all this is just extraordinary. It's a great human achievement, and as with so many areas in the scientific enterprise it's not that I want to make little of it, not remotely, but I do want to say, 'remember what you are doing, what you are assuming.' And remember too that the pressure to create narrative is always going to be really strong, and that will take you beyond what science itself really justifies.

RT: Yes. And narrative can look quite unnarrative-like. If it is, as it were, a narrative of physical laws, it looks empty of meaning; if it is a narrative of material causes it looks empty of meaning. It actually should be an embarrassment for people who have an atheistic viewpoint such as my own, because there is a very strange idea that whatever happens has somehow to be *made* to happen. The divine origin of events, of things, and so on and so forth, is visibly vulnerable, but the assumption that somehow things are *made* to happen, within the non-theistic world picture, is also equally challengeable. Laws don't make anything happen. In a way, at best they are the railway lines along which things go, they are not the engine. But causes are very strange. And I think causes in many ways share an embarrassment with special divine action. God descends from being a general principle that informs and drives the world, to actually intervening in history. In science we have general laws which don't produce any kind of singular events, and so we invoke the notion of cause in order, as local 'oomph', to make this or that happen. Do you think that analogy is a reasonable one?

RW: It's a very interesting analogy, I think. Very interesting because, again, it illustrates our need not to see events as arbitrary.

There's a story that can be told, and it's a story which doesn't have any surd elements in it, any completely vacuous, back-groundless aspects to it. And I think it's interesting that, in the earliest philosophical discussions of causality, like Aristotle, you already have a recognition, that talking about 'cause' is an analogical thing. There are lots of ways in which we can use the word 'cause'. We can talk about material cause; what actually triggered this as a matter of ordinary material process; what's it for, where's it going; what's the intelligible shape of the transaction we're talking about? And I find that, appropriately translated, that's quite a helpful model. 'Cause' is not just one set of questions, and knowing the answer to the question 'Why this?' can take you in a number of interestingly different directions. The trouble is that we all like to have this idea that, at bottom, all there is is some one process, one story that will just do all the work. And whether it's a particular rather simple notion of God, or whether it's 'cause', I think you are right, there is a comparable desire to get it down to 'What's Really Going On' (capital W, capital R and so on).

RT: And that's related very much to reductionist notions that whatever happens at the manifest level ultimately, within science, boils down to interactions between elementary particles, general forces and so on. But it's interesting, what you say about causes, because it seems to me that science does privilege the efficient cause, the *vis a tergo*, the push from behind, and very much frowns upon final causes, the notion of the pull from the front, the teleological notion of why things unfold the way they do.

RW: And where this, I think, is most difficult is simply in making sense of the distinction between the sciences. Is all biology really chemistry, all chemistry really physics, all physics really maths? Well, in one sense, yes, because you can trace a line going right through to some fundamental story to tell. On the other hand, how on earth is it that you get from an equation to a wombat or a potato, let alone a Raymond Tallis?

RT: Whose location in that particular ontology ...!

RW: Yes! It's the hierarchy question really. In what sense can you talk about the form that's more than the sum of its parts exercising some sort of causal shaping on those parts? That's something which sheer reductionism doesn't seem to me to help very much with.

RT: And we would have on our side an unusual witness, Richard Feynman, Nobel Prize-winning physicist, who said, basically, the Schrödinger wave equation doesn't tell us whether there will be music, morality and frogs, or indeed whether they would never exist at all. He argued that we need new equations, he said 'qualitative equations', although that does seem to me to be a contradiction in terms.

RW: I'd like to see one of those.

RT: Exactly. And in that sense, he was aware of how, in many ways, you could boil things down to absolute fundamentals, but you would then have trouble boiling them up again to the kind of manifest world we live in and see.

RW: Yes, yes, that's right. And that, I think, goes back to the question about the analogical nature of cause. There are several different ways of answering this question, for these purposes it will be very important to get the maths right, for certain other purposes that's not going to be the question you ask. One of the things I occasionally say, when I'm asked to talk about the rationale of higher education, is that it ought to be the creation of communities where you always recognise that somebody else's questions are as interesting as yours.

RT: That is a fantastic definition. It's profound charity in a sense – the notion that you open yourself up to other people's interests and to other people's answers.

RW: Yes.

RT: You mentioned science and indicated that of course there are many natural sciences, and there are human sciences. If we think of a science as something that's driven by a methodology that delivers objective, reliable, repeatable and generalisable knowledge, then of course there are human sciences, where one does talk about aims and ends and purposes, whether it's economics or social sciences and so on. And I suppose our shared worry about reductionism is not the privileging of sciences in the broader sense, but the privileging of physical sciences – objective quantitative sciences.

RW: And behind that, I think, is the deeper question of what we think counts as knowledge. Because we are encouraged, I think, to imagine a distinction between hard knowledge and fuzzy knowledge – real knowledge, which is what the so-called exact sciences deliver, and a sort of impressionistic swamp where bright ideas emerge and common sense occasionally prevails, but it's not like the real thing. And that seems to me a very odd way of looking at knowledge. I am fascinated by the way in which we actually learn to know things, which is as *bodies*. I learn the shape of my environment as a baby by bumping into things. I learn, somehow or other, to map my world around me. The German philosopher and theologian Edith Stein talks about the self as 'the zero point of orientation'. In a very physical sense we map the world around ourselves, we discover where we can't go, we shape, we imagine, we project points of view onto others, and it's all very much how the body fits itself into an environment. That's how we start knowing things and people. And I think that to reduce hard knowledge to the set of right answers to a set of physical questions – it's not like the way we actually work.

RT: I entirely agree with you. And the sort of 'zero' she was talking about was not, as it were, a 'zero, zero, zero' of coordinate space, but a centre of egocentric space. And it seems that we transcend our bodies in many ways. As an atheist, I do feel we continually transcend our bodies as part of the community of minds, and so on, but we are absolutely inseparable from our bodies. At the very least my body is a necessary condition of my being Raymond Tallis, and if you chop my head off my IQ falls precipitously and the conversation comes to an end. But it does seem to me that there is a difficult situation here, because, clearly, true knowledge cannot be confined to that which arises out of our being tethered to one particular place, to the 0,0,0 of the centre of our biological being. One of the extraordinary aspects of humanity is that we are able to transcend our bodies, so that my feeling warm becomes 'that it is warm' and ultimately the notion that there is a sun which is heating my body, and so on and so forth. So it's getting the right balance between the knowledge that is rooted in our egocentric bodily existence, knowledge which is rooted in qualitative experience, on the one hand, and on the other hand the knowledge that transcends that – factual knowledge, propositional knowledge that x is the case.

RW: Yes. And I suppose this is where you have to talk about the collaborative dimension to learning. The ego, left to itself, if that's even imaginable or conceivable, is not going to know very much actually. It can't, in and of itself, metaphorically speaking, see the back of its head. It can't imagine itself even as a body without the map of other bodies, other perceptions, the sense of criss-crossing lines of perception. And of course, what crystallises that in actual human relations is language, and this, as you know, is something I am very very interested in indeed – the way in which we learn and we operate, we know in language, and our transcendence is, in a sense, bound up with our linguistic capacity. I'm using 'linguistic' very generally, not just exchanging words, but all the life of the imagination and the communicative patterns and ritual patterns that we use. I think that if we want to talk about knowledge, we are bound somewhere along the line to talk about human collaboration. I hesitate to use the word 'community', that begs a few questions, but certainly collaboration. And it's not just a matter of lots of people doing the same thing, but an acknowledgement that, because of my bodiliness, because of my finitude, I will always be learning from another perspective, even by myself.

RT: We inhabit a world that has been woven together by a trillion cognitive handshakes, don't we, and only some of them explicitly linguistic.

RW: Yes, exactly that.

RT: Some of them are sublinguistic, all the exchange of smiles with a child and its mother and so on. I actually quite like the notion of a community of minds, as the ultimate locus of our being. We have two loci – one is our bodies, inescapable, but the other is the way we transcend our bodies and are disposed into a community of minds. And it brings me back to religious notions and to the sociologisation of religious notions. For Durkheim, religion was our way of expressing our sense of something greater than ourselves, namely the society in which we live. I wondered how you felt about that interpretation of religion.

RW: I think that religion works in a number of different ways. One of them is certainly the Durkheimian sense of giving substance to the priority, shall we say, certainly the otherness of the order we are in, and sacralising it in that sense. But of course, the other strand in religious behaviour and language is that it sometimes comes in to unsettle or destabilise those sacral orders, so that a Christian martyr in the Roman Empire can say, 'Well, actually the social order is not sacred, because there is a truth or a power that is not subject to Caesar, and that's where I stand, and that's what I'll risk my life for.' And right through every religious tradition I can see there is that very complex toing and froing between 'yes, this is what guarantees order, stability and the ultimate environment' and 'yes, this is also what relativises any particular claim to stability or order in the name of something more.' And I think that because, ordinarily speaking, the Abrahamic religions have had a slightly more unsettling and tumultuous sense of how that works, they have tended to drive rather more critical social developments, for good and ill.

RT: So, in many ways, there seem to be two aspects of religion. One is as an affirmation of the collective tradition and the other is quite subversive and undermining. And there is an inevitable drive, you feel, towards subverting the tradition, that religion is always potentially – is always essentially – stirring things up.

RW: I'm cautious about any statement that religion is essentially … .

RT: No, of course.

RW: But, granted the point, I don't think you can, let's say, give an account of religion that will really do the work it needs to without somehow coming to terms with the fact that it stirs things up, that it gives people a place to stand, a place of leverage over against the social order.

RT: An Archimedean point.

RW: Yes, an Archimedean point. And I think of people I've met in the old South Africa or in Latin America, people who really have found it necessary to find that Archimedean point, and to be able to say, 'So what they do to me doesn't matter.' There are many grounds for saying that, but religion certainly is one of them.

RT: Basically, there's something within me that can't be touched.

RW: Exactly that. And that's precisely the language that I've heard used by people I've met in those circumstances – something that can't be touched. Which means, I suspect, again, not a some 'thing', not a little ghost in me, but that there is some dimension of my awareness, my language, my imagination, which does not answer to what is convenient or comfortable.

RT: Monday, Tuesday, Wednesday and the temporal powers and so on. For an atheist, my Archimedean point is my own corpse. I try and look upon my life from the standpoint of my corpse, look upon this organism, look upon Mondays and Tuesdays and all the things that the corpse, before it became a corpse, got up to, and so on. It's a pretty weak Archimedean point compared with the one that you're describing, but we definitely all need that point, don't we? It's certainly true we need to wake up out of Monday, Tuesday and Wednesday and to have somewhere outside, a massive outside, an eternal outside perhaps, an outside that goes beyond the transience of ephemera.

RW: Yes. This is what worries me most, I think, about some of those who gleefully embrace either a physicalist determinism or a sort of postmodern 'jouissance' – 'everything goes'. I don't see how you could distil an Archimedean point from either of those. Because if it's all just 'I can say what I like and that's it', that's an odd claim. It appears to give you a distance from determinism and all the rest of it, but what it actually delivers is a world of isolated wills, who have no particular reason for cooperating, loving, working – just mid-air. And both of those distortions worry me.

RT: And also, I think they are probably self-deceptive because the 'I' in question gets its intelligibility for itself, borrows it, from the outside world.

RW: Exactly, in all the ways we have discussed already. Yes, the 'community of minds' thing.

RT: I only make sense of myself using the language of the community.

RW: Yes, and I think what puzzles me about some of the strong determinist, physicalist arguments is that they boil down to saying something like, 'I cannot mean what I say.'

RT: They certainly do. It seems to me that if I deny free will, clearly my action in denying it would be as unaccountable as a pebble falling through a gravitational field. It just happens.

RW: Yes, it just happens.

RT: And if I say I actually believe that I have no margin of free will, my assertion likewise becomes just another material event in a material world. It seems to me that you've got to have an awful lot of free will in order to deny that you are free. It's analogous to the situation with the self: you have to have quite a lot of self to deny that you are a self. Raymond Tallis's assertion that his self was an illusion would seem to require quite a bit of the said self to be mobilised in order to arrive at that conclusion.

RW: Yes. So there would be a story, a narrative. You would be telling a story of how you, Raymond Tallis, had learned over a long period of time that you were an illusion.

RT: Exactly.

RW: Something strange about that.

RT: It would include coming to understand the concept of 'illusion', which means the difference between how things are and how they appear to be and so on.

RW: Yes, we agree very much about this. The whole consciousness debate in a lot of contemporary philosophy seems to me an absolute quagmire of nonsense.

RT: And I feel confident and secure in agreeing with what you have just said, particularly in relation to materialist accounts of consciousness. If we look at the properties of matter as described in the most authoritative way, which is physics or chemistry, there is nothing in those properties that would generate a creature like myself and like yourself that is (a) aware of itself and (b) able to put the word 'matter' in inverted commas.

RW: Yes.

RT: I find knowledge and the growth of knowledge deeply mysterious. One caricature of the difference between science and religion is to say that science is always looking for answers and it begins with questions, and that religious viewpoints often begin with answers and try to make sense of them – in other words, if you like, work backwards, to see what questions they can solve. That is a caricature, but can we explore that a bit?

RW: Yes we can. I think that's a really interesting set of questions because a lot of traditional theology, I suppose, did begin from the propositions and worked backwards. If you study the history of theology, of course you do see how the other thing happens, you see the processes by which people test out ways of saying things. They begin with a sense that the world has changed somehow. That sense is expressed in, say, the New

Testament, by hymnody, by exaltation, by prayer, and a sort of 'primal soup' of theological understanding. Then people begin to say, 'so, if we're saying x, y and z, can we sum it up like this?' and, like a chair at a meeting, who suddenly looks round and begins to see the heads shaking and the eyes narrowing ...

RT: (*Laughs*) Thus speaks the voice of experience ...!

RW: ... you find, 'yes, that looked like a promising formulation, but it won't quite do because it doesn't quite get it all in.' And so you begin to get formulations in the early church which are an attempt to keep as many items in play as possible. And, on the whole, the things that fall off the edge and get stigmatised as heresy or whatever are the things which, in the eyes of the majority, leave out some crucial bit that needs to be in there somehow, even if you're not quite sure how you keep it. Now, I think that's not a bad model for how theology advances. That is, in trying to find formulations that keep as much as possible of the practice, the imagery, in play, from time to time you get a moment where it becomes quite important to say 'actually, that formulation, that style of behaviour, that set of conclusions really won't live with where we are now.' So, whether it's a fifth century council saying 'We can't be doing with Eutychianism', or Aphthartodocetism or one of those prevalent heresies, or whether it's the church in South Africa in the 1970s saying that apartheid is a heresy, or the anti-slavery movement, or whatever, there is a kind of progress that goes on. It's not entirely a matter of givens. You can, I think, believe that doctrine gets you somewhere, so long as you have that sense of how it gets there. It's learning again – the story of how you learn.

RT: That's interesting. What you've described could almost be echoed in science, in the structure of scientific revolutions. You have a paradigm, and it accommodates new and novel facts and it gets more and more uncomfortable, and then finally it goes pop. But what is true also in science and I think in theology is, 'OK it goes pop, but we mustn't exaggerate the extent to which the paradigm goes pop.' For example, what Archimedes discovered still stands up. Newton's laws still stand up – they have just been shown to have limited application, and not true if we take the finite speed of light and so on. That's why we talk about heresies in science as well. The big heresy of my own medical career was related to the causation of peptic ulcers. If in 1970 I'd said that peptic ulcer was caused by an infection, I would have been invited to return the following year to resit the exam. By 1983 it had been discovered that peptic ulcer was caused by an infection. It took fifteen years for that to be accepted, and Nobel Prizes awarded, and so on. So there is a kind of resistance, a certain tensile strength within the paradigms, and then they go pop, but I think, as you say, not to the extent that some seemed to think Kuhn implied, that nothing is left standing. Einstein built on Newton and I guess in many ways contemporary theology still draws on the very earliest Christian tradition or whatever.

RW: That's right. It doesn't simply repeat it. Take one very concrete example from the last twenty or thirty years, and that's the way that theology has engaged with environmental issues. Prior to the mid-twentieth century, I presume there was hardly anybody who really thought about that, as they hadn't thought much about the environmental question as a whole. Now, bit by bit, elements of an earlier theology are squeezed out, and you say 'yes, actually, given this challenge, this question, maybe theology has some perspective on this. If we put *a*, *b* and *c* together, we can construct a theology of environmental responsibility.' There's been quite a bit of that. Interestingly, some of it's come from the Eastern Orthodox world which, in many ways, is doctrinally very conservative, but has a historic investment in the idea of transfigured matter in a way that doesn't always work in the Western Christian tradition. So there's been something that has kind of rumbled along there in the background. As well as the 'failed formulae from the chair' metaphor, I also like the 'slow fuse' metaphor – that Christianity lights some very long fuses, that eventually explode in its face, sometimes.

RT: Does that then feed into the notion that we have to be – for all creatures great and small, the beautiful and the less beautiful and so on – stewards rather than consumers of what is available? Does that fit with the Orthodox tradition?

RW: Very much so, yes. Because there is this picture of the created order as a speaking order, not literally obviously, but as a meaningful whole which communicates something about the nature of what's beyond creation, exemplified in the language that one of the Greek theologians uses about every particular bit of the created order being a 'logos', a word, a distillation of order and harmony and convergence in itself.

RT: 'Logos', for me, is a cue to explore something else, which is the mystery of the intelligibility of the world.

RW: Yes.

RT: I think it was Einstein who said that the greatest mystery is the fact that the world makes sense, and to me an even greater mystery is that we appear to be making expanding sense of the world. In one sense we are understanding more and more, although I have to say there are three big headline things which I do not understand and don't feel confident that I will understand. One is why there is something rather than nothing, another is how life arose – I think all the accounts of that are pretty empty – and the third is how self-conscious life, life that is an issue for itself, arose. I suppose those remain mysteries for you.

RW: Yes, I would put those three exactly in the place you do. Because actually if you try to construct a comprehensive physicalist account of things, there will be no intelligible way of phrasing those questions. You can't phrase those questions in such a way that you can get an answer within those terms.

RT: In other words, what piece of matter would turn upon itself and ask about its own nature and origin?

RW: Once you have defined matter in the way you need to for these purposes, you are defining it so that you cannot raise the question of consciousness. Once you define time and the universe in the way you need to for cosmology, you cannot raise the 'something rather than nothing' question, and so on. And it worries me a bit that the simple philosophical intractability of those questions isn't flagged up a bit more firmly by some of our contemporaries.

RT: Exactly.

RW: But, that being said, I think it is important to understand that our knowledge of the workings of our environment is indeed cumulative. That is to say, it's not that we have great breaks between paradigms and we crumple up the paper and throw it away, but we have – and this is something that I am fascinated by – we have the notion of a *mistake*. And to have the very notion of a mistake is to have a very important philosophical idea, because it allows you to say, 'I now see where the story branches off the line. I now see where the argument fails, or the observation fails. I've been building up confrontation with a number of unsolved issues and there are now so many unsolved issues that I see that we have got to recast the question.' And the idea of a mistake is the idea of confrontation with something that gently but inexorably presses me to some new formulation.

RT: It is an extraordinary capacity, the human capacity to think that we may be mistaken. It is connected with the character of thought as active uncertainty – I think it was Quine who said 'Man is the species who invented doubt' – where you deliberately say, 'I am not certain, and there is something to be resolved here.' But dealing with the big questions – why there is something rather than nothing, where does life come from, and so on – to some extent do your religious beliefs mitigate your sense of ignorance about that? Many people who have religious beliefs feel that they greatly mitigate the mystery of those questions. Do you feel that's a simplification?

RW: I feel that it's a bit of a simplification if the answer is just, 'well God stepped in.' But I think if you have a rather broader metaphysical picture in which you say 'intelligence and intelligibility are somehow fundamental categories for understanding anything', then it's perhaps not massively or apocalyptically surprising that there is something rather than nothing, that there is the possibility of continuous mental or intellectual effort, that there is consciousness. So it's more a matter of saying, within that metaphysical framework, you can see why all this makes some kind of sense. You don't then, I think, need to say 'so God steps in and fiddles with the screws and the levers at this point.' You say that there is overall an order of intelligence which moves, crystallises, takes shape, in these ways in finite life.

RT: But it's an unusual use of the word 'intelligence' in a way. It's an extrapolation. One doesn't want to think of God as an entity with an IQ of 45 billion, say. He's not on that scale and, in a way, it's very difficult to escape from the notion of 'intelligence' in that sense ...

RW: I know, and there's a famous anecdote, I think in one of C. S. Lewis's letters, where he and his friends are having an argument about God's understanding and somebody looks up a classical work of theology and says, 'ah, the point is, God doesn't understand anything.' Meaning that you take it out of that sort of discourse.

RT: Yes, because understanding is a rather lowly faculty to have.

RW: Yes, and it's 'intentional', that is, it's object-directed.

RT: Yes, it's local.

RW: So that's where, if you follow this through, you have to go into, on the one hand, the traditional disciplines of negative theology – 'when I say "intelligence", I don't mean "a case of"...' – but also, in some traditions, you'd want to say that the relation of God to God, the self-understanding of God, is the ultimate prototype of all other intelligence, which is something you find in Platonic theology, something you find also in some forms of Hinduism. *Sat Chit Ananda* – Being, Understanding, and Bliss – the circuit of perfect life. It doesn't answer the questions, and every time I use the word 'intelligence' I am uncomfortably aware that the way we habitually use it is precisely 'coming to terms with a given environment', 'struggling to understand', all of that, which presumably we don't want to apply to God – or I don't.

RT: Picking up what you were saying, it does tend to have a local application, as 'understanding' does. And it reminds me of the physicist Lee Smolin, who has written very critically about a lot of contemporary physics, when he talks about 'the cosmological fallacy', the mistake of applying to the whole of the cosmos laws that have been discovered within parts of the cosmos. And he feels it's a fatal arrogance of much contemporary physics to extrapolate physical laws, which are in some sense local, to the totality of things. I guess you would be very sympathetic to that.

RW: I would, yes. There's a massive act of faith involved, I think, in applying laws like that. It seems to me that the whole quantum principle – that cause and effect are not necessarily proximate in the ways we have habitually taken for granted – that at least makes me think that some of these problems of language are not just the preserve of theologians.

RT: No, absolutely not. And clearly, if you look at the philosophy of causation, it's in a total muddle – partly because 'cause' is a very untidy concept. It serves all sorts of purposes. It embraces a multitude of ideas: the exchange of energy, the push and pull of mechanics, transmission of information, and rational explanation. It's such a muddle. No wonder the philosophy of causation is in a rather poor state, to the point where causes are often emptied of any kind of content, of the 'oomph' that brings things about, as they are in theories of causes as counterfactuals. This stripped-down version of causation reminds me, very indirectly, of the stripped-down, non-interventionist God – the apophatic God of certain theologies – who offers little in the way of explanation of why things happen. That is a very modest idea of God, modest almost to the point of extinction, almost to the point of atheism. I just throw that out as an exploratory thought.

RW: Simone Weil said that she had to try to believe in a God who was like the real God in all points except not existing. Let me try and unscramble that; it's complicated. What Simone Weil is saying is: we constantly refine and elaborate notions of God to the point of an abstraction that is on the edge of disappearing. And that can lead us to think that what we're talking about is, as you say, minimal. The tradition of apophatic theology, getting your answer in negatives, is of course surrounded by a set of disciplines of prayer and receptivity, which attempts to say at the same time 'this is plenitude.' It's not that there's so little we can say, but there's far too much to say. And again, the Buddhist way of holding together emptiness and plenitude, the fact that nirvana is not simply a cancellation sign in Buddhism – the image is of what happens when a flame is extinguished, which is not that some 'thing' comes to an end, but some energy is unfolded, released.

RT: I think it was Hegel – he may have been quoting someone else – who said, 'Omnis determinatio est negatio' – that when you give something a definition you negate it. And so to give God a set of properties is already to diminish God in some sense.

RW: Yes, you're breaking down something which is, by concept, unthematisable, something which is an unconditioned agency, something for which we only have the words, we don't have any idea. We break it down into adjectives we can use about God that are not complete nonsense – 'good', 'intelligent', 'loving', whatever – and hope for the best.

RT: For many people, in a sense, arguments about God are pointless. It primarily is an experience, of fire in the head, or whatever you want to call it; and arguments, in a sense, are rather 'after the fact', a matter of defending your experience against somebody who hasn't shared that experience. The reason I'm saying this is because, in many ways, I worry as an atheist that I just simply haven't had the experience, rather than that I have a very good argument against the existence of God.

RW: Well, indeed. If good arguments against or for the existence of God were as good arguments as they think they are, then the world would either be full of people like Richard Dawkins or it would be full of people like – whoever else you want to name. And because the world isn't full of complete idiots, presumably there's something else going on here than just argument. Wittgenstein says, doesn't he, that people adopt or lose religious faith not because of argument but because of ways they live their lives, and he says specifically suffering at a particular level. And I think that religious people have always said that suffering can either intensify the sense of the sacredness of God, or it can crush it and destroy it. Simone Weil says that any concept of God that could have survived, say, the genocide of the American Indians would have to be a radically different concept of God from what you started with, because something had happened which so broke down easy notions of protection and providence that you might come up with something but it would not be where you started. So there is something about this 'experience' thing. And the reason I like Wittgenstein's formulation, and Simone Weil's formulation, is that they are not talking about an experience of God in the sense of something going 'ping' in your head – you know, 'oh, that's God, I'm having a Religious Experience, capital R capital E.' It's much more: as I digest and live with this kind of experience, this kind of suffering, this kind of ecstasy, and I listen to how religious people talk about it, I think, 'yes, actually that's what rings the bell, that's where I want to align.'

RT: I remember you said, at our previous discussion, you saw people who had beliefs and you said, 'I want a bit of that.'

RW: Yes, something like that.

RT: And that did strike a bell with me. But one of the strange things is that you and I are sitting side by side, and each of us has a different conception of the future after we die. I know the idea of 'eternity' doesn't imply something literally in the future, but that is quite a profound difference, isn't it? I have thought about eternity quite a lot in a very amateurish sort of way. For many people that is very important – what religion delivers is some massive restitution of some sort for whatever happens in life. It's something that I find very difficult, in my very literal-minded atheist way, to imagine, because one can either have an eternity in which one is re-embodied, which brings all sorts of problems, or the more likely eternity in which one is disembodied, where one has no location in space, in time, no needs, no future, no past, not much going on. I just wondered how important it is for you to populate the idea of eternity with any content at all, or whether it's much more profound than that.

RW: I think it's inevitable that we who are believers try to populate it, at least to this extent, that whatever the future is, in some sense I remain a node or a nexus of relationship, and therefore, secondly, I have a relationship with God. I think Christians particularly have had very diverse understandings of what that might mean, and there are those for whom post-mortem existence is the existence of some aspect of us that survives death. Most theologians, I think, would say, 'no, that can't be right', because again the soul, the spirit, is not a bit of me, it's the meaning, or the shape, or the form of my bodily life.

RT: You're an embodied subject.

RW: Exactly. So, whatever future there is – and I share your unease about the word 'future', but let's use it for the time being – whatever future there is is a future that is intelligibly a life of a subject that has been embodied, at the very least. And, because of that, I suppose the flesh I'd want to put on it is something to do with relatedness, something to do with memory, something to do with, ultimately, that continuation of a growth in understanding, of our openness to the infinite. More than that, I am not particularly interested in saying or thinking, because it seems to me that this is language that characteristically belongs in the realm of hope, of prayer, rather than theory. That relationship which I now have to the ultimate truth which is God, I hope and pray will go on growing and not stop growing, even when aspects of myself, of my bodily self, have stopped growing.

RT: Even when one of the *relata*, as it were, in this binding relationship with God, even when one of the *relata* is either utterly transformed or in fact disappears.

RW: Indeed – which I can't imagine either.

RT: No, quite.

RW: Which is why, as I say, I don't try and theorise too much about it.

RT: To me as an atheist, the very fact we have the concept of eternity keeps the door slightly open, actually, because we must be very strange creatures to have the concept of eternity – indeed, to have the notion of time. All objects live in time, whether pebbles, trees or philosophers, but only one object has the concept of time and, against that, the concept of eternity. So, in a way, that to me is definitely an 'ajar of uncertainty'.

RW: Yes, I can resonate with that, because I think having the concept of time is having the concept of growth. In the context I've been outlining, I think the notion of a growth that doesn't have an obvious term to it – a growth in Being, Understanding and Bliss – makes some kind of sense. And it takes us back yet again to this question of being the sort of beings who construct narratives, who tell stories about where they come from, and connect up their experiences, because to me that is one of the things about time. You said that we are the only beings who have the notion of time – because we connect, because we remember, we say 'my fifteen-year-old self, my twenty-five-year-old self, my thirty-five-year-old self, embarrassing as those memories may be, I know I was that.' Much as I'd rather not!

RT: I was going to say exactly that. I think it was Dostoevsky who says you can be walking down the street and be arrested with shame at something you did thirty-five years ago. And I can vouch for that.

RW: And the Buddhist teaching that what we face in growth and meditation is 'old selves' – that makes a lot of sense in that context. We're a lot of the time recycling old patterns, old stories. We haven't actually moved in time as we should have done. We're stuck with the selves we have created along the way – and yet there is one story going through.

RT: And because of the fact of the story's 'going through', living isn't a matter of successive instants. We have temporal depth, and it seems to me that, in that respect, we are unlike anything else, including our primate cousins the chimps. We have an explicit past and an explicit future and we have episodic memories for specific things, and that is completely inexplicable, as far as I'm concerned, in material terms. As Einstein says, we believing physicists know that past, present and future are just stubborn illusions, because there is nothing in physics, in our notion of matter, that would accommodate tensed time. It seems to me that tensed time is one of those most extraordinary underrated aspects of our life. And it's against that, I suppose, that the notion of eternity is an outgrowth of our sense of future, even though it isn't located in the future, it's not an endlessly extended future. And it's because we are tensed creatures that we never really get to know ourselves. We can look back on our earlier selves with astonishment as well as a deep familiarity. So that your twenty-five-year-old self still causes your sixty-year-old self embarrassment, as mine does. Or (very occasionally!) joy.

RW: Or joy, yes. And again, the whole notion that we learn, that the correlate of tensed time is learning, not only telling myself a story about myself, but saying 'I can see the increment, I can see that I've moved.' The self I was is now part of my knowing, and goes on being, so what I've just said becomes part of my agenda to change things.

RT: There is sometimes a sense of loss as well, though, isn't there. As we age, there isn't so much dew on the consciousness as there was when one was younger. One was more sharply aware of things. Do you feel you have progressed in knowledge and understanding over time? Presumably you must feel that, and I guess I have the illusion likewise.

RW: Yes, I do believe that. But of course what I know and understand is unfortunately largely my own incompetent way of understanding. We get better at knowing how little we know.

RT: And of course, the present me – the survivor of the fifteen-year-old, twenty-five-year-old Ray – has the latest word, the survivor's, the victor's, version, so it is natural to assume that one is wiser than one's previous selves.

RW: Fortunately, we don't have to battle it out with our selves, or we would be deeply dismayed.

RT: But there is this interesting tension, particularly in relation to the sort of ideas that very much have dominated your life, which are ideas that in themselves are eternal, unchanging, standing for fixed values, while your own experience of them is evolving, and you hope to be getting clearer about them. I suppose, in my own case, I hope I've improved a bit and understand more, and my consciousness has to some extent widened, but there isn't perhaps the notion that I'm catching sight of something that was already there. Am I talking rubbish?

RW: No, I see the question, I think. I would say, I think, that the growth in knowledge or understanding, which I hope goes on, is somehow getting more acclimatised to a perspective on myself that is nothing to do with me or with the ensemble of human consciousness, but is a perspective of truthfulness.

RT: And this is this 'outside' again, this Archimedean point, or whatever.

RW: Yes. So you could say 'slowly becoming a soul', you could say 'slowly aligning with God', and in my tradition and discipline, of course, it's assumed that at the moment of death you will almost certainly get a very nasty shock as to how very little you have aligned with God, how very little you have become a soul, how minuscule you are in the face of the truth. That's why, to me, one of the most interesting imaginative constructs about life after death is the sort of thing represented by George Herbert's poem *Love*. Suddenly, when you think you've got to the point where maybe you've got it sorted, something utterly beyond your ken, utterly, radically different, not recognisable, steps in, and you think, my God, I know nothing! 'My soul drew back, guilty of lust and sin.'

RT: Well, we are at our most intelligent when we feel at our most stupid, aren't we? When we feel that we know nothing. Because one of the things that concerns me in this trajectory of gradual understanding is that, as a doctor, I've been terribly aware of dementia, and other such things, and one could end one's days in a state of totally curdled misunderstanding, utter confusion. That spoils the story, doesn't it, of deepening wisdom?

RW: It does, yes.

RT: I'm terrified of that. I guess you are as well. I guess we all are. And that suddenly makes one's knowledge, or one's assumption of knowledge, seem shockingly contingent on one's bodily state. A bang on the head is enough to knock all the philosophy out of me. How would you relate that to the narrative of somebody growing in understanding, growing towards God?

RW: It's very hard to. I mean, if you've been alongside family members or friends with dementia, this is just the most challenging thing about it. I've been in that position several times. And I suppose what I believe is that somewhere deep under the surface there's a capacity that still lies open. It's buried deep, it's curdled, and I suppose it comes through in those unbearably fleeting moments, with people with dementia, where you just catch a glimpse in an eye, or a gesture, or a flicker of expression, and you think, yes, something's still there. I find it very hard to believe that that is just cancelled, overlaid. There's an image in a novel by Hilda Prescott, *The Man on a Donkey* – it's a great novel about the sixteenth century – describing the death of Robert Aske, who is one of the heroes of the novel, one of the leaders of the Pilgrimage of Grace, and he's being hanged in chains in York. She spends several pages describing his dying – it's horrific – until finally he is not conscious except for flashes of pain, and she says, '[t]here is something like a worm under the soil turning towards the light.' And I suppose, when you see people in the depths of the humiliation and loss represented by dementia or whatever, something of that is what I want to say ...

RT: It's a bit like 'that which cannot be touched', in the courageous political prisoners we were thinking about.

RW: Something like that, yes. Because as soon as you say it's gone, something about your present relationship changes radically, and I think those of us who've sat with people dying in that condition would find it a bit difficult simply to say, it's gone, there isn't a relationship.

RT: One's utter dependency on one's body, and on social and historical circumstances, and the utter contingency of what you might read, who you might know, what you bump into, what education you've had, in determining the pilgrimage you have through life – well, it seems almost a mockery that it should hang on such accidental, sometimes quite little, things.

RW: It can seem a mockery. It can seem, of course, from the opposite point of view, an extraordinary kind of carnival. The fact that our eyes met across a crowded room, the fact that it could have been otherwise and it wasn't. Sometimes celebratory as well as painful.

RT: There is certainly something about embracing the contingent, isn't there, and making it, as it were, retrospectively necessary and saying 'I've embraced this, I've chosen this.' It's true most of all when one chooses one's marital partner, or whatever. One embraces contingency.

RW: One embraces contingency.

Part II

Knowledge and language

The remaining chapters have been divided into three main sections – 'Knowledge and Language', 'Ethics and Values' and 'Diversity and Dialogue'. These are intended as a useful way of identifying and classifying the topics, while acknowledging that many of the chapters deal with issues falling under more than one of those headings.

The chapters in the present section deal with questions about *beliefs*. Do religious people and atheists misunderstand one another's beliefs, perhaps as a result of misconceptions of the language in which those beliefs are expressed? How can they rationally assess one another's beliefs, and is there any prospect of reaching agreement?

Nick Spencer (Chapter 2) examines the language of religious beliefs, emphasises the prominence of metaphor, and invites non-believers to recognise that metaphorical language is not unique to religion but pervades our ways of talking about the world and ourselves.

Julian Baggini (Chapter 3) suggests that there remains a core of literal factual beliefs which most religious people hold, that there is limited prospect for convergence between the beliefs of atheists and the religious, and that the search for common ground between them should look elsewhere.

Stephen Law (Chapter 4) looks at why it is that religious believers and atheists may see one another's beliefs as irrational and how they might explain this apparent irrationality, and offers some thoughts on how debate and argument between them should proceed.

Jonathan Rée (Chapter 5) suggests that such debates can be more profitable when atheists separate their atheism from oversimplified historical claims about the inevitability of progressive enlightenment.

Fiona Ellis (Chapter 6) argues that rather than disagreeing about the existence or non-existence of 'the supernatural', religious believers and atheists can share a framework of what she calls 'expansive naturalism', that this is needed if atheists are to recognise the existence of values, and that it can therefore serve as a more useful framework for the religion/atheism debate.

Fern Elsdon-Baker (Chapter 7) warns against an oversimplified opposition between 'science' and 'religion', and suggests that the relation between them can be better understood by looking at how science and religion are not just sets of theoretical beliefs but enter into people's lives in varied and complex ways.

Part II

Knowledge and language

2 Signifying nothing?

How the religious and non-religious can speak the same language

Nick Spencer

In an interview in 2014, on the topic of his book *The Edge of Words: God and the Habits of Language*, former Archbishop of Canterbury Rowan Williams talked about something called 'tight-corner apophaticism'. This, in his words, is a 'turning to negative theology or language about mystery whenever things get difficult'.[1] It is, in effect, an intellectual Get Out of Jail Free card played whenever the game gets tough, allowing the panicky theologian to slip off the pitch with his dignity intact, even if at the cost of leaving the lingering impression that there is in fact nothing more to theology than metaphysical smoke and mystical mirrors.

'Tight-corner apophaticism' and, in particular, the overhasty and lazy use of the word 'mystery' has rightly been a long-standing atheist critique of religion. You need not read very far through the screeds of new atheist polemic to drag up the accusation that recourse to mystery is not much more than a Hogwartian invisibility cloak, something that is perhaps entirely appropriate to those whose academic work might as well include Charms, Potions and the Defence against the Dark Arts.

Two kinds of rejoinder tempt those theologians who deign to respond (many don't, some citing theological reasons for doing so but almost invariably sounding haughty or afraid in the process). The first is to engage in the battle as it presents itself, the second is to reach for a different trump card, namely metaphor. This essay argues, in essence, that the first response is defective and the second is partial.

The first response engages in a battle in which the field and weapons are already chosen, in such a way as pretty much to guarantee defeat. If you cede a certain 'literal' or 'substitutionary' model of language – one in which only words identifiable with something demonstrably real in the world are meaningful, and in which all other linguistic practices (such as metaphor) are an improper and unnecessary distraction or substitution from the meaning of the statement – before you begin a battle about what words mean and how they should be understood, you should not be surprised if you fail to make your case.

The second response feels more secure – after all, 'metaphor' is a more respectable card than 'mystery'. However, all too often, when people hear that something was meant metaphorically, they understand it to mean '*only* metaphorically', a gentler, and more intellectually respectable way of saying 'not true' or, at the very least, 'not true enough to be important'. Moreover, to admit the significance of metaphor in one particular area of discourse only is to fail to recognise its ubiquity.

Instead, this essay argues that a better response for those faced with this criticism – which, it should be already clear, is a serious criticism meriting a genuine response – is to take the battle back to the aggressor (if such combative metaphors may be excused in a volume dedicated to bridge-building), and to question the premises of the critique. Language, it turns out, is not simply tilted against the religious but against (or conceivably towards) all those who want to say anything meaningful about anything of deep significance; the field of combat is rutted and uneven, and threatens to trip anyone up. It is not just the theological who need to watch their step.

A brief history of the accusation

The 'literal criticism' of theological language has a long prehistory. In mid-fifteenth-century England, one Thomas Semer was accused of being a Lollard. The word itself probably derived from a medieval Dutch word meaning 'mumbler' or 'mutterer', and although the term seems to have been deployed derisively and indiscriminately of anyone deemed to be a heretic, there is a linguistic tinge to the accusation. Lollards demystified the theology and practice of the late medieval church. According to Semer, there was no such thing as the soul, heaven, hell or purgatory. Christ, he claimed, was nothing but a man born of Joseph and Mary, and the Eucharist was nothing more than bread.

Semer may have been an extreme example – it is never easy to tell which opinions alleged Lollards held and which they were simply accused of holding – but the literalising of religious claims and practices deemed to be unbiblical, irrational or oppressive was even then (and was certainly later) to flourish as a mainstay of anticlerical and then anti-Christian criticism.

Thomas Hobbes was one of its most conspicuous advocates. An education at Magdalen Hall in Oxford turned the young Hobbes against scholasticism for life. Absurdity, he wrote in *Leviathan*, is caused by 'names that signifie nothing; but are taken up and learned by rote from the Schools, as *hypostatical*, *transubstantiate*, *consubstantiate*, *eternal-Now*, and the like canting of Schoole-men'.[2] Hobbes escaped the already crumbling prison of early modern scholasticism and entered the service of William Cavendish, soon to be Duke of Devonshire, with whose family he remained connected for seventy years. As tutor to Cavendish's son he had access to several great libraries, and met a number of leading thinkers, including Marin Mersenne, Pierre Gassendi and Galileo Galilei, on educational tours of Europe. It was on one of these that, according to his biographer John Aubrey, Hobbes chanced upon proposition 47 of Euclid's *Elements*. He duly fell in love with geometry – curiously, Euclid had the same effect on Charles Darwin two centuries later – which appeared to offer Hobbes a literal clarity and certainty that was conspicuously absent from the canting schoolmen.

Mathematics and by association 'science' – although the term was several centuries away from denoting the practices and assumptions we associate with it today – offered precisely the kind of exact, positive, quantifiable and incontestable knowledge that theology did not. Its words actually meant something. According to Hobbes, what we think is objective talk of God is really subjective talk of ourselves:

> We understand nothing of *what he is*, but only *that he is*; and therefore the Attributes we give him, are not to tell one another, *what he is*, nor to signifie our opinion of his Nature, but our desire to honor him with such names as we conceive most honorable amongst our selves.[3]

Religious language was autobiography dressed up in colourful fripperies.

Even were revelation from and about God a possibility – and readers of *Leviathan* could be excused for thinking its author did not think it was – there would be insurmountable problems over its means of transmission. 'How God speaketh to a man immediately, may be understood by those well enough, to whom he hath so spoken,' Hobbes wrote, 'but how the same should be understood by another, is hard, if not impossible to know.' In reality, it was impossible rather than merely 'hard'. 'If a man pretend to me, that God hath spoken to him supernaturally, and immediately, and I make doubt of it, I cannot easily perceive what argument he can produce, to oblige me to believe it.'[4] The language of revelation, even if it could be assumed to stretch from God to man, invariably broke down from man to man.

Leviathan was called 'a farrago of Christian atheism' within months of its publication and Hobbes' ensuing reputation – to be a Hobbist was effectively to be an atheist in later seventeenth century – lent his arguments a certain risqué quality. Nevertheless, the rather more respectable John Locke deployed a similar argument in book 3, 'Of Words', in his *Essay concerning Human Understanding*. In chapter 10, entitled 'Of the Abuse of Words', Locke wrote:

> if we would speak of things as they are, we must allow that all the art of rhetoric, besides order and clearness; all the artificial and figurative application of words eloquence hath invented, are for nothing else but to insinuate wrong ideas, move the passions, and thereby mislead the judgment; and so indeed are perfect cheats.[5]

Locke, like Hobbes, eschewed rhetoric and 'artificial' speech as obfuscatory: at best a misleading complication, at worst a deliberate attempt to obscure the truth.

Locke's own sincere, if vaguely deistic, Christian faith retarded such ideas from being deployed in anti-Christian polemic in eighteenth-century Britain.

They were, however, used much more commonly in this way in France. The French *philosophes* who gathered round the table of Paul-Henri Thiry, Baron d'Holbach, from the early 1750s had as much, if not more, reason than Hobbes to detest Christianity. They deployed a range of weapons in their guerrilla war – historical, cosmological, biological, ethical – among them the linguistic attack. In Holbach's mind, words only meant anything when they correlated with identifiable sense experiences. The rest of the time they were abstract to the point of being (literally) meaningless. 'Every time that a word or its idea does not furnish any sensible object to which one can refer it,' he wrote, 'this word or this idea is derived from nothing, is void of sense; one should banish the idea from one's mind and the word from the language, since it signifies nothing.'[6] Supreme among those that merited banishment were, of course, theological ones.

This was a view popular around Holbach's table, in particular with Claude Adrien Helvétius, former farmer-general (essentially national tax collector) turned philosopher, to whom we shall return. It never really caught on in Britain, where, quite apart from Locke's own influence, Christianity was intellectually and politically both more tolerant and respectable, thereby drawing the argument's teeth among potential atheists. The main exception was Jeremy Bentham who seemed to be temperamentally ill-disposed towards any kind of belief. In his essay 'Of Ontology', Bentham discussed the existence of God within the wider context of logic and language, separating out the categories of fictitious and real entities, and then subdividing the latter into perceptible real entities and inferential real entities. In as far as God could be said to be real at all, he was inferentially real. All inferential knowledge, however, Bentham reasoned, was imperfect and uncertain, and since there was nothing to be lost from not inferring this divine reality, Bentham concluded that God might as well not exist. This, note, did not mean God definitely did not or could not exist, but rather that because, within Bentham's system, language only made sense in as far as it was rooted in the physical world, all God-talk, indeed all metaphysics, was impossible. In the words of one scholar, 'Bentham did not have a theology because, according to his theory of logic and language, there was none to be had.'[7]

These views, meandering through Hobbes, Locke, the *philosophes* and Bentham, reached their climax in that spectacular twentieth-century philosophical firework known as logical positivism. It is a tale oft and well told. Not long after Ludwig Wittgenstein published his *Tractatus Logico-Philosophicus* in 1921, a number of philosophers in Vienna took up (what they thought were) the key ideas from the book and developed them into a self-conscious philosophical movement, for which they even issued a manifesto. This Vienna Circle of logical positivists, as it became known, was resolutely anti-metaphysical. They adopted from Wittgenstein the idea that philosophy did not contribute to knowledge about the world so much as clarify statements of what was already, supposedly, known. Such statements fell into two groups: mathematical claims, which could be tested logically, and scientific ones, those claims about the world that were made through the process of the natural sciences and which could therefore be verified (or perhaps only falsified). All other statements were meaningless. In one fell swoop, all religious claims were dismissed as nonsense.

The Vienna Circle remained largely closed until its thought was introduced to the Anglo-Saxon philosophical world by the young English philosopher A. J. Ayer. Ayer met Wittgenstein in 1932 and then Moritz Schlick, professor of philosophy of science and the Vienna Circle's de facto leader, who invited him to join them. He embraced and popularised the group's ideas in his book *Language, Truth and Logic* which was published in 1936, in which he argued that, as all religious language was unverifiable, it was all basically nonsense. Because it couldn't be verified one way or the other, the statement 'there is a God' was effectively meaningless. Ayer rejected the label atheist just as he did theist, as to do otherwise would, in his mind, have been to grant God-talk a legitimacy it didn't have.

> To say that 'God exists' is to make a metaphysical utterance which cannot either be true or false. And by the same criterion, no sentence which purports to describe the nature of a transcendent god can possess any literal significance.[8]

This was arguably the apex of the 'literalism' argument, the logical (as it were) terminus of a train of thought concerning the meaningfulness, or otherwise, of religious language that stretched back to Hobbes and even beyond. Eschewing any arguments about the existence or otherwise of God, it simply asserted that the word was meaningless, on account of having no verifiable or falsifiable content.

The problem with this criticism

Logical positivism dropped dead suddenly in the 1970s. When asked by philosopher Bryan Magee in mid-70s what he now thought were the defects of the movement, Ayer famously admitted that 'I suppose the most important defect was that nearly all of it was false.'[9]

The seeds of this decline were there long before its inception, however, and it is by looking at these, in, for example, the thought of Helvétius that we can understand the inadequacy of the 'literalism' critique and move towards a more fruitful field for dialogue.

Helvétius, although no more sympathetic to Christianity than his more famous dinner host, was less interested in savaging the institution than in erecting an alternative. His best known publication, *De l'esprit*, was notorious not so much for its author's scepticism concerning religion, as his attitude to free will. The book took a rigorously empirical view, which was of a piece with the author's anti-Christian sentiments, arguing that the mind comprised nothing but a flow of sensations that combined with a store of 'continuing images' which constituted memory. These phenomena were ordered and grouped into classes, with vocabulary and grammar providing labels for them, treating each as if it were real. This meant that many problems in philosophy were caused by simple misunderstanding of grammar (logical positivism *avant la lettre* in effect). Abstractions like beauty, for example, were simply grammatical constructs, with no actual existence outside language. Once this was realised, a whole universe of metaphysical – and, of course, theological – claims and counterclaims could be swept away.

It also meant that the human capacity to determine its own ends was an illusion. Helvétius believed he had discovered the laws of human nature, just as Newton had discovered those of the physical world. In both cases, they were rigid and deterministic. Humans were the way they were on account of the vast panoply of sticks and carrots that was their environment. Their own beliefs and motives were irrelevant. This view fed Helvétius' belief in human malleability and the omnicompetence of education and legislation, a view that would lead Isaiah Berlin to label him as one of his six 'enemies of human liberty' in his 1952 lectures on the subject. In Berlin's words, by Helvétius' logic

> scientists know the truth, therefore scientists are virtuous, therefore scientists make us happy … What we need is a universe governed by scientists, because to be a good man, to be a wise man, to be a scientist, to be a virtuous man are, in the end, the same thing.[10]

The socio-political consequences of Helvétius' view are of less concern to us here than their coherence or alleged comprehensiveness. If only clearly identifiable phenomena could legitimately be named and manipulated, everything else was nonsense. This was the way the *philosophes* (or some of them) dismissed God. Helvétius, however, followed his linguistic logic through (as did his less philosophical but more scientific near-contemporary Julien Offray de La Mettrie) in a way that he judged to be supremely hopeful, and Berlin supremely worrying. Helvétius argued that not only talk of God was meaningless, but so was talk of human freedom, and indeed the human mind. Clinging to the literal theory of language meant that Helvétius had to let go of other commitments and ideas without which we are left with, at best, an unrecognisably attenuated vision of human nature; or, in the title words of La Mettrie's most famous and most controversial book, *L'Homme machine* or *Man a Machine*.

Seeing as: articulating a response

This brings us towards a response to the literal criticism of language. Put bluntly, most language is in some way metaphorical because we are incapable of representing or navigating the world otherwise. In Janet Soskice's words, 'there are many areas where, if we do not speak figuratively, we can say very little'.[11]

This can be illustrated through trivial examples, such as wine. In spite of the fact that humans find it very difficult to agree with any precision about the smell and taste of wine, no one doubts that wines smell and taste of something. There is 'something there' about which we can talk meaningfully, if hesitantly. Wine is, as it were, open to a critical realist account. That acknowledged, the most perfunctory examination of a sommelier's vocabulary shows how overwhelmingly metaphorical it is: wines are crisp, dry, firm, flat, heavy, meaty, sharp, sinewy, supple, tart and velvety. None of those terms is literally true ('dry' wine?). All are metaphorical. But, that does not mean they are 'only' metaphorical or that our metaphorical language is not really describing, albeit tentatively, reality.

If we cannot talk about wine without resorting to metaphor, one wonders how much less we can talk about the inner states that we recognise as being essential to our being human. This is obviously the case for our moral, psychological, emotional or spiritual states – I often feel shamefaced or blue or disheartened or bitter or neglected or stirred or inspired or overjoyed – but the same applies to physical states, as anyone who has ever had a dull ache or a stabbing pain or a splitting headache or just feels generally rundown will testify. One might jettison such language, à la Helvétius, in preference for strict adherence to a literal model, but it is at the cost of describing, and therefore recognising, what it is to be fully human.

There is, however, a more subtle reason for metaphor in human speech than straightforward need. Humans are, to borrow Wittgenstein's famous phrase, 'seeing-as' creatures. Contrary to Locke, we can't see or speak of things 'as they are'. We don't just see the world but we see it 'as' something. Minds are formed by language and not simply language by minds. Metaphorical language is not merely a substitution for the real thing, a decorative ornament taking the place of what we really want to say. Rather, it is foundational to the way we 'see' the world. In Janet Soskice's words, '[i]n almost all areas of abstract thought ... the very frames within which we work are given by metaphors which function in structuring not only what sort of answers we get, but what kind of questions we ask.'[12] Metaphor gives us new ways of seeing the world. Because we are seeing-as creatures, metaphor is an intrinsic and inescapable part of being human.

In some areas of discourse, such as when I ask you what you had for breakfast or how your journey to work was, metaphor is unlikely to have a major role, although it might make a profitable appearance if your toast was burnt or your train was excruciatingly slow. But it is liable to be particularly important when it comes to the kind of things theology is interested in. If the simile is allowed, to do theology without confident recourse to metaphor would be like doing mathematics without being able to count. Such is how theologians might want to respond to the literal language critique: not by sheepishly admitting that what they were saying was 'only' metaphorical but by bullishly stating that the only possible lexical response to what they are talking about is a metaphorical one.

For all Hobbes' legitimate health warnings about how this can degener-
ate into incomprehensible and obfuscatory discourse, this argument is not,
I humbly submit, simply sophistry. Indeed, it has its roots deep within the
Christian tradition. After all, who imagines that the biblical writers didn't
realise that God wasn't a shepherd or a rock or a tower, or that he didn't
have wings, or that Jesus wasn't a lamb or bread or light or a door or a
vine. It is always brave or foolish to proclaim that the biblical writers *really*
or *actually* meant this or that, but it is a safe bet that when they spoke or
penned the various statements alluded to above they believed themselves to
have been speaking metaphorically *and* truthfully.

Scientific metaphor

One of the pleasing aspects of this argument is that it applies just as much
to a seemingly more 'literal' discipline, like 'science', as it does to religion.
This might be observed in at least three ways. First, many now-mundanely
ordinary scientific words and phrases, such as cells and cyberspace, natural selection and neural circuits, big bang and computer viruses, find their
origins in metaphor. Science adopts metaphorical words and phrases and
integrates them very well into its family. Second, a great many scientific
terms necessarily designate non-observable entities and events, thus inevitably reaching beyond the literal model of language, such as hard-wired
brains, streams of data, charmed quarks, and parallel universes. Third, and
most interestingly, scientific language seems invariably to have recourse to
metaphor to describe and explain what is going on, such as with currents of
electricity, junk DNA, string theories, or elegant equations. Scientific models of understanding often naturally gravitate towards metaphor.

This can sometimes get science authors into trouble, perhaps most
famously over the question of whether genes are selfish. This idea was well
popularised by Richard Dawkins, although in a way that seemed to spawn
rather than clear up possible ambiguities. Dawkins ended his eponymous
book by saying that humans should 'try to teach generosity and altruism,
because we are born selfish', although he subsequently insisted that his use
of the selfish metaphor was to describe the behaviour (metaphor intrudes
again) of the gene and not of the people it built (and again).[13] He was subsequently taken to task by the philosopher Mary Midgley for his careless
use of the word 'selfish' to describe genes, in a paper that was notoriously
bad-tempered and somewhat ill-argued. That admitted, Dawkins' reply a
few months later was instructive. 'Provided I define selfishness in a particular
way,' he wrote, 'an oak tree, or a gene, may legitimately be described as
selfish.'[14] Such a view was not a one-off. Indeed, criticised for his use of
the word 'robot' to describe human beings in *The Selfish Gene*, Dawkins
replied, '[p]art of the problem lies with the popular, but erroneous,
associations of the word "robot"', before going on to tell people what they
should understand from the word.[15] This kind of excuse not only puts one
in mind of Humpty-Dumpty, who proclaimed in Lewis Carroll's *Through*

the Looking Glass, 'When I use a word, it means just what I choose it to mean – neither more nor less', but is every bit as slippery as the 'tight-corner' apophaticism with which we started.

However legitimate or otherwise this particular example of selfishness is, the key point is that these are not examples of 'pure' or 'literal' scientific concepts. Metaphor is central to how we understand what exists and what is going on. Metaphorically true does not mean literally false.

Questions of truth

This leaves us with one final, if enormously important point. Legitimising metaphor in this way will frustrate those of a more literalist persuasion who may justly say that it now becomes fiendishly difficult to prove anyone wrong (or, for that matter, right). Admitting the inherently metaphorical nature of all such discourse not only admits metaphysics back into the feast but simultaneously denies us the tools by means of which we might eject it again. How, if all this talk is metaphorical, can you ever say that it's wrong?

In one sense, the answer is you can't, a conclusion that should be as discomforting to those who think you can prove 'religion' right, as to those who think you can prove it wrong.

In reality, however, this is not as much of a problem as it seems. After all, how can you prove whether a gene is selfish, or the universe is elegant, or man is a 'machine'? You cannot but that does not mean that the different metaphors aren't more or less successful and acceptable.

The key is the fit. Each of these metaphors introduces a conceptual framework or model that purports to elucidate and explain better the phenomenon under discussion. Some such models fit better than others. The cogs, levers and pulleys so favoured by biologists in the eighteenth century as a means of explaining the human body did not, it transpired, fit the growing evidence as to how the body actually functioned and so fell into disuse. Some metaphors, such as the networked nature of neural activity within the brain, do, presently, seem to do the trick and remain in favour. Others, such as the allegedly selfish nature of genes, are, it seems, underdetermined by the available evidence and therefore remain contested. It is not, therefore, that metaphor can just claim the right of a truth claim to be taken seriously while avoiding the responsibility of allowing its truth claims to be measured. Metaphor may not be readily proved true or false like a more straightforwardly literal proposition, but the extent to which the conceptual, 'seeing-as' model it presents us with actually fits with the evidence available to us serves the same effect.

As with scientific, so with religious metaphors: Thomas Fawcett wrote in *The Symbolic Language of Religion* that:

> the theologian … requires models which are primarily valuable for their existential contents. Religious models exist to give a symbolic picture of reality of such a kind as to provide man with a way of orienting his life

in the world ... in addition to being apprehended as an It the world may be apprehended as a Thou.[16]

A Christian would argue that these metaphors and models are derived primarily through the revelation of God as recorded in the pages of scripture. Experience and apprehension alone are not enough. However, people's experience and apprehension do play a key role in ascertaining the fit of those models. The biblical witness to the work and person of God is that God grounds the metaphors of, among others, 'living water' and 'love'. The extent to which those metaphors are legitimate and appropriate is then assessed (if not adjudicated) by the extent to which people actually sense that they experience God at all and, in particular, as 'living water' or 'love'. Just as the proof of the scientific metaphorical pudding is in the observation and experiment, so that of the religious one is in the life lived.

Conclusion

The argument of this chapter is not that theology can't be meaningless (it really can). It is that it doesn't have to be literal to be meaningful and indeed, given the subjects with which it engages, it is highly likely to need to be metaphorical. Theology deals with metaphor but not metaphor that is 'only' metaphor.

Crucially, however, while this could be read as simply a version of the metaphorical defence cited at the start, my point has been that all serious discourse – meaning talk of anything emotionally, psychologically, morally, spiritually and even physically or scientifically serious – invariably reverts to metaphor. If theologians naturally find themselves taking shelter in metaphor, they should find a whole host of others there too. In the fashion of Monsieur Jourdain in Molière's *The Bourgeois Gentleman*, we all find ourselves proclaiming that we've been speaking in metaphor without knowing it.

Recognising this should help the theist–atheist discourse in two ways. First, it should encourage atheists finally to slay the 'literal' accusation as found in Hobbes, Helvétius, Vienna and Ayer, the ghost of which is continually threatening to rise from their graves. In doing so, it should help theists and atheists communicate by realising that they don't actually speak two different languages – literal and metaphorical – but that they are both, of necessity, bilingual.

Second, it should also encourage religious believers to be a little more humble in their claims, irrespective of how absolutely they hold them, if simply because those claims will naturally have recourse to metaphor, which will always by its nature be inadequate, revisable, tentative – the best fit available rather than the unqualified, incontestable and eternal truth. Given that this, however, is more or less exactly what the Bible itself says – 'What shall we say the kingdom of God is like, or what parable shall we use to describe it? It is like a mustard seed ... a sower ... treasure hidden in a field ...' – one hopes that shouldn't be too much of a problem.

Notes

1 'It's Intelligence All the Way Down', interview with Rowan Williams, Theos website, 20 October 2014, <http://www.theosthinktank.co.uk/comment/2014/10/20/its-intelligence-all-the-way-down>.
2 Thomas Hobbes, *Leviathan* (Oxford: Oxford World's Classics, 1998), 31 (1.5).
3 Hobbes, *Leviathan*, 262 (3.34).
4 Ibid., 196 (3.32).
5 John Locke, *Essay Concerning Human Understanding* (London: Penguin Classics, 1997), 398 (3.10).
6 Quoted in Michael Hunter and David Wootton (eds), *Atheism from the Reformation to the Enlightenment* (Oxford: Oxford University Press, 1992), 280–1.
7 Philip Schofield, 'Political and Religious Radicalism in the Thought of Jeremy Bentham', *History of Political Thought* 20 (1999): 272–91, at 281.
8 A. J. Ayer, *Language, Truth and Logic* (New York: Dover Publications, 2002), 83.
9 Bryan Magee, *Men of Ideas: Some Creators of Contemporary Philosophy* (New York: Viking Press, 1978), 131.
10 Isaiah Berlin, *Freedom and Its Betrayal*, ed. Henry Hardy (London: Pimlico, 2003), 24.
11 Janet Soskice, *Metaphor and Religious Language* (Oxford: Oxford University Press, 1987), 96.
12 Soskice, *Metaphor*, 63.
13 Richard Dawkins, *The Selfish Gene* (Oxford: Oxford University Press, 1989), 3.
14 Richard Dawkins, 'In Defence of Selfish Genes', *Philosophy* 56 (1980): 556–73.
15 Ibid., 270. As Andrew Brown has observed, '[t]his lofty condescension – "popular, but erroneous" – is difficult for a popular writer to maintain. Who is he to tell us what the erroneous associations of the word "robot" are?'. Andrew Brown, *The Darwin Wars: How Stupid Genes Became Selfish Gods* (London: Simon & Schuster, 1999), 40.
16 Thomas Fawcett, *The Symbolic Language of Religion* (London: SCM Press, 1971), 80.

3 The myth of *mythos*

Julian Baggini

People drawn to 'interfaith dialogue' or faith/non-faith dialogue often see themselves as part of a 'coalition of the reasonable'. They believe that although there may be fanatics on all sides of the debate, there is a quiet majority (or at least large minority) who are not dogmatic and do not see the worldview they endorse as having a monopoly on truth and wisdom. They hope that if we can bring other like-minded people together, they can counter the illusion that our beliefs about religion inevitably divide us.

I am certainly drawn to the idea of a coalition of the reasonable, since the alternatives are hardly palatable: a coalition of the unreasonable or a divided band of the reasonable. However, I have come to think that many of us have perhaps been working with a false assumption of what that coalition looks like. Some of us – perhaps most, but certainly nowhere near all – assume that under the surface of doctrinal discord lies what we might call a liberal understanding of religion and belief, in which headline issues such as the infallibility of the Qur'an or the divinity of Christ turn out to be not such important matters after all. Religious belief is taken to be paradigmatically relaxed in matters of creed, non-literal in matters of interpretation, and pluralistic in relation to difference. I think this picture is largely wrong. However, I do not believe that spells the end of any hope for the coalition of the reasonable. Rather, this coalition must be built on something other than a shared liberal approach to orthodoxy.

The importance of *doxa*

Debates about the nature of religious belief, agnosticism and atheism are often hampered by participants being too swift to assume they know what other people believe, including those who are, on the face of it, on their side of the debate. This is partly a problem of overgeneralisation: talking about the religious, Christians or atheists as though they were all of one voice. If we never allowed ourselves to talk in such general terms we'd end up burdened by so many qualifications and caveats we'd never say anything at all. At the same time, the absence of sufficient specificity is a more common problem than its excess.

A less obvious problem is that people may accept there are lots of views out there, but they are very confident they know what the genuine version of any given belief looks like, which is usually how the speaker wants it to look. For instance, atheists sometimes feel they don't need to address subtler forms of non-literal religious belief because that's not really what religion is. For instance, in an interview, A. C. Grayling once told me that 'your gentle, moderate Sunday Christian' is 'confused, or they're cherry-pickers, or they are hypocrites, or they haven't really thought about it, or they don't really know what they believe'.[1] On this view, true religion involves belief in mythical beings and anyone who says otherwise is no true believer. At the same time, others claim that the proper way to view religion is as practice not doctrine and that it is those who maintain otherwise who are just wrong.

The central question here is whether religion in its true form is primarily a matter of practice or of belief, ethics or creeds, *praxis* or *doxa*. One problem with this is that there are two senses of 'true religion' bouncing around here: what we think it *ought* to be, in its best form, and what it actually, usually *is*. It is possible that most religion is as the atheists describe it but that, in its best form, it is not like this at all. Whatever the truth here, it seems to me that both sides are at least in part describing as well as prescribing, and that their claims are mere assertions. And so the debate about whether religion really requires literal belief in divine beings and realms has become another pantomime, with some shouting 'oh no it isn't!' while the atheists in the audience cry back 'oh yes it is!' But what we should really be shouting is 'behind you!' If only we'd look, we'd see a better way to resolve the dispute: evidence. You cannot decide a priori what actual religion really is. To know you need to see what people actually believe and do.

I know of no systematic and conclusive research that would settle these issues. But I have at least conducted a reasonably large survey of the beliefs of Christian churchgoers, both through a number of churches in Bristol, England and online. The results make for interesting reading, despite the obvious limitations of the methodology. The online version was taken by a self-selecting sample of 767 churchgoers, the majority of whom were recruited through and read the *Guardian's Comment Is Free* blog at least occasionally and who were mostly aged 18–35. This is not a representative sample of typical practising Christians. The paper version was completed by 141 churchgoers in Bristol, covering a broad range of denominations and areas but again not randomly sampled. However, these apparent limitations in some ways make the results even more interesting, because you'd expect the sample group in both instances to be more educated and liberal than the average. We can then be fairly confident that the surveys would not overstate the extent to which people held conventional, some might say more simplistic, versions of Christian doctrine.[2]

Nevertheless, it is essential to stress that I take these surveys to be no more than indicative. And as the survey was exclusively about Christianity, what we can extrapolate about the likely beliefs of people in other religions is especially limited. So I see these results as being no more than highly suggestive and would like to see more rigorous work done to test what the reality is.

So what is the headline finding? It is that whatever some might say about religion being more about practice than belief, more *praxis* than *doxa*, more about the moral insight of *mythos* than the factual claims of *logos*, the vast majority of churchgoing Christians appear to believe orthodox doctrine at pretty much face value. They believe that Jesus is divine, not simply an exceptional human being; that his resurrection was a real, bodily one; that he performed miracles no human being ever could; that he needed to die on the cross so that our sins could be forgiven; and that Jesus is the only way to eternal life. On many of these issues, a significant minority were uncertain but in all cases it is only a small minority who actively disagreed, or even just tended to disagree. As for the main reason they go to church, it is not for reflection, spiritual guidance or to be part of a community, but overwhelmingly in order to worship God.

This is, I think, a firm riposte to those who dismiss atheists, especially the 'new' variety, as being fixated on the literal beliefs associated with religion rather than ethos or practice. It suggests that they are not attacking straw men when they criticise religion for promoting superstitious and supernatural beliefs. Of course, you can define 'supernatural' in such a way that turning water into wine isn't supernatural after all, but when atheists use this word, their argument is not based on an unjustified linguistic or metaphysical stipulation. They are simply pointing out that religions maintain that things happen which cannot be explained simply in terms of physical laws and human agency, and on this it appears most churchgoers agree.

There are some areas where the mainstream belief is not quite traditional. Most accept that although the Bible refers to God as 'He', God is neither male nor female. Only a minority – albeit a very large one – believe in biblical infallibility, which is not the same as its factual accuracy, since most reject a reading of Genesis as history. Nonetheless, even in these areas liberals might be less pleased that these are no longer majority views than disturbed by how many still hold them.

One objection I heard more than once to my survey was that some questions were ill-formed and contained false assumptions, and so there was no way of giving a meaningful answer. In fact, I made it clear at various points in the survey that people should not answer questions if they felt unable to do so and it turns out the vast majority felt they could provide meaningful answers. So those who complained they couldn't answer the questions as they stood were speaking for themselves, not the majority of Christian churchgoers.

It seems to me that these results, if truly indicative of what people actually believe, are highly significant for the present debate about religion. The challenge to the likes of Karen Armstrong is to accept that when they claim religion isn't really about literal belief, they are advocating a view about how religion *ought to be in its best form* which just doesn't describe the reality on the ground. They are defending an ideal of religion, a possibility that is not the normal actuality. Therefore when responding to atheist criticisms, the accusation cannot be that they misrepresent religion. The best that can be said is that atheists focus too much on religion as it is most usually found and should pay more attention to the better forms.

I accept, however, that there may be ways of defending the idea that *mythos* is as a matter of fact more important than *logos* despite what believers themselves might say, and I've found a possible one in book 42 of the apocryphal *Gospel according to Monty.*

The parable of the allotments

1   One day as Jesus was walking through the marketplace, a scholar came up to him and asked: 'Teacher, what should I believe?'

2   Jesus turned to him and said: 'Once there were three neighbouring allotments, tended by three people, Thea, Alf and Flo.'

3   'There he goes off on one of his stories again', whispered Judas to Peter. 'Why can't he just give a straight answer?'

4   'Ssshh!' Peter replied. 'The stories are good. People remember them. And the faithful that follow us will make good use of their ambiguity as they adapt to new times and places.'

5   'One day, an environmental scientist walked past the allotments', continued Jesus, a little miffed that not all his disciples were concentrating, 'smiled happily at the enthusiasm and effort of the gardeners, and asked them why they were working so hard.

6   '"Because the organic food we produce here is cheaper, healthier and better for the planet", they replied as one.

7   'At this, the environmental scientist's face fell. "Alas, it is not true", he said, explaining at length that the small, inefficient nature of their endeavours did not result in cheaper or less resource-intensive food than could be bought in shops, and nor was there any evidence home-grown food had any significant health benefits.

8   'They continued to discuss this for several hours, after which, all were persuaded that their convictions had been wrong. They packed up their tools, went home and resolved never to return.

9   'A month later, the scientist was again walking through the allotments. He saw that Thea's patch remained untended but Alf and Flo were both working their earth as industriously as before. "Did you change your views back after we talked?" he asked them.

10   '"No", replied Alf. "We stayed at home the next day, but then we both realised that what we really loved about the allotment was the contact with the ground, seeing the food grow, being outside, watching the changing of the seasons, the camaraderie of our fellow gardeners."

11   '"We sincerely thought that what we believed about organic allotments was the reason we came. But when that belief went, we realised it wasn't about that at all", added Flo. "Although it was for Thea."

12   'Several months later, the scientist passed by again, and this time he saw that only Flo was at work, and Alf's allotment had become overgrown. "What happened to your friend?" he asked Flo.

13   '"He continued for a while", she replied. "Yes, he enjoyed all the things we said we enjoyed last time. But working an allotment is

hard work and over time it transpired that these rewards weren't enough. Without the belief that it really was healthier, greener and cheaper, he simply did not have a strong enough incentive to persist."

14 '"But you?" asked the scientist. "For me, the activity is enough."' Jesus fell silent and it was clear the parable was over.

15 'And the moral of the story?' asked the scholar. 'There's always a moral.' Jesus shrugged his shoulders. 'People can be mistaken about how important their own beliefs are.'

16 'I see', said the scholar. 'So, metaphorically speaking, they all believed at the start that their "religion" rested on a whole set of beliefs. For Thea, that was true, for Flo it turned out not to be. Alf agreed with Flo in principle but found that without belief he was not motivated enough to do the practice.'

17 Jesus nodded gently. 'Do you think there are more Theas, Alfs or Flos in this world?' he asked.

18 'I don't know', replied the scholar. 'But isn't the main question not how many of each type there are, but which one I should be?'

19 'You can lead a man to gardens, but you cannot make him dig', replied Jesus, and he set off on his way. 'Hey! Where do you think you're going?' shouted the scholar. 'I need a better answer than that! We all need answers!'

20 'Grow your own', replied Jesus, without turning his head.

What religious elites really think

Whatever the theological reality on the parish ground, as it were, there is still some unclarity about the actual beliefs of people who accuse atheist critics of religion of dealing only with the simple, highly literal forms of belief, while ignoring more nuanced, intellectual understandings of religion. For example, in an exchange with me a few years back, the theologian Theo Hobson said:

> a huge proportion of believers inhabit this grey area between 'literal' and 'metaphorical' belief – in a sense all believers do. Atheists call this muddle and hypocrisy – they want every believer to be two-dimensional, so as to bash them all with a two-dimensional critique.[3]

I have a great deal of sympathy for the view that it is possible to have religion without primitive superstition. However, it is rarely clear to me exactly what is being offered in its place, other than a rejection of the idea that religion requires belief in anthropomorphic supernatural beings. Furthermore, there seems to me to be an intriguing ambiguity in the argument that religion is not essentially about the supernatural. Is it the case that religion *need* not or *should* not include literal, supernatural beliefs? 'Should' not implies an acceptance that atheist critics are actually right to say that belief in gods, heaven and such like is silly, but wrong to think that intelligent religious people actually embrace such absurdities. All that 'need not' means is that it is possible to do away with the supernatural if you so wish. But that is compatible with the view that not only are supernatural beliefs an acceptable part of religion, they may, as a matter of fact, remain central for most believers.

I can't help suspecting that many people who stress the non-supernatural aspects of religion are actually still very much wedded to the spooky bits, but too embarrassed to volunteer the fact. For instance, I've had many an interesting discussion with a believer about how religious language is not the same as scientific language, only to discover that, when pushed, the faith of my otherwise modern, intelligent and sophisticated interlocutor rests on a belief in Christ's empty tomb.

So I wanted to test how many of a sample of religious elites – senior clergy and theologians – really did embrace the kind of religious faith that explicitly rejects the kinds of things atheist critics think silly. To do this I formulated four 'articles of twenty-first-century faith': beliefs that I think would make religion entirely intellectually respectable, even to the hardest-nosed atheists. They are neither so vague that anyone could put their name to them, nor so specific that people who are broadly sympathetic should feel unable to do so. They are brief and minimalist, stating clearly and concisely only as much as needs to be stated to establish the legitimacy of superstition-free belief. Here they are:

> Preamble. We acknowledge that religion comes in many shapes and forms and that therefore any attempt to define what religion 'really' is would be stipulation, not description. Nevertheless, we have a view of what religion should be, in its best form, and these four articles describe features that a religion fit for the contemporary world needs to have. These features are not meant to be exhaustive and nor do they necessarily capture what is most important for any given individual. They are rather a minimal set of features that we can agree on despite our differences, and believe others can agree on too.

> 1   To be religious is primarily to assent to a set of values, and/or practise a way of life, and/or belong to a community that shares these values and/or practices. Any creeds or factual assertions associated with these things, especially ones that make claims about the nature and origin of the natural universe, are at most secondary and often irrelevant.
> 2   Religious belief does not, and should not, require the belief that any supernatural events have occurred here on earth, including miracles that bend or break natural laws, the resurrection of the dead, or visits by gods or angelic messengers.
> 3   Religions are not crypto- or protosciences. They should make no claims about the physical nature, origin or structure of the natural universe. That which science can study and explain empirically should be left to science, and if a religion makes a claim that is

incompatible with our best science, the scientific claim, not the religious one, should prevail.

4   Religious texts are the creation of the human intellect and imagination. None need be taken as expressing the thoughts of a divine or supernatural mind that exists independently of humanity.

I sent these to a handful of selected atheists, agnostics and liberal believers for their comments. I anticipated that many would simply refuse to state clearly whether they agree or not. They would complain, for example, that the wording forces them to choose between two equally unpalatable alternatives. But this would be to deny a simply logical truth that if you do not agree with a statement, you disagree with it. For instance, if you cannot say you agree that 'religious belief does not, and should not, require the belief that any supernatural events have occurred here on earth', then it follows that you think religion *does* require the belief that some supernatural events have occurred here on earth. Either it requires such beliefs or it does not. For sure, there is much more that would have to be said about just what is meant by 'supernatural' and so on to work out from this precisely what a person who agrees or disagrees thinks. But that they agree or disagree should be clear.

So we need to be clear that to reject these articles of faith would mean to maintain their contradictions, namely:

1   Religious creeds or factual assertions are neither secondary nor irrelevant to religion.
2   Religious belief requires the belief that some supernatural events have occurred here on earth.
3   Religions can make claims about the physical nature, origin or structure of the natural universe. That which science can study and explain empirically should not be left to science, and if a religion makes a claim that is incompatible with our best science, the scientific claim need not prevail.
4   Human intellect and imagination are insufficient to explain the existence of religious texts.

So the stakes were high. Rejecting the articles of twenty-first-century faith means admitting many of the things that are claimed of religion by 'crude and simplistic' new atheist critics. However, I actually found very few of the people I approached able to endorse them.

First, those willing to sign up. Since Karen Armstrong has been the most prominent advocate of seeing religion as *mythos* not *logos*[4] – roughly speaking, as about values and practices, not beliefs about what exists or has happened on earth or beyond – it was not surprising she agreed with the first article, which asserts that creeds or factual assertions are at most secondary and often irrelevant to religion. She also agreed – with some reservations about the wording – with the second, that religious belief does not, and should not, require the belief that any supernatural events have occurred here on earth, and the third, that religions are not crypto- or protosciences.

Although she said that she agreed that 'religious texts are the creation of the human intellect and imagination', she said 'your wording is prohibitive' because it

> would antagonise a lot of people. It is too bald and needs nuance. There needs to be some acknowledgement that the 'supernatural being' is only a symbol of transcendence – something that many religious people understand intuitively – even though they might not express it explicitly. That religious language is essentially symbolic – pointing beyond itself to what lies beyond speech and concepts.

I have to say I can't see why my wording makes any of this problematic. Still, with caveats, Armstrong was basically with me.

Also on board was agnostic ex-priest Mark Vernon, again with some reservations about wording. The prominent atheist blogger and philosopher Massimo Pigliucci said, 'I would not object to religions based on those four tenets, though I do wonder what the point of a religion would be if people actually agreed to them, particularly the second and fourth ones.'

Finally, faith-friendly atheist John Gray found it all very reasonable, but wouldn't actually 'sign up' to the articles for various reasons, one being that too many complexities can't 'be captured in a short list of propositions' and another being that 'I tend to be sceptical of anything that's credal, even when it's as reasonable as this.' Qualified support, then, but only from a confirmed atheist who is unusually supportive of religion, an agnostic ex-priest, an ecumenical former nun who has rejected all dogma, and another atheist. I would compare this to discovering that central state socialism has its defenders, it's just that none are actual central state socialists. People who do not at all represent real, existing religion are defending it by appealing to characteristics it doesn't actually have.

If the articles of faith are to provide any hope of establishing the existence of the kind of reasonable faith I think should be possible, we need to get support for them from people who are actually actively and self-consciously religious. But that was not forthcoming. Theo Hobson, for example, a self-described 'liberal' theologian, said, 'I'm afraid I don't really sympathise with this. Christianity can't be reformed by the neat excision of the "irrational"/supernatural. It is rooted in worship of Jesus as divine – the "creed" side is an expression of this.'

Nick Spencer, research director at the eminently reasonable public theology think tank Theos, was even clearer in his rejection, saying, for instance:

> Although religious texts are indeed created by human intellect and imagination, that doesn't mean they can't be taken as expressing the thoughts of the divine ... I don't see what's left of the Abrahamics if you do take this out of the equation in this way.

Spencer also provided little hope of finding too many other supporters out there, adding that 'there would be precious few Christians I know ... who could sign up to all your points. To take just the most obvious example: according to mainstream Christian thought, Christianity is founded on a belief in the physical resurrection.'

Giles Fraser, even though he is a radical cleric who resigned as canon chancellor of St Paul's Cathedral over the treatment of anti-austerity campaigners camped outside the church, said this was 'tricky' and 'I'm not sure I can assent to any of these. Which is not to say that I agree with their opposite either. These are just not the terms in which I do God.'

Even one leading atheist couldn't agree with me that assenting to the four articles would make religious belief reasonable. A. C. Grayling said the articles

> leave out the crucial bits about religious belief, which are that there is powerful supernatural agency or agencies active in or upon the universe, with ... responsibility for its existence, an interest in human beings and their behaviour, a set of desires respecting this latter, etc.

For Grayling, it's not worth asking the hypothetical question of whether religion in the form I described would be reasonable because he doesn't think religion could be understood in those ways.

One source of understandable resistance was that the articles were expressed as beliefs when for many, the whole point is that we need to move away from putting beliefs at the centre. Hence Gray would have preferred the second article to talk of 'religious practice' not 'religious belief', while Hobson said 'believing in God' is 'rather unhelpful' and that it's 'better to talk of "doing God"', which is just the phrase Fraser used when expressing his reservations.

But I find this all too evasive. As I have argued, it is not forcing a false choice on anyone to ask if they agree with a statement or not unless you compel them to choose between two options which do not exhaust the possibilities. It's also true that you cannot reject certain propositions without, by simple logic, committing yourself to what they negate. What's more, the claim that religion is not about belief is itself a belief, which reflects the fact that there are plenty of beliefs about religions to agree or disagree with, even if you think the religion is more about doing than believing.

Hence the rejection of the articles suggests that either most liberal religious commentators and leaders are inconsistent or incoherent; or that they ultimately do believe that when it comes to religion, creeds and factual assertions matter; belief that supernatural events have occurred here on earth is required; religion can make quasi-scientific claims; and that human intellect and imagination are not enough to explain the existence of religious texts.

It's worth noting that the focus of my discussion so far has entirely been on the monotheistic Abrahamic faiths. It is often argued that things are different when you head further east, with Buddhism especially tempting.

Although there is no space to address this fully here, my own view is that very similar problems emerge here too. Just watch Werner Herzog's documentary *Wheel of Time*, in which – to take just one example – crowds of pilgrims go crazy to catch dumplings tossed by monks that are supposed to bring good fortune, and you'll be disabused of any notion you might have that Buddhism is not up to its neck in superstition. Or visit the first Tibetan Buddhist centre to be established in the West, Kagyu Samye Ling in Dumfriesshire, where there are not only electric-powered prayer wheels, but for a minimum donation of £500 you could have your remains buried in the Stupa, which is supposed to contain a grain of the Buddha's bone.

The coalition of the reasonable

What I have said so far might seem rather negative for a book which is supposed to be about fruitful religion/non-religious dialogue. But I think it is actually extremely important to be clear about difference if we are to find any common ground.

There are two equal and opposite pathologies of the common ground. One is the refusal to share any, to maintain clear divisions between yourself and those you disagree with. The other is to pretend or imagine people have more in common with you than they do, latching on to any kind of similarity as evidence of sameness.

To find the right mean between the two we need to be honest about what our similarities and differences are – but, more fundamentally, be clear as to what the point of trying to establish common ground is. If we seek shared territory because we want the world to be a lovely, friendly place where deep disagreements are rare and no one holds beliefs we judge to be stupid, ignorant or deluded, then I suspect we are not so much looking for common ground as to expand the territory of our own.

Whatever our psychological motivations, I think there are two sets of good reasons for at least trying to establish a common ground, ones that help identify where it is to be found. The first set is pragmatically political and social. It's just not good to have families, streets, neighbourhoods or nations divided by faith, or lack of it. It's worth trying to find something in common even with those we totally disagree with, simply to grease the wheels of social interaction. This is fine as far as it goes, but when tolerance, engagement and respect are based on nothing other than our need to get on, the peace that results is unstable, lacking deep roots.

There is, however, another set of considerations that can provide a firmer basis for coexistence. It starts from a recognition that we are all flawed human beings with prejudices formed from our social backgrounds, and limitations created by our education, intellectual weaknesses and other cognitive blind spots. Of course, this is in some sense true of psychopaths, obsessives and lunatics, people we could never hope to find common cause with. So a real common ground also needs some common central ethical and intellectual values that prove others are engaged in the same project as us. In the search for such a common ground in the religion debate, I suggest the virtues of sincerity, charity and modesty can do this work.

By sincerity, I don't mean simply that people genuinely believe what they say. Rather, they make a genuine effort to discover the truth and are able to question honestly the beliefs they were brought up with or have adopted in adult life. As some put it, they are fellow seekers.

By charity, I mean the effort to try to understand the views and arguments of those we disagree with in the most sympathetic form we can, being critical of their strongest versions, not their weakest ones or straw-man caricatures.

By modesty I simply mean some real sense that we are all limited in our understanding and that no matter how sure we are, we could be mistaken. Even when others go very wrong indeed, we can recognise that there for either the grace of God or the luck of chance go I. This kind of modesty is not incompatible with having strongly held beliefs and certainly doesn't require agnosticism.

In looking to form a 'coalition of the reasonable' of atheists and religious believers, it is to virtues like these that we should look, not more substantive beliefs about how the world is or what religious belief is 'really' like. One of the most important things I have learned over recent years is that attempting to forge an alliance between people of 'liberal' faith and atheists based on shared beliefs results in a very small club indeed: worth joining, but unlikely to make much impact.

Although it's probably true that almost everyone claims the virtues of sincerity, charity and modesty for themselves, in practice many fall short. We should ask of those who claim to be part of the coalition of the reasonable: do they take any individuals or texts to be infallible sources of knowledge? If the answer is yes, they fail the test of sincerity. Do we see the principle of charity at work in how they actually criticise and discuss people of other faiths or none? And do they show any sign of genuinely being open to being wrong?

One reason why this coalition matters is for the political goal of coexistence. I don't think anyone who genuinely embraced sincerity, charity and modesty could support an intolerant or divisive *polis*. On the other hand, those who do not display these virtues are just the kind of people who would advocate separate schools for people of different faiths, demonise those with different views, and see compromise as an inexcusable sell-out of principle.

Of course, in reality there is no neat divide between the reasonable and the unreasonable: it's a case of more/less, not either/or. But divisions are real even when the boundaries between them are fuzzy, and I really do think that the most important divide in the religion debate is not between believers or non-believers, but between those who show the virtues of reasonableness and those who do not. That's why I've often had more fruitful dialogues with some Catholics and evangelicals than I have with some fellow atheists. Our allies should be all those who don't just proclaim the virtues of reasonableness, but live by them, whether atheist or agnostic – or any stripe of religion.[5]

Notes

1 Unpublished transcript. Extracts from this interview can be heard on the July 2009 Baggini's Philosophy Monthly podcast at the *Microphilosophy* website, <www.microphilosophy.net/july-podcast-3/>.
2 Full data of the survey can be found at the *Microphilosophy* website, <www.microphilosophy.net/churchgoers-survey/>.
3 'Theo Hobson v Julian Baggini', *Guardian*, 3 November 2008, <www.theguardian.com/commentisfree/2008/nov/03/religion>.
4 See Karen Armstrong, *The Case for God* (London: Bodley Head, 2009), esp. 2–4
5 This chapter is adapted from a series of articles for the *Guardian's Comment Is Free* blog called 'Heathen's Progress', published between 30 September 2011 and 25 March 2012. Links to all these can be found at the *Microphilosophy* website, <www.microphilosophy.net/category/heathens-progress/>. My thanks to Andrew Brown for commissioning the series.

4   Why do religious believers and non-believers see one another as irrational?

Stephen Law

How reasonable is it for the religious to believe the central tenets of their respective religions? According to many atheists: not very. Atheists usually suppose it is in each case unreasonable for Christians, Jews, Muslims, Hindus, Baha'is, Quakers, Mormons, Scientologists and so on to believe what they do.

The religious person usually takes a different view of at least their own religious belief. They suppose science and reason do not significantly undermine, and may indeed support, the core tenets of their own faith. The same is true of non-religious theists who consider their brand of theism is reasonably, or at least not unreasonably, held even if no particular religion is. Indeed, many consider atheism unreasonable.

Even when participants in discussions between atheists on the one hand and defenders of some variety of religious or theistic belief on the other include intelligent, philosophically sophisticated and well-informed people striving to think carefully and objectively, they still often arrive at strikingly different conclusions regarding the reasonableness of their respective beliefs. Consider this hypothetical discussion between Peter and Ada, which I take to represent fairly standard views on either side.

Peter is an intelligent, educated, contemporary Christian. Central to Peter's faith is his belief that the Judaeo-Christian God exists and that Jesus was resurrected. Ada is an intelligent, educated contemporary atheist. Ada believes there is no God, and that there was no resurrection. Peter and Ada engage in lengthy and detailed discussion of my central question: how reasonable is it for Peter to hold the Christian beliefs he does? Together they carefully consider Peter's Christian beliefs, the various arguments he offers in their support and Ada's arguments against them. Peter and Ada do their level best to come to a fair and impartial assessment of the reasonableness of Peter's Christian belief. Nevertheless, they arrive at very different conclusions. Peter concludes, on the basis of the considerations he explores with Ada, that his Christian belief is reasonable, or at least not unreasonable. Ada, on the basis of the same considerations, concludes that Peter believes unreasonably, notwithstanding both the arguments at Peter's command and his claimed religious experiences. Ada's assessment is shared by many atheists, including myself.

Let's also suppose what is quite likely to be true: that Peter and Ada disagree about how reasonable it is for Ada to believe atheism is true.

Ada maintains it is reasonable for her to embrace atheism. Peter concludes that Ada's atheism is unreasonable.

I begin by focusing on some of the explanations Peter might offer for (as Peter sees it) Ada's error in judging that Peter believes unreasonably. Though I focus here specifically on Christian belief, the points made below in many cases carry over to many other varieties of religious belief.

I'll now sketch three answers to the following question: if atheists like Ada are mistaken in supposing Christians like Peter believe unreasonably, what explains their error?

(1) Wishful thinking. Atheists like Ada reject Christianity and condemn it as unreasonable not because it is unreasonable, but because they don't want it, or theism more generally, to be true.

Those who attempt to explain mistaken assessments of the reasonableness of Christianity as a product of wishful thinking sometimes quote atheist philosopher Thomas Nagel, who in his book *The Last Word*, says:

> It isn't just that I don't believe in God, and naturally, hope there is no God. I don't want there to be a God; I don't want the universe to be like that.[1]

This may be the view of some atheists, but is it the view of many? Surely the Christian message is one of hope. It provides numerous attractive reassurances, especially about death and justice. In particular, it promises we can be reunited with our loved ones beyond the grave, that people will ultimately get their just deserts, and so on. These are appealing beliefs for most of us.

Indeed, that Christianity is not, as a rule, the sort of thing people *want* to be true is fairly obviously contradicted by the manner in which Christians tend to promote it. They often place at least as much emphasis on how wonderful it would be if Christianity were true as on any intellectual case in its support.

But perhaps we've overlooked some of the less attractive aspects of Christian belief, aspects that might yet motivate someone like Ada to condemn it as unreasonable when it's not? Consider the following variant of the wishful-thinking explanation.

(1.1)   Atheists don't want to believe in eternal damnation.

In his book *The Last Superstition*, the philosopher Edward Feser quotes Nagel in support of the view that many secular intellectuals reject religion because they don't want it to be true. Feser then adds:

> Atheism, like religion, can often rest more on a will to believe than on dispassionate rational arguments. Indeed, as the philosopher C. F. J. Martin has pointed out, the element of divine punishment – traditionally understood in the monotheistic religions as a sentence of eternal damnation in Hell – shows that atheism is hardly less plausibly

motivated by wishful thinking than theism is. For while it is hard to understand why someone would want to believe that he is in danger of everlasting hellfire, it is not at all hard to see why one would desperately want not to believe this.[2]

On Feser's view, the presence of this unappealing thought in Christianity – that divine punishment awaits unbelievers – shows that people are just as likely to disbelieve Christianity as a result of wishful thinking as they are to believe.

Feser is fairly obviously mistaken, I think. It may be true, as a general rule, that the unappealing character of a thought makes it less likely to be believed. However, there's an obvious exception. An exception is when the unappealing thought takes the form of a threat: believe *or else*.

I once received an email chain message claiming that if I forwarded the message to two friends I would receive good fortune, but if I failed to forward the message I would be cursed with bad luck. The appealing thought that I would receive good luck if I did as I was instructed was obviously intended to incentivise me to pass the message on. But then so too was the unappealing threat of bad luck if I didn't. The email waved both a carrot and a stick at me, the stick providing me with at least as much incentive to act as the carrot.

A recipient of Feser's traditional Christian message is presented with a vastly more impressive carrot-and-stick combination. The carrot includes the promise of everlasting life for those who truly believe; the stick includes the threat of eternal damnation for those who don't.

Feser is correct that an atheist like Nagel won't want it to be true that hell awaits those who fail to believe. But then neither do I want it to be true that, as a result of my failing to forward that email message, I will receive bad luck. It does not follow, in either case, that the unpleasant character of the threat functions, on balance, as a disincentive – making it *less* likely that recipients of the message will believe what they are being asked to believe. On the contrary, the inclusion of such a threat typically makes it *more* likely the recipient will accept the belief, not less. I discarded that email message not because of the unappealing threat it contained, but despite the threat.

There is a further limitation to this particular diagnosis of why it is that atheists fail to recognise the reasonableness of theism or Christianity. Many Christians, including theologically sophisticated Christians, reject the doctrine of eternal damnation. So, even if the thought of eternal damnation were off-putting, it would only put people off those varieties of theistic belief that involve the doctrine.

Here's another variant of the wishful-thinking explanation.

(1.2)   Atheists don't want to submit themselves to God's moral authority.

Some Christians suggest that those who reject Christian belief as unreasonable do so because they do not want to submit themselves to any external, objective moral authority. They want to be able to pursue their own selfish agendas unfettered by the thought that what they are doing is against God's will.

This explanation is also implausible. Most atheists believe that they have objective moral duties. They believe it's an objective fact that they ought not to steal, lie and so on. So it's untrue that atheists, as a rule, have a problem with acknowledging the existence of objective moral constraints on their behaviour. That can't be the explanation for their assessment that Christian belief is unreasonable.

Indeed atheists do not, as a rule, have any particular difficulty holding beliefs requiring them to act in ways that are not in their own self-interest. They usually strive to behave in accordance with what they take to be their moral duties, even when such behaviour is disadvantageous to them personally. This fact significantly reduces the plausibility of the suggestion that atheists are moved to reject Christianity/theism because Christian belief prohibits them acting in their own self-interest.

No doubt there are aspects of mainstream Christian teaching that are particularly off-putting to some. Take traditional Christian sexual teaching for example. It's not implausible that gay people will be more likely than others to reject the widespread Christian belief that gay sexual relationships are sinful. However, most atheists aren't gay, so a desire to engage in such relations can't explain their failure to believe. Further, most actively gay atheists are aware that they are welcomed by – and can even be married within – at least some religions (including even some Christian denominations). This still further reduces the plausibility of the suggestion that even their atheism is largely motivated by wishful thinking.

Wishful-thinking-based explanations for the failure of individuals to appreciate the reasonableness of Christian belief also run into obvious trouble with those tortured individuals who struggle valiantly to keep their faith but lose it nonetheless. Their rejection of Christianity does not appear to be motivated by wishful thinking. Quite the opposite.

To summarise: wishful thinking may play some role in producing atheists like Ada, but what evidence we possess regarding the beliefs and desires of atheists provides little reason to suppose it plays any significant role. Indeed, we might plausibly suppose that Ada would, on balance, actually much prefer it if Christianity was true, not false. As a matter of fact, so would I.

(2) Atheists fail to recognise the reasonableness of Christian belief because they are ignorant of the *Christian* message and/or the strength of the intellectual case in its favour.

Is this true? One recent US study found that those self-identifying as atheists and agnostics scored better on average on a general religious knowledge quiz than did the religious. They also had a better knowledge of Christianity, on average, than did those self-identifying as Christian.[3] It does not appear to be *ignorance* of the Christian message that accounts for widespread lack of belief, at least not in the US.

Might non-belief or disbelief be better explained by a *failure to appreciate the power of the arguments* both for the existence of God and the truth of Christianity? Most professional philosophers and philosophy graduate students possess at least a passing knowledge of those arguments. They also have considerable training and expertise in assessing the cogency of arguments. Yet a recent PhilPapers survey indicated that, globally, only 14.6 per cent of professional philosophers and philosophy graduate students favour or lean even towards theism, let alone Christianity.[4]

The above statistic might prompt some Christians to claim that the proportion of theists is at least higher among those specialising in the philosophy of religion (perhaps about 70 per cent, most of whom are Christian[5]) and that this in turn supports the view that a greater familiarity with the arguments for theism, and indeed Christianity, does indeed lead to an increased likelihood of belief. However, even if it were true that a higher percentage of philosophers of religion are theists and Christians, that would not, as it stands, support the conclusion that this is a result of them having acquired a better appreciation of the strength of the case for theism and Christianity. Philosophy of religion is more likely to attract committed theists and Christians in the first place. Indeed, a recent survey of philosophers of religion revealed that while philosophical training and engagement did indeed lead to belief revision among the 151 respondents, 'the direction of this revision was most frequently in the direction of theism to atheism'.[6] This suggests greater familiarity with the arguments for theism and Christianity doesn't increase belief, but, if anything, tends to decrease it.

Setting aside these more general worries with the above explanation of atheist belief, there remains the obvious problem that the explanation does not apply in Ada's case. We stipulated that Ada is a philosophically sophisticated individual familiar with Peter's Christian beliefs and the arguments at his disposal.

(3) Atheists reject Christian belief because they have a faulty God-sense.

A third explanation for the failure of atheists like Ada to recognise the reasonableness of Christian belief begins with the thought that some people can know directly that God exists by virtue of their possessing a reliable *sensus divinitatis* or God-sense. Such individuals need not infer that God exists. God just directly makes himself known to them via this additional, reliable, God-given faculty. According to Alvin Plantinga, it may be 'perfectly sensible' for such an individual to believe in God. Plantinga says:

> [suppose] I have a rich interior spiritual life ... it seems to me that I am in communion with God, and that I see something of his marvelous glory and beauty, that I feel his love and his presence with me. Then

(unless I've got some powerful defeater, and we need not hypothesize that I do) a response that involves believing that there is such a person is clearly perfectly sensible.[7]

So why do atheists like Ada fail to have direct awareness of God's existence and consequent reasonable belief? According to Plantinga, because their *sensus divinitatis* is malfunctioning as a result of sin:

> Were it not for sin and its effects, God's presence and glory would be as obvious and uncontroversial to us all as the presence of other minds, physical objects and the past. Like any cognitive process, however, the *sensus divinitatis* can malfunction; as a result of sin, it has been damaged.

According to Plantinga, the failure of atheists reasonably to believe in God is, at least in part, a result of their possessing a faulty, sin-corrupted God-sense.

Plantinga might offer a similar explanation for the failure of atheists reasonably to believe the great truths of the Christian gospels. On Plantinga's extended A/C (Aquinas/Calvin) model of how such beliefs might be warranted, knowledge of and reasonable belief in such truths, including the truth of the resurrection, might be had through the internal instigation of the Holy Spirit (IIHS). When a Christian reads the gospels, the Holy Spirit illuminates what is read and causes the Christian to recognise that it is true. But why, then, on reading the same biblical passages, does the atheist not benefit from a similar revelation? Presumably, because sin somehow smothers or blocks their epistemic access.[8]

How plausible is the sin-blocked-*sensus*/IIHS explanation for the failure of atheists to recognise the reasonableness of Christian belief? Most religious people concede that many atheists are virtuous, moral people – sometimes at least as moral as many of their Christian counterparts who nevertheless appear to enjoy such revelatory experiences. So why, assuming these atheistic individuals are not significantly more sin-ravaged than their Christian counterparts, do they not similarly enjoy the benefits of a reliably functioning *sensus divinitatis* and the revelatory activity of the Holy Spirit when reading the gospels?

Suppose Peter claims to enjoy just the sort of revelatory experiences that Plantinga supposes a reliably functioning *sensus divinitatis* and the IIHS might deliver. Ada lacks these experiences. Yet, like many atheists, Ada doesn't appear particularly sinful. We might plausibly suppose she appears at least as virtuous as Peter. Perhaps more so. But then the sin-based explanation for the failure of Ada reasonably to believe what Peter reasonably believes seems to fail in this case.

What if the sin-blocked nature of the mechanisms that might otherwise provide an atheist with reasonable belief in both God and the great truths of the gospels is accounted for not by that atheist's own personal sin, but by the sin of others? Perhaps, as a result of the general damp environment in which it's currently located, Ada's car won't start. Similarly, because of the sin-filled environment in which she is currently located, Ada's *sensus divinitatis* won't work. It's not her own personal sin that's caused the malfunction, but her sin-filled environment.

We've rescued the sin-based explanation for Ada's failure reasonably to believe in God and Christianity, but only by introducing more puzzles. Given that Ada and Peter occupy much the same environment, why does its sin-filled character cause Ada's *sensus divinitatis* to malfunction, but not Peter's?

We might similarly wonder why it is that the virtuous members of other religions who have heard the gospel message also fail to recognise its truth. Presumably it's not their own personal sin that is blocking the IIHS. But if it's our more general sin-filled environment that's responsible for the blockage, why is it that Peter receives full epistemic access via the IIHS while neither Ada nor, say, Peter's virtuous Muslim colleague sitting next to Peter in the same library and reading the same gospel passages does not?

Of course, if the only sin that really matters – the only sin that blocks an individual's epistemic access – is that of not believing in the existence of God and the truth of Christianity, then atheists like Ada as well as those of other religious faiths are indeed all sinners in the requisite sense. Peter, by contrast, though he might in other respects be less virtuous than Ada, would be, in this vital respect, sin-free. That, we might suppose, is why Peter enjoys these revelatory experiences while both Ada and Peter's otherwise equally virtuous Muslim colleague do not. But notice that if that is how we understand Ada's *sensus divinitatis*- and IIHS-blocking sin, we can't now explain Ada's failure to believe as a consequence of her sin. For our explanation would then be circular. Our explanation for Ada's failure to believe would be that she fails to believe.

In summary, what evidence there is concerning the way in which immorality, belief and such revelatory experiences are distributed tends not to support such sin-based explanations for the failure of atheists to recognise the reasonableness of theistic and Christian belief but, if anything, to undermine them.

I'll digress here briefly to examine a variant of the sin-blocking explanation offered by philosopher William Lane Craig. According to Craig, when the Holy Spirit works in atheists to reveal the truth of Christianity, they deliberately block this activity:

> when a person refuses to come to Christ it is never just because of lack of evidence or because of intellectual difficulties: at root, he refuses to come because he willingly ignores and rejects the drawing of God's Spirit on his heart. No one in the final analysis really fails to become a Christian because of lack of arguments; he fails to become a Christian because he loves darkness rather than light and wants nothing to do with God.[9]

Notice that Craig's diagnosis of how sin can block or smother the internal activity of the Holy Spirit brings us back to the first of our four popular explanations: wishful thinking. On Craig's view, the atheist in whom the Holy Spirit has been at work does, at some level, know that God exists and Christianity is true. However, the atheist *deliberately suppresses or rationalizes away this knowledge* because they don't *want* to have to face it overtly.

Craig's variant of the wishful-thinking explanation runs into much the same difficulties that plague other wishful-thinking-based accounts. Most obviously, it's clear many atheists and agnostics really do desperately want Christianity to be true, and struggle valiantly, if ultimately without success, to retain their faith.

Explanations and 'just-so' stories

The explanations outlined above aren't supposed to be exhaustive, but they're intended to illustrate something of the range of explanations available to Peter. Peter might suppose Ada's failure to recognise the reasonableness of Peter's Christian belief is due to (i) some intellectual weakness of hers (e.g. Ada is ignorant of, or lacks the intellectual ability to appreciate the strength of, the case for considering Peter's Christian belief not unreasonable), (ii) her own emotional or spiritual resistance to that case, or (iii) something else blocking or interfering with mechanisms that might otherwise deliver that recognition. These explanations might be employed individually or in combination.

However, the explanations examined have various drawbacks. The first two explanations don't apply to someone like Ada who, we are supposing, is as intelligent and aware as Peter of the claims and the case for Christianity and who does not find Christianity unattractive.

Of course, Peter might suggest Ada and other atheists who say they don't find Christianity unattractive are deluding themselves. They *say* they don't find it unattractive, but deep down they do. That may be a *possibility*. Still, this suggestion faces an obvious drawback: it's a 'just-so' story. There is little in the way of independent evidence to suggest that it is actually true.

The sin-blocked *sensus divinitatis*/IIHS explanation suffers the same flaw. Perhaps we can know that, if God exists and Christianity is true, it is likely God would both furnish us with a *sensus divinitatis* and also make the truth of Christianity known by some similar mechanism. However, even if we can know that, if God exists and Christianity is true, then such mechanisms probably do exist, what independent evidence is there not only that such mechanisms exist, but that the failure of atheists like Ada to recognise that belief in God and Christianity is not unreasonable is due, even in part, to their sin-blocked nature? Little, if indeed any.

Notice that the kind of explanations offered by Peter tend to be offered not just to account for the failure of sceptics to recognise the reasonableness of other religions, but also to account for the failure of sceptics to recognise the reasonableness of belief in various other New Age and fringe belief systems. Suppose Sally believes in the existence of disembodied spirit guides, on the basis of testimony of others and her own subjective sense that such things exist and communicate with her. She finds that many are sceptical and think she believes unreasonably. To explain this, she might appeal to a combination of wishful thinking (people don't want to be distracted by other-worldly considerations from their selfish pursuit of material wealth and power; also, they often find unattractive the thought that they inhabit a world in which invisible beings monitor their every move, stripping them of all privacy), ignorance (people are unaware of the good evidence that exists for such beings), a blocked spirit-sense (it has been corrupted by worldly concerns, or perhaps the spirits can see some individuals are not yet ready to receive their spiritual wisdom), or the activities of other, less benevolent disembodied beings who have an interest in blocking our spiritual development and who consequently work to blind people to the reality of spirit guides. Notice these explanations suffer much the same drawbacks as Peter's. Wishful thinking? But many sceptics would like to believe in spirit guides. Ignorance? But many sceptics are by no means ignorant of the evidence Sally finds compelling. And of course, Sally's last two explanations are also just-so stories: they *might* be true, but there's little if any independent reason to suppose they *are* true.

X-claims

I turn now to explanations atheists like Ada might offer for the failure of a Christian like Peter to recognise the unreasonableness of his religious belief. In fact, I'll stick to just one explanation, which I call the X-claim explanation.

Humans have a remarkable capacity for generating false but nevertheless impressively rich and seductive systems of belief. One variety of false belief to which we are particularly prone is belief in *hidden agency*. We're quick to appeal to hidden, extraordinarily or supernaturally gifted agents when presented with a mystery. When we couldn't understand why the planets moved in the way they do, we concluded they must be agents – gods. When we couldn't otherwise explain natural diseases and disasters, we supposed they must be the work of malevolent agents, such as witches and demons. When we couldn't explain why the seasons rolled by, or why plants sprang back to life in the spring, we supposed that these events must be the responsibility of sprites, or nature spirits, or other agents. As a result of this natural tendency to reach for hidden agents when presented with a mystery, humanity has hypothesised countless hidden beings and developed remarkably rich and complex narratives about them.

Often associated with belief in hidden agents is a belief in superpowers and superfaculties. The hidden agents themselves often possess such powers and faculties. Superfaculties – spirit-senses, god-senses, psychic powers and so on – are often also invoked to explain how our knowledge of and communication with the hidden agents is possible. So, for example, mediums claim the uncanny ability to psychically communicate with the dead, and some religious claim to have a *sensus divinitatis* or god-sense.

Our susceptibility to these kinds of belief system is well-documented. Many intelligent, educated people have proven vulnerable to some of the most outlandish examples (indeed, the sophisticated often prove more adept at providing rationalisations for holding beliefs to which they have already been powerfully drawn – research suggests the sophisticated are more prone than the average person to confirmation bias in such circumstances[10]). Sir Arthur Conan Doyle, creator of that quintessentially rational fictional character Sherlock Holmes, believed in fairies, and was successfully hoaxed by two little girls armed with nothing more than paper cut-outs and a film camera. Millions of people, many smart and well-educated, believe the absurdities of Mormonism and Scientology, and some 130 million US citizens believe in a God that miraculously created the entire universe some time within the last 10,000 years.

Very often, these beliefs systems are rooted in a combination of *testimony* – anecdotes supposedly originating with eyewitnesses to miracles, precognition – and *subjective experience* – people claim to 'just know' their dead auntie is in the room with them, that they have a guardian angel, or that God speaks to them, for example.

Let's call *X-claims* such claims concerning the existence of such mysterious hidden agents and associated magical and/or extraordinary powers, faculties, objects and events. X-claims are claims about which we are notoriously unreliable. There are a great many false-positive beliefs. Indeed, such claims, even when they might initially seem extremely well supported, are regularly successfully debunked.

Given these facts about X-claims, *we should be very cautious about taking them at face value.* This is not to say that no X-claim is true, or could ever be reasonably believed. But, knowing of our remarkable proneness to false positive belief in X-claims when that belief is grounded in some combination of testimony and subjective impression, it's surely unwise to accept any X-claims on just that sort of basis.

Let's now turn to the question – how likely is it that someone like Peter might come to believe that a belief system like Christianity is reasonable even if, in reality, it's unreasonable?

The answer is, of course, quite likely. Christianity, as understood by someone like Peter, is built around a core of X-claims – claims about a god, angels, miracles and so on. And, as we should all know by now, human beings have an impressive track record of being convinced about the truth and reasonableness of such beliefs quite irrespective of their actual reasonableness. There's every reason to expect a belief system like Christianity or Islam or Judaism to appear reasonable to a great many people even if it is not, in fact, reasonable.

So an atheist like Ada can easily explain why someone like Peter might consider Christianity reasonable even if it is not. For Christianity is an example of a variety of belief – X-claim belief – about which we are *notoriously unreliable judges of reasonableness.* Notice that this explanation of

Peter's error is also not a just-so story. There really is excellent evidence that we are highly prone to misjudge such beliefs as reasonable when they're not.

Conclusions

What conclusions can we draw from the above observations? We shouldn't conclude that there really is no adequate, non-just-so, currently available explanation for why many atheists like Ada might misjudge the reasonableness of Christian belief. For there remains at least one obvious candidate explanation that I have yet to mention. The fact is that disagreements about the reasonableness of positions are widespread across many arenas, including the political, philosophical and even the scientific. We humans are fallible, and even the best and most informed of us regularly make mistakes, including mistakes about what's reasonable and what's not. So Peter can explain Ada's supposed error in this way: it's a consequence of this all-too-common human fallibility that we're already very familiar with. Ada and atheists like her have just made an honest mistake. And this explanation is also no just-so story – our human fallibility is a well-established fact.

However, I noted already that a majority of professional philosophers tend to be atheist, with less than 15 per cent even *leaning towards* any sort of theism. There has been a dramatic collapse in religious belief among professional philosophers over the last century or so. Why so, if not because they have figured out that such beliefs are, in fact, pretty unreasonable? Even within philosophy of religion, where professional philosophers tend to be Christian, it appears that, in so far as philosophers change their opinions in light of argument, more tend to shift in the direction of atheism. So, while Peter might perhaps not implausibly explain Ada's supposed error by appealing to common-or-garden human fallibility, I think even this sort of explanation is far more plausibly applied by Ada with respect to Peter's supposed error.

I now want to draw five morals in light of the above discussion concerning how Peter and Ada might usefully approach each other in debate and argument.

1   There's a tendency among the religious to take offence at comparisons drawn by atheists between religious belief and other supernatural beliefs such as belief in ghosts, fairies, etc. No doubt some atheists do just want to belittle and bait the religious by making such comparisons. However, it seems to me that, *given that the X-claim explanation of why Peter fails to recognise the unreasonableness of his Christian belief looks fairly plausible and certainly is no just-so story, drawing such a comparison can be very appropriate.* I certainly intend no offence by drawing it. I don't think the religious should take offence.

2   Atheists should not suggest that religious folk are stupid. Unfortunately, many do. While there is some evidence that a lower IQ correlates with

increased religiosity, the fact is that most popular religions – even the most absurd – can boast adherents at least as smart as myself. I count among my close friends Christians with impressive intellects. They aren't fools.

3 I suggest honesty is the best policy. Christians who, like William Lane Craig, suppose the sin of rejecting God is so momentous that deathbed atheists really deserve to burn in hell ought not to attempt to hide that opinion for fear of causing offence (Craig doesn't do this, of course). First off, most atheists have thick skins. We know we're a highly distrusted minority (more Americans would rather have a pot-smoking president than an atheist one, for example). Secondly, I for one would much rather understand what my intellectual opponent *really* believes about me than have them disguise it. After all, if a Christian really believes that, as an atheist, I am hell-bound, they surely have a moral duty to warn me. I understand and appreciate that. I think we atheists should be similarly honest. I consider Christian belief of the sort defended by Peter to be pretty ludicrous: scarcely less ludicrous, in fact, than many other religious belief systems that Peter himself would probably find ludicrous (such as Mormonism and Scientology, for example). I think I should be honest about that, rather than disguise my opinions for fear of 'causing offence'. For obvious reasons, dialogues between belief systems where the participants try to disguise their beliefs and deal in half-truths are unlikely to be helpful in terms of *getting at the truth*. Nor am I convinced such deceit is even the best policy when the aim is merely *getting along*. If Peter tells me he believes that, being an atheist, my moral depravity is so deep as to qualify me for eternal damnation, I'll be a little shocked. But I'll be happy to discuss that with him. If, on the other hand, he chooses to hide this assessment from me, then there is a good chance that I'll nevertheless detect his attitude. If you'd feel sullied after having shaken hands with a mass murderer like Pol Pot, imagine how sullied Peter may feel after shaking hands with me. I doubt Peter could keep such moral revulsion entirely under wraps. And my detection of his deceit is, in turn, likely to make me suspicious and distrustful of him.

4 A little mockery and leg-pulling is, in some circumstances, entirely appropriate. No one should abandon a belief because others laugh at it. Nor should any religious person or atheist be mocked merely to cause them distress. However, while humour should not take the place of rigorous criticism, it can enhance the latter's effectiveness by breaking the spell of deference and 'respect' that belief systems are capable of casting over us. In Hans Christian Andersen's *The Emperor's New Clothes*, the small boy who points and laughs breaks the spell: he allows everyone else watching the naked Emperor to see they have been duped, to recognise the absurdity of their situation. Of course, some authoritarians (be they religious or atheist) who revel in pomposity and demand overweening respect are aware that humour can unmask them, which explains why they are particularly fearful of it (I am now thinking of *Charlie Hebdo*). I am more than happy for others to pull my leg. I hope they won't mind if I sometimes pull theirs.

5   Atheists should understand the often good motives of those who evangelise. After all, Christian evangelists really are trying to save us atheists. The stakes couldn't be higher. If I could only save someone from a dangerous fall by rudely grabbing them and shouting my warning in their face, I would. I will generally forgive those who strive, by behaving with similarly urgency, to save me from a fate literally worse than death. I certainly don't expect the religious to keep their beliefs to themselves.

Notes

1   Thomas Nagel, *The Last Word* (New York: Oxford University Press, 1997), 130.
2   Edward Feser, *The Last Superstition* (South Bend, IN: St Augustine's Press, 2008), 10.
3   Results of a 2010 survey conducted by the Pew Forum on Religion and Public Life – results summarised in 'US Religious Knowledge Survey', executive summary, Pew Research Center, 28 September, <http://www.pewforum.org/U-S-Religious-Knowledge-Survey.aspx>.
4   Results of the PhilPapers survey are at *PhilPapers Surveys*, Preliminary Survey results, <http://philpapers.org/surveys/results.pl>.
5   In the English-speaking world just over 70 per cent of those who specialise in philosophy of religion are theists according to two studies. Most of them are Christian. See David Bourget and David Chalmers, 'Correlations with: AOS:Philosophy of Religion', in *PhilPapers Surveys*, 2009, <http://philpapers.org/surveys/linear_most_with.pl?A=profile%3AAOS%3APhilosophy%20of%20Religion>; and Helen De Cruz, 'Confirmation Bias or Expertise? The Prevalence of Theism in Philosophy of Religion', *Prosblogion: The Philosophy of Religion Blog*, 25 February 2012, <http://prosblogion.ektopos.com/2012/02/25/one_of_the_stri/>.
6   Preliminary report of results from the 2013 British Academy-funded survey are available online from Helen De Cruz, 'Results of My Qualitative Study of Attitudes and Religious Motivations of Philosophers of Religion', *Prosblogion: The Philosophy of Religion Blog*, 31 December 2013, <http://prosblogion.ektopos.com/2013/12/31/results-of-my-qualitative-study-of-attitudes-and-religious-motivations-of-philosophers-of-religion/>.
7   Alvin Plantinga, 'Reformed Epistemology', in Philip L. Quinn and Charles Taliaferro (eds), *A Companion to The Philosophy of Religion* (Oxford: Blackwell, 1997), 387.
8   Plantinga's account of how firm and certain knowledge of the great truths of the gospels can be had by means of a process of belief formation instigated by the Holy Spirit (a process that brings about belief in those truths in response to the reading of scripture, etc.) is presented in his *Warranted Christian Belief* (Oxford: Oxford University Press, 2000), see ch. 8.
9   William Lane Craig, *Reasonable Faith: Christian Truth and Apologetics* (rev. edn; Wheaton, IL: Crossway, 2008), 35–6.
10 See Charles S. Taber and Milton Lodge, 'Motivated Skepticism in the Evaluation of Political Beliefs', *American Journal of Political Science* 50, no. 3 (2006): 755–69.

5   Atheism and history

Jonathan Rée

Scratch a modern atheist, and the chances are you will find a historian: not a studious archive-sleuth, but a broad-brush anecdotalist, regaling you with stories about the steady decline of religion and the irresistible rise of secular enlightenment. Or perhaps I should say *historicist* rather than historian: someone motivated not so much by curiosity as to what actually happened as by a determination to see the past as a journey towards a definite and desirable destination. Either way, we atheists seem not to be content with arguing against the existence of God: we have difficulty getting through our intellectual lives without telling ourselves that we are on the side of progress and our ultimate triumph is inevitable. Our atheism has a secret affinity with history, it seems: we may not know it but it does.

Take the self-declared sceptic David Hume. He never quite outed himself as an atheist, but he was notorious for his hostility to Christianity and his refusal to countenance a personal deity or a supernatural afterlife. In the summer of 1776, when he was close to death, he received a visit from James Boswell, who begged him to think again. 'I went to see Mr David Hume, who was … just a-dying', Boswell recalled, and to his surprise he found him 'placid and even cheerful'. Hume seems to have taken pleasure in winding Boswell up: he told his friend that 'the morality of every religion was bad', and that 'when he heard a man was religious, he concluded he was a rascal'. Hume was expecting to be 'annihilated' within a day or two but, according to the incredulous Boswell, he 'persisted in disbelieving a future state even when he had death before his eyes'.[1]

In some ways, however, Hume was still a believer – even a believer in a 'future state' – though not in the way Boswell meant. In his lifetime he was more famous for a six-volume *History of England* than for his works of philosophy, and he was admired for spinning elaborate narratives showing how, in politics at least, things never work out quite as anyone expects. When it came to the history of religion, however, he seems to have been some kind of determinist, believing that religious faith was bound to wither away as time went by. He had no objection to dying, but he told his friends that he would like to put it off for a while: he wanted to live long enough to gloat over the collapse of 'prevailing systems of superstition', and to 'have the pleasure of seeing the churches shut up, and the clergy sent about their business'.[2]

Hume's confidence in the historical inevitability of atheism was part of a broad movement in eighteenth-century thought, known at the time as *histoire raisonnée* or 'conjectural history'. The movement was based on John Locke's project of tracing all ideas to their sources in experience, but transposed from the history of the individual mind to that of humanity as a whole. Montesquieu, Rousseau and Condillac were amongst the pioneers of conjectural history, and while they all set about the task in different ways, they agreed in trying to draw an a priori line starting from a primitive 'natural' state and leading up to the ultimate summit of civilisation. They placed the prehistoric 'origin' of history several thousand years back, and then traced a steady development as humanity took itself in hand and propelled itself through a succession of stages, each less natural and more artificial than the last, and passing through the present on its way to an even better future.

In 1748 Hume's friend Adam Smith launched his career as a teacher by taking up conjectural history in a series of public lectures in Edinburgh. He began by considering 'the origin and progress of language', imagining what must have happened when 'two savages met together' to devise the world's first system of verbal communication. They would have started with proper names, according to Smith, before moving on to general nouns, followed by adjectives and then verbs. The primeval 'contrivers of language' were not 'very abstract philosophers', however, and when it came to representing relations they loaded their verbs with 'inflections', and the 'original' languages of humanity – Hebrew, Old Slavonic and Greek, for example – were therefore involved in a mass of unnecessary complications. But in due course different classes of ideas came to be distinguished more clearly, and assigned to dedicated parts of speech: efficiency improved, and the languages of the world started to 'make advances a good deal similar to those in the construction of machines'. The path of subsequent progress could be traced from the introduction of prepositions and auxiliaries into Latin, and their increasing prominence in French and finally their proliferation in English which, if it was 'more prolix' than other languages, was also much more efficient. Having constructed a conjectural history of language, Smith turned his attention to astronomy, philosophy, morality and the organisation of human labour, and wherever he looked, he was pleased to find a steady evolution from natural idiocy to rational efficiency.[3]

Hume had already been thinking on similar lines, and in 1757 he published a succinct essay on *The Natural History of Religion*, promising to track religious ideas to their 'origin in human nature', five or six thousand years ago. 'Polytheism or idolatry', Hume said, 'was, and necessarily must have been, the first and most ancient religion of mankind.' At the beginning of history, the 'ignorant multitude must first entertain some grovelling and familiar notion of superior powers' – the savage mind 'deifies every part of the universe', according to Hume, and 'conceives all the conspicuous productions of nature, to be themselves so many real divinities'. But then, in accordance with the 'natural progress of human thought', the mind 'rises gradually, from inferior to superior', and embarks on a steady progress towards monotheism: rival anthropomorphic deities are gradually amalgamated into a single God, conceived as 'pure spirit, omniscient, omnipotent and omnipresent'. But the development has been uneven, and Catholicism, with its doctrine of the real presence of Christ's body and blood in holy communion, was clearly still in thrall to prehistoric superstition. 'In a future age,' Hume said, 'it will probably become difficult to persuade some nations, that any human, two-legged creature could ever embrace such principles', and though he did not say so, his readers might guess that he thought much the same about Protestantism. 'Ignorance is the mother of devotion', as he put it: and he left us to wonder why, if the number of acknowledged gods had already dropped to three, two and eventually one, it might not fall in due course to zero.[4]

If Hume had been granted his wish to live another hundred years in order to gloat over the decline and fall of religion, he would have been terribly disappointed. In the second half of the nineteenth century, religious belief was still rampant in Britain, Europe and America, and it was perhaps more passionate and militant than it had been in Hume's lifetime. Atheism was as rare as ever amongst the population at large, and in any case its character had changed. Eighteenth-century infidels like Hume had imagined that the decline of religion would release human intelligence from the fetters of superstition, allowing it to emerge magnificent and proud and free; but to their successors a hundred years later, it appeared to involve a grave wound to human self-confidence. Religion was seen as a fool's paradise or a collective delusion of grandeur, and the triumph of atheism was also a tragedy, leaving us facing the grim fact that humanity is no more than an accidental efflorescence on the surface of a cooling planet, awaiting cosmic death and signifying nothing.

The shift from cheerful atheism to depressive atheism can be dated to the publication of Charles Lyell's *Principles of Geology* in 1830. Lyell argued that the history of the earth needs to be reckoned not in thousands but in millions of years, thus making humanity a late arrival on earth rather than its first possessor. Lyell's arguments provided Charles Darwin with the timescale required for a theory of the development of human life from primeval slime, and when, after much hesitation, Darwin published *Origin of Species* in 1859, he concluded with a peroration about the 'forms most beautiful and wonderful' that have evolved on our planet as it went 'cycling on according to the fixed law of gravity', and he tried to assure his readers and himself that 'there is a grandeur in this view of life'.[5]

But that was not how everyone saw it. 'Old ladies, of both sexes, consider it a decidedly dangerous book', as T. H. Huxley wrote in an early review of *Origin*. Huxley suggested that Darwin was the nineteenth-century equivalent of Copernicus: his theory of the evolution of human life through natural selection was, he said, a challenge to cosy human illusions about the cosmic significance of humanity, just as Copernicus's idea of the earth as a planet going round the sun had been back in the sixteenth century.

> The myths of Paganism are as dead as Osiris or Zeus, and the man who should revive them, in opposition to the knowledge of our time, would be justly laughed to scorn; but the coeval imaginations current among the rude inhabitants of Palestine … have unfortunately not yet shared their fate. … Extinguished theologians lie about the cradle of every science as the strangled snakes beside that of Hercules; and history records that whenever science and dogmatism have been fairly opposed, the latter has been forced to retire from the lists, bleeding and crushed, if not annihilated; scotched, if not slain.[6]

Darwin relished the comment about 'extinguished theologians' – '*splendid*', he called it – and while he himself had no wish to antagonise the church, he did nothing to discourage his self-appointed disciple.[7]

The idea of Darwin as a second Copernicus soon took on a life of its own. The flamboyant German atheist, Ernst Haeckel, writing in 1868, insisted on regarding Darwinism as 'only a small fragment of a far more comprehensive doctrine' – a doctrine of 'monism', 'realism' or 'scientific materialism', which recognised that the universe as a whole was no more than a vast impersonal machine, sublimely indifferent to the happiness or indeed the existence of the human race.[8] Ten years later he elaborated on the parallel between Darwin and Copernicus: just as Copernicus had overthrown the 'geocentric idea of the universe,' he claimed, so Darwin had overthrown the 'anthropocentric idea … that man was the centre of the life of earth'.[9] Thanks to the efforts of the National Secular Society, founded in Britain in 1866, and of similar organisations all round the world, a certain idea of Copernicus and Darwin was built in to the foundations of twentieth-century atheism, and science itself was imagined as a stern disciplinarian, intent on cutting our aspirations down to size.

Sigmund Freud brought the story up to date in 1917 by applying it to the practice and theory of psychoanalysis.

> In the course of centuries the naïve self-love of men has had to submit to two major blows at the hands of science. The first was when they learnt that our earth was not the centre of the universe … . The second blow fell when biological research destroyed man's supposedly privileged place in creation and proved his descent from the animal kingdom. … But human megalomania will have suffered its third and most wounding blow from the psychological research of the present time which seeks to prove to the ego that it is not even master in its own house.[10]

But you did not have to be a Freudian to credit the figure of science with imperious cruelty. Bertrand Russell insisted on the point on many occasions, starting with an essay on 'A Free Man's Worship', first published in 1903. He spoke there of 'the savage' who is 'willing to prostrate himself before his gods, without inquiring whether they are worthy of his worship'. But then, he said, 'gradually, as morality grows bolder, the claim of the ideal world begins to be felt', only to find itself confronted by the hard world of fact, as described by what he called 'Science' (with a capital S). 'The world which Science presents for our belief', Russell said, is 'purposeless' and 'void of meaning'.

> Amid such a world, if anywhere, our ideals henceforward must find a home. That Man is the product of causes which had no prevision of the end they were achieving; that his origin, his growth, his hopes and fears, his loves and his beliefs, are but the outcome of accidental collocations of atoms; that no fire, no heroism, no intensity of thought and feeling, can preserve an individual life beyond the grave; that all the labours of the ages, all the devotion, all the inspiration, all the noonday brightness of human genius, are destined to extinction in the vast death of the solar system, and that the whole temple of Man's achievement must inevitably be buried beneath the debris of a universe in ruins – all these things, if not quite beyond dispute, are yet so nearly certain, that no philosophy which rejects them can hope to stand. Only within the scaffolding of these truths, only on the firm foundation of unyielding despair, can the soul's habitation henceforth be safely built.[11]

Many readers have felt stirred by Russell's portentous pathos – of all his works, 'Free Man's Worship' is still one of the most popular – but there is something rather contrived about it all the same. William James put his finger on it in an essay on 'The Will to Believe', where he voiced doubts about what he called the 'manly school of science' whose members (Huxley being a prime example) liked to imagine that their approach to knowledge was 'absolutely impersonal'. But that was a fatuous dream, according to James: our choice of what to believe is determined by what we want as well as what we know – and Russell was 'one of the finest exemplifiers I know'. James agreed with his friend Canning Schiller when he claimed that Russell's hatred of religion was 'at bottom emotional', and that, like all those who tried to make a drama out of their atheism, he was himself the victim of a virulent will-to-believe – namely, a 'will to believe whatever seems the harsher possibility'.[12] The anti-sentimentalist cult, from Huxley and Haeckel to Russell and Freud was, it would seem, an example of unbridled sentimentalism.

I don't know if we will ever learn to make a case for atheism without hitching it to some version of history, but I hope we will. I hope we will give up trying to define atheism in terms of an effort to put a distance between ourselves and the 'savages' postulated in their different ways by different philosophers – by Hume, for example, with his cheerful anticipation of an age of moderate scepticism, or by Russell with his sentimental cult of 'unyielding despair'. I hope we will stop thinking that we need to speculate about historic trends in public opinion before deciding what we ought to believe. And perhaps there are one or two precedents from which encouragement can be drawn.

The logician Frank Ramsey was in many ways a follower of Russell, and like him he was impressed by two great forces that he believed to have dominated intellectual life in the nineteenth century: 'one is the advance of science', he said, and 'the other the decay of religion'. But like James, he found Russell's rhetoric unpersuasive. 'Where I seem to differ from some of my friends is in attaching little importance to physical size', he wrote in 1925,

> I don't feel the least humble before the vastness of the heavens. The stars may be large, but they cannot think or love; and these are qualities which impress me far more than size does. I take no credit for weighing nearly seventeen stone. ... My picture of the world is drawn in perspective, and not like a model to scale. The foreground is occupied by human beings and the stars are all as small as threepenny bits. ... In time the world will cool and everything will die; but that is a long time off still, and its present value at compound discount is almost nothing.[13]

How you respond to the prospect of cosmic annihilation is, as Ramsey realised, a matter of mood rather than doctrine, or choice rather than fate, and it is perhaps more suited to poetry than to inflated philosophical prose.

Thomas Hardy is exemplary. He learned his atheism in the 1860s, from Hume, Darwin and Huxley amongst others; and while critics liked to call him a 'pessimist', he never accepted the description. He was impressed by the contingency of human existence, both individually and collectively, but he contemplated it not with raging gloom but with good-humoured equanimity: 'we are too old in apathy', as he put it in an early poem: 'mankind shall cease—so let it be.' He opened one of his last collections with a miniature poem called 'Waiting Both', which portrays a star looking down on an earthbound human being, and asking 'what do you mean to do?' The human being, impressed by the triviality of earthly existence and the majesty of the star, can see no prospect but to 'wait, and let time go by, till my change come.' But it turns out that the star is equally overawed: 'just so', the star says: 'so mean I.' History may be on our side, or it may not, but either way, as Hardy once said: 'one dares not prophesy.'[14]

Oddly enough, we atheists persist in prophesying in spite of everything. We may pride ourselves on our evidence-driven rationality, but we still like to presume that religious belief is bound to disappear with the passage of time. We help ourselves to a notion that began as a philosophical conjecture in the eighteenth century – a notion that may once have seemed to reflect real developments in modern industrial cultures, though it has been decisively falsified in the past fifty years by the rise all round the world of dogmatic religiosity. But the fact that it happens to be false is not the worst thing about the atheist sense of history: even more damaging is the way it encourages us atheists to confine ourselves to an intellectual ghetto. It encourages us to presume that the entirety of non-atheist thought can be dumped in a bin called 'superstition', and to imagine that atheist enlightenment sprang fully armed from immaculate fact and reason, rather than emerging from massive networks of discussion in which, as a matter of historical fact, it is often impossible to draw a line between religionists and their opponents, or to work out which insights belong to which side. As we struggle to make sense of our tangled intellectual inheritance, we ought to recognise that we are all in it together.

Notes

1 James Boswell, 'An account of my last interview with David Hume, Esq.', in *Private Papers of James Boswell*, ed. Geoffrey Scott and Frederick A. Pottle, 18 vols, privately printed, vol. 12 (1931): 227–32.
2 'Letter from Adam Smith, to William Strahan, Esq.', in *The Life of David Hume, Esq., written by himself* (London: W. Strahan and T. Cadell, 1777), 37–62.
3 Adam Smith, *Lectures on Rhetoric and Belles Lettres*, ed. J. C. Bryce, from student notes made in 1762 (Oxford: Oxford University Press, 1983), 9–13 (lecture 3).
4 David Hume, 'The Natural History of Religion', *Four Dissertations* (London: A. Millar, 1757), edited by J. C. A. Gaskin, in *Principal Writings on Religion* (Oxford: Oxford University Press, 1998), 134–6, 150, 168, 185.
5 Charles Darwin, *On the Origin of Species by means of Natural Selection, or the preservation of favoured races in the struggle for life* (London: John Murray, 1859), 490.
6 [T. H. Huxley], 'Darwin on the Origin of Species', *Westminster Review* (April 1860): 541–70, at 541, 569, 556.
7 Darwin to Huxley, 14 April 1860, Darwin Correspondence Project, electronic resource, Cambridge University Library, <https://www.darwinproject.ac.uk/letter/?docId=letters/DCP-LETT-2760.xml;query=Huxley%2014%20April%201860;brand=defaul>.
8 Ernst Haeckel, *Natürlichen Schöpfungsgeschichte* (Berlin, 1868), translated as *The History of Creation* by a 'young lady', revised by E. Ray Lankester, 2 vols (London: Henry S. King, 1876), vol. 1, at 1–2, 35, 37.
9 Ernst Haeckel, *The Pedigree of Man: and Other Essays* (1878), trans. Edward B. Aveling (London: Freethought Publishing Co., 1883), 52; the theme was later promoted by Emil du Bois-Reymond, who got into trouble for a lecture on 'Darwin und Copernicus' at the Berlin Academy of Sciences in 1883; see Gabriel Finkelstein, *Emil du Bois-Reymond: Neuroscience, Self, and Society in Nineteenth-Century Germany* (Cambridge, MA: MIT Press, 2013), 254–5.
10 *Introductory Lectures on Psychoanalysis* (1916–17), trans. James Strachey (1920; Harmondsworth: Penguin, 1971), 326 (lecture 18); the same point is made in 'A Difficulty in the Path of Psychoanalysis' (1917), *Standard Edition*, vol. 17: 137–44.
11 'A Free Man's Worship' (1903), in *Mysticism and Logic* (London: George Allen & Unwin, 1917).
12 William James, 'The Will to Believe', in *The Will to Believe, and Other Essays in Popular Philosophy* (New York: Longmans, Green, 1897), 7 (first published in *New World* 5 (June 1896): 327–47); letter from Russell to James, 22 July 1909; James to F. C. S. Schiller, 19 December 1909; and Schiller to James, 19 December 1909, in *Correspondence of William James*, ed. Ignas K. Skrupskelis and Elizabeth M. Berkeley (Charlottesville: University Press of Virginia, 2004), vol. 12, at 294, 393.

13 Paper read to Cambridge Apostles, 28 February 1925, printed as 'Epilogue' in Frank Plumpton Ramsey, *The Foundations of Mathematics and Other Logical Essays*, ed. R. B. Braithwaite (London: Kegan Paul, Trench, Trubner & Co., 1931), 287–92.

14 'I said to Love', *Poems of the Past and the Present* (1901), in *The Collected Poems of Thomas Hardy* (London: Macmillan, 1939), 103–4; see also 'God's Funeral', *Satires of Circumstance, Lyrics and Reveries* (1914), in *Collected Poems*, 307–9; 'Waiting Both', *Human Shows, Far Phantasies, Songs and Trifles* (1925), in *Collected Poems*, 665; 'Apology', introduction to *Late Lyrics and Earlier* (1922), in *Collected Poems*, 532.

6 Atheism and naturalism

Fiona Ellis

Preliminaries

It has long been supposed that atheism and naturalism stand in the closest connection.[1] Thus, John Herman Randall Jr, writing in 1944, tells us that 'there is no room for any Supernatural in naturalism – no supernatural or transcendental God and no personal survival after death', and that the position 'finds itself in thoroughgoing opposition to all forms of thought which assert the existence of a supernatural or transcendental Realm of Being and make knowledge of that realm of fundamental importance to human living'.[2] More recently, and in similar anti-supernaturalist vein, we are told that 'the most familiar definition is in terms of the rejection of supernatural entities such as gods, demons, souls, and ghosts';[3] that '[n]aturalism on any reading is opposed to supernaturalism', supernaturalism involving 'the invocation of an agent or force that somehow stands outside the familiar natural world and whose doings cannot be understood as part of it';[4] and that '[e]xcluded by anti-supernaturalism are such things as immaterial minds or souls, vital forces, and divine beings'.[5]

So the naturalist – or at least, the typical naturalist – is opposed to supernaturalism, and this involves a rejection of supernatural entities like gods, demons, souls, and ghosts. This leaves us with 'the familiar natural world' in which we live and move and have our being, and we are encouraged to suppose that the position is both eminently sensible and intellectually superior. As James Griffin has put it, it is an admirable and deep motive force behind naturalism that we do not need

> any world except the ordinary world around us – mainly the world of humans and animals and happenings in their lives. An other-worldly realm ... just produces unnecessary problems about what it could possibly be and how we could learn about it.[6]

The implication here is that the naturalist is simply removing from our ontology a superfluous and problematic *something else* – a supernatural realm of being which, for the unenlightened amongst us, is of fundamental importance both to reality in general and human living in particular. Small wonder that naturalism 'has become a slogan in the name of which the vast majority of work in analytic philosophy is pursued',[7] featuring 'what many believe to be the strongest and most promising achievements of twentieth century Anglo-American philosophy'.[8]

We have a sense of what the naturalist is seeking to avoid, and an equal sense that its underlying motive is to be applauded. After all, it is surely a good thing to be removing from our ontology realms and items that we do not need. What is less clear is how we are to determine what stands to be eliminated in this way. Ghosts, demons, and gods seem reasonable enough contenders, but what about vital forces and what about God? Are these things superfluous and problematic? And how can we legislate upon what counts as such without first having a clearly defined conception of the nature and limits of the supposedly familiar and unproblematic natural world?

The naturalism in the name of which the vast majority of work in analytic philosophy is pursued has tended to be defined in exclusively scientific terms. Thus we are told by Randall that the naturalist's creed presupposes 'reliance on an unrestricted scientific method and the consequent rejection of any form of supernaturalism',[9] and the editors of a recent collection claim that the position involves 'a commitment to an exclusively scientific conception of nature' (the ontological theme), and 'a reconception of the traditional relation between philosophy and science according to which philosophical enquiry is conceived of as continuous with science' (the methodological theme).[10]

The question of the limits of science is no less problematic than that of the limits of nature, and it is understandable that there has been disagreement over what it could mean to commit to an exclusively scientific conception of nature and an unrestricted scientific method. According to one way of thinking, we should all be reductive materialists or materialist naturalists. As Thomas Nagel puts it, 'among the scientists and philosophers who do express views about the natural order as a whole, reductive materialism is widely assumed to be the only serious possibility'.[11] Reductive materialism admits of various characterisations, ranging from David Armstrong's 'the natural world contains nothing but the entities recognised by physics'[12] to John Dupré's more recent 'if there is only material stuff in the world (no spooky stuff), then the properties of stuff must ultimately explain everything'.[13] Dupré challenges Nagel's account of the position's supposed prevalence, objecting that it expresses a once popular view which has been 'almost entirely rejected by philosophers actually engaged with the physical and biological sciences: it simply has no interesting relation to the diversity of things that scientists actually do'.[14] We are to suppose that the scientists themselves have moved beyond this paradigm, although Dupré claims elsewhere that its reductive spirit continues to animate philosophical thought,[15] and a recent interview in *Scientific American* finds the physicist George Ellis bemoaning the fact that many of his fellow scientists remain 'strong reductionists'.[16]

The strong reductionist takes the measure of nature to be physics. A more moderate naturalism defines this measure with reference to a broader conception of science (Why just physics? How on earth could that explain everything? And what reason could be given for insisting upon this restriction?); and an even more moderate position challenges the assumption that the offending restriction can be lifted only in terms which are themselves restricted by science (Why just science? How on earth could that explain everything? And what reason could be given for insisting upon this restriction?). It is in the context of giving expression to these anti-scientistic complaints that we find John McDowell recommending that we 'discourag(e) this dazzlement by science' which leads us to suppose that 'genuine truth is restricted to what can be validated by their methods'.[17] It should go without saying that this is not a rejection of science.

The atheist and scientist Richard Dawkins has been suitably and familiarly dazzled. Thus, he insists that 'God's existence or non-existence is a scientific fact about the universe ... the presence or absence of a creative super-intelligence is unequivocally a scientific question';[18] his professed aim being to 'attack ... God, all gods, anything and everything supernatural, wherever and whenever they have been or will be invented'.[19] For Dawkins then, the scientific fact about the universe is that God is absent from its domain, and he concludes on this basis that atheism must be embraced. His attitude would be embraced by those naturalists who insist that the limits of nature are to be circumscribed by science, and they express a similar antipathy towards 'anything and everything supernatural'. As noted, however, the limits of science are themselves in question, and even supposing that we have a relatively clear grasp upon what counts as science and what does not, there is no justification for launching the kind of attack Dawkins has in mind. For if 'supernatural' is the logical complement of 'natural' in the scientific sense, then the astounding claim is that what comes under attack is anything which does not fall within the explanatory domain of science.

McDowell and Griffin reject scientistic naturalism, but they are happy to describe themselves as naturalists. After all, naturalism is motivated by the admirable thought that we do not need any world except the ordinary world around us, and that an other-worldly realm just produces unnecessary problems about what it could possibly be and how we could learn about it. It should be clear from what has been said that the distinction between what is intra- and other-worldly is ill-defined, and that the more liberal or expansive naturalist rejects the scientific naturalist's conception of these notions. That is to say, he denies that the scientist has the monopoly on nature/world, and must deny therefore that an other-worldly realm comes into play whenever these scientistic strictures are dropped. So the expansive naturalist is a supernaturalist from the perspective of scientific naturalism, for he insists that we precisely *do* need something more than the world as comprehended by science. However, he would deny that this 'more' is to be located in a second, supernatural, realm, for his conception of nature exceeds the limits of scientific naturalism, granting him the right to say that it is *this* world – the familiar ordinary world – which is to be comprehended in these more expansive terms. As Griffin puts it, 'the boundaries of the "natural" are pushed outward a bit, in a duly motivated way'.[20]

The natural world thus conceived incorporates value, an important focus of these naturalists being the moral values which come into play when beings like ourselves make moral distinctions and respond accordingly. It is granted that science has some role to play in explaining the relevant responses, the human sciences being of particular significance in this context.[21] What is denied, however, is that it can cover all the explanatory ground – a concession which becomes rather less daunting once it is allowed that there is more to explanation and reality than what the scientist comprehends.

Value is an essential part of the expansive naturalist's picture, but he agrees with his scientistic opponent that the natural world must be shorn of any reference to gods and God, and we are encouraged to suppose that a move in either of these directions is both unnecessary and problematic. The charge is familiar, and in what follows I want to grant with the naturalist that we should be resisting unnecessary and problematic expansions, but deny that it follows from this that naturalism must be atheistic. In short, I shall argue that the expansive naturalist is operating with a deficient conception of God, namely, one according to which God is an unnecessary and problematic *something else,* that such items merit rejection, but that it does not follow from this that we must reject reference to God. As I shall spell out below, my argumentative strategy in this context involves following the structure of the expansive naturalist's response to the charge that his own expanded conception of nature raises similar difficulties, my claim being that *his* objection to theistic naturalism invites an analogous response. To put it another way, I am suggesting that there is scope for allowing that nature is God-involving as well as being value-involving, that this move can be defended on (liberal) naturalistic grounds, and hence, that the expansive naturalist has every reason to take this option seriously.

Naturalism and God

McDowell is too good a philosopher to insist upon the truth of atheism, and we find him using the imagery of darkness to refer to that which exceeds the limits of his more relaxed conception of nature – 'the region of darkness' as he describes it.[22] It is here that we are returned to his own preferred conception of the meaning of 'natural', namely, 'not supernatural (not occult, not magical)', and he adds that:

> [t]here is no need for me to take a stand on whether *everything* is natural in that sense (thereby, among other things, giving needless offence to people who think respect for modern science is compatible with a kind of religious belief that preserves room for the supernatural.[23]

The imagery of darkness would suit the apophatic theologian, but McDowell is no such thing – intentionally at least – and seems to believe that this mysterious dimension, such as it is, could have no bearing upon nature and our natural human being. It is, after all, 'occult' and 'magical', and it calls to mind the 'rampant platonism' he criticises elsewhere, with its implication that our lives are 'mysteriously split, somehow taking place both in nature and in some alien realm – in "Plato's Heaven" perhaps'.[24]

McDowell's criticisms of the supernatural are structurally equivalent to those of the scientific naturalist when he objects to the values which form part of the expansive naturalist's ontology on the ground that they, too, are 'occult' and 'magical' (the word 'spooky' is the more usual term of abuse). Thus, we find Peter Railton, in the context of a dialogue with David Wiggins, bemoaning the 'worrisome ontological expansion' which ensues if we exceed his own preferred social-scientific terms, to which he adds that that we can explain everything that needs to be explained about value without making this problematic move – the relevant entities just produce unnecessary problems about what they could possibly be and how we could learn about them.[25] The refrain is getting familiar.

What does this have to do with God? Well, the expansive naturalist's conception of 'religious reality' (to coin a phrase) turns it into something occult and alien – i.e. supernatural in the pejorative sense. But what if this conception can be challenged in the way that *he* challenges the scientific naturalist's understanding of his own preferred conception of value? The expansive naturalist could try to block this parallel by objecting that the two cases are completely different – God is 'occult' and 'alien' in a way that value is not. Yet this response simply begs the question against the possibility of an alternative framework – one which challenges the assumption that God must be viewed in these pejorative terms and hence, that nature must exclude Him.

Does this not lead to a form of pantheism? After all, the naturalist is committed to a one-world position, and I seem to be suggesting that God can be accommodated within such a framework. The theist is no pantheist, but he denies that God sits alongside nature to create the unnecessary problems to which Griffin refers – as if it is a matter of adding an irrelevant and alien realm to the familiar natural world.[26] Rather, it is *this* world which is God-involving, God being actively present in all things. So God is rescued from 'some alien realm', but He is not reducible to the world in which He is present, for He is its source and sustainer, and, as such, to be distinguished from anything within it, or indeed, beyond it.[27] The theist will claim further that we can enter into loving fellowship with this actively present God, that our receptivity in this context brings personal transformation, and that this transformation is expressed most significantly at the level of morality. Indeed, we shall find Emmanuel Levinas claiming that being moral is the *only* way of relating authentically to God, anxious as he is to deflate the cognitive pretensions of those for whom God is a mere object of theory.[28]

Levinas offers a salutary reminder of our cognitive limitations in this context, and his example will be important when we consider what it could really mean to be a theistic naturalist. I am certainly not suggesting that there is an easy route to theism, nor that the difficulties it confronts are not genuine. My aim at this stage is simply to make clear that the typical naturalist's conception of these difficulties can be challenged, and that once we move beyond the unduly restrictive parameters of scientism, there is scope for questioning the assumption that an expansion in the direction of God is bound to be philosophically disastrous. If the expansive naturalist has shown us anything at all it is that the limits of nature are entirely unclear.

A worry and a response

The limits of nature may well be unclear, but there is a further reason for resisting the kind of move I am recommending, namely, that it goes against the prevalent assumption that naturalism and theism are logically incompatible. After all, it is standard in philosophy of religion today to define 'naturalism' in a way that excludes the existence of God or gods.[29] It is standard also to suppose that naturalism is equivalent to scientific naturalism, and my response to this worry takes us back to what has been said already. The scientific naturalist does not have the monopoly on the meaning of this term, and recent philosophy testifies to its pliability. So its meaning is hardly fixed, and those who have embraced the term to their own particular ends have done so with an eye to the advantages it procures. In particular, it gives their philosophical endeavours the seal of empirical respectability. This meaning has not been stretched in a theistic direction – at least not by contemporary naturalists – and reservations on this score are therefore understandable.[30] However, this does not rule out such a move, and if I am right then there are naturalistic arguments to this end – on a suitably expanded conception thereof. The virtues of this move should be apparent. For we are in a position to challenge the conclusion – common to most naturalists – that talk of God belongs to the realm of idle metaphysics, that it comprises an esoteric discipline which is irrelevant to what really matters, and that it has no bearing upon the question of nature and of our natural human being.

A further notable advantage of my approach is that it offers the prospects for defending a theistic framework using philosophical resources which can genuinely appeal to an atheist – at least, one who has moved beyond the limits of scientistic naturalism. This point has been of particular significance to me. I have long been persuaded that there is nothing remotely pernicious or embarrassing about metaphysical enquiry per se, and that reference to Plato's heaven or the Kingdom of God need not spell inevitable philosophical disaster. At the same time, however, I am aware of how problematic these notions can sound to contemporary philosophical ears. What better way to vindicate them than by reference to a metaphysical framework which demands no more than a resistance to scientism, a spirit of open-mindedness, and a preparedness to go where one's arguments lead? I also find it ironic and amusing that the best philosophical defence of the position towards which I have been gradually moving should come from a way of thinking which, at one level at least, will have nothing to do with God. Of course, this refusal concedes nothing to the vitriolic tendencies of the militant atheist – understandably so given that the philosophers in question have no particular axe to grind, and have seen through the fundamentalist faith which tends to drive such attacks. Rather, and in true phenomenological spirit, they seek to return us to the things themselves, guarding against the imposition of frameworks which preclude the possibility of meeting such an aim. It is in the context of appreciating this methodological stance that we can begin to appreciate the theistic significance of their claims. Or so I contend.[31]

Atheism, theism, and Levinas

This is all very well, but I have said next to nothing about God, other than to make clear what He is not, and to claim that He is actively present in all things without being reducible to them. I have also made a point of mentioning Levinas's worries about saying anything at all in this context, and his idea that we relate to God *only* at the level of morality. The idea that we relate to God *only* at this level must surely compromise the possibility of moving in the direction of theism. After all, the secular expansive naturalist operates at the level of morality, and his framework does not involve God. It remains open that the secular expansive naturalist is wrong about this, but if we add to the equation that God-talk is excluded, then it is difficult to see how the relevant difference can be made out. It is surely a condition upon defending a theistic form of naturalism that it can be expressed.

Levinas counts as a theist in the sense that he operates with a God-involving conception of reality, and he makes no bones about this dimension of his position. However, he is suspicious of the cognitive pretensions of theology, and anxious to distance himself from the invented gods of our wishful and egoistic thinking.[32] He would object that these inventions make for the most pernicious form of atheism, pernicious in the sense that it is so easily mistaken for its opposite, offering easy canon fodder to those who see theism as a position for the intellectually challenged – witness the diatribes of Dawkins and his ilk. It is in the context of appreciating this point that we can see the significance of a kind of atheism which, for Levinas, has more profound theistic significance, namely, that which 'void[s] ... the child's heaven' so that we are no longer beholden to the offending idols. God is said to 'retire ... from the world' in this sense, and to 'hide His face'. All the better to be revealed, we are to suppose, the revelation in question involving 'a God who renounces all aids to manifestation, and appeals instead to the full maturity of the responsible man'.[33] It is Levinas's contention that we relate to God – and know Him – by being moral, the implication being that this is the *only* such way:

> Ethics is not the corollary of the vision of God, it is that very vision. Ethics is an optic, such that everything I know of God and everything I can hear of His word and reasonably say to Him must find an ethical expression ... to know God is to know what is to be done.[34]

Levinas exposes the limitations of any position which treats God as just one more item within or beyond the world, applauding the removal of the familiar and offending other-worldly realms. So he agrees with the naturalist that we should be anti-supernaturalists in this sense, but he denies that this involves rejecting God, God being revealed in our moral interactions with others. As he sees it then, atheism is not invariably opposed to theism, and theism is most authentically expressed at the level of morality.

If this is right, then the secular expansive naturalist is a closet theist, and the move I am recommending we make on his behalf has already been completed. It seems equally plausible, however, to protest that the theism at issue here is indiscernible from atheism, and that such a theism is unworthy of the name. This sceptical response is understandable, but it presupposes that the question of value is closed, that it has nothing to do with God, and that it is entirely clear in any case what it means to bring God to the equation. The themes with which we began – the nature and limits of nature and value – make it clear that all of these questions remain open, the central issue here being whether there is a conception of God which improves upon the crude supernaturalist model to which the typical naturalist is in thrall. It would therefore beg the very question at issue to insist that we know exactly what it means – or could not mean – to describe nature in God-involving terms.

But don't we need to say something about God himself rather than simply focusing upon our moral responses? And wouldn't *this* offer a more fruitful way of clarifying the distinction between atheism and theism? I have already acknowledged Levinas's reservations about theology, while noting that he is happy to describe his position in God-involving terms. So there is a clear enough sense in which he is talking about God, and it is no part of his position that the God to which he refers is a mere idol (i.e. something less than God). Crucially, however, he believes that there are limits to what can be said if we are to avoid these lesser gods, and that whatever we do say in this context must be commensurate with the reality we are struggling to comprehend. Levinas is prepared to acknowledge that this reality is both infinite and moral, but he denies that it can be adequately appreciated in theoretical terms. Why? Because God cannot be reduced to an object of theory, and His irreducibly moral dimension must be reflected in our knowledge: to know God is to know what is to be done. Or as he puts it elsewhere, '[t]he infinite is not "in front of me"; it is I who express it'.[35]

All of this is to say rather a lot about God, and Levinas goes on to make further claims which are problematic even by theistic lights.[36] What is significant about his position from my point of view is the knife edge which separates it from secular expansive naturalism, and the questions it raises for an understanding of the atheism/theism debate. There are certainly no knock-down arguments in the offing – in either direction, it must be stressed. However, this follows from the nature of the case at hand, it being fundamental to the question of God that hard and fast conclusions are excluded. The dogmatic atheist should bear this in mind, and bear in mind also that the position to which he so desperately clings may not be the end of wisdom even if it is the beginning.

Notes

1 Some of these claims are developed in chapter 1 of my *God, Value, and Nature* (Oxford: Oxford University Press, 2014).
2 John Herman Randall Jr, 'Epilogue: The Nature of Naturalism', in Yervant H. Krikorian (ed.), *Naturalism and the Human Spirit* (New York: Columbia University Press, 1944), 358.
3 Mario De Caro and David Macarthur, 'Introduction: The Nature of Naturalism', in Mario De Caro and David Macarthur (eds), *Naturalism in Question* (Cambridge, MA: Harvard University Press, 2004), 2.
4 Barry Stroud, 'The Charm of Naturalism', in Mario De Caro and David Macarthur (eds), *Naturalism in Question* (Cambridge, MA: Harvard University Press, 2004), 23.
5 John Dupré, 'How to Be Naturalistic without Being Simplistic in the Study of Human Nature', in Mario De Caro and David Macarthur (eds), *Naturalism and Normativity* (New York: Columbia University Press, 2010), 290.
6 James Griffin, *Value Judgement: Improving our Ethical Beliefs* (Oxford: Oxford University Press, 1996), 43–4.
7 De Caro and Macarthur, 'Introduction: The Nature of Naturalism', 2.
8 Richard Bernstein, 'Whatever Happened to Naturalism?', *Proceedings and Addresses of the American Philosophical Association* 69, no. 2 (November 1995): 57–76, at 58.
9 Randall, 'Epilogue: The Nature of Naturalism', 358.
10 De Caro and Macarthur, 'Introduction: The Nature of Naturalism', 3.
11 Thomas Nagel, *Mind and Cosmos: Why the Materialist Neo-Darwinian Conception of Nature is Almost Certainly False* (New York: Oxford University Press, 2012), 4.
12 D. M. Armstrong, 'Naturalism, Materialism, and First Philosophy', in *The Nature of Mind and Other Essays* (St Lucia: University of Queensland Press, 1980), 156.
13 John Dupré, review of *Mind and Cosmos: Why the Materialist Neo-Darwinian Conception of Nature is Almost Certainly False*, by Thomas Nagel, *Notre Dame Philosophical Reviews* [online journal], 29 October 2012, <https://ndpr.nd.edu/news/35163-mind-and-cosmos-why-the-materialist-neo-darwinian-conception-of-nature-is-almost-certainly-false/>.
14 One of the clearest and most decisive challenges to such a position is to be found in Barry Stroud's 'The Physical World', *Proceedings of the Aristotelian Society*, n.s., 87 (1986–87): 263–77.
15 See John Dupré, 'The Miracle of Monism', in Mario De Caro and David Macarthur (eds), *Naturalism in Question* (Cambridge, MA: Harvard University Press, 2004), 46–7.
16 Interview with John Horgan, 'Physicist George Ellis Knocks Physicists for Knocking Philosophy, Falsification, Free Will', *Scientific American*, 22 July 2014, <http://blogs.scientificamerican.com/cross-check/2014/07/22/physicist-george-ellis-knocks-physicists-for-knocking-philosophy-free-will/>.
17 John McDowell, 'Responses' (response to Charles Lamore), in Nicholas H. Smith (ed.), *Reading McDowell on Mind and World* (London: Routledge, 2002), 295.
18 Richard Dawkins, *The God Delusion* (London: Bantam Press, 2006), 50–8.
19 Dawkins, *God Delusion*, 36.
20 Griffin, *Value Judgement*, 51.
21 See chapter 2 of my *God, Value, and Nature* for a detailed discussion of the human sciences in this context.

22 John McDowell, 'Responses' (response to Fink), in Jakob Lindgaard (ed.), *John McDowell: Experience, Norm, and Nature* (Oxford: Blackwell, 2008), 217. I take this part of the discussion from chapter 4 of *God, Value, and Nature.*

23 McDowell, 'Responses' (response to Fink), 218.

24 John McDowell, 'Two Sorts of Naturalism', in *Mind, Value, and Reality* (Cambridge, MA: Harvard University Press, 1998), 177.

25 Witness Railton: '[i]f for example, moral facts are identified with – or otherwise reducible to natural facts, then there is no special mystery about what sort of thing they are, or how we come to have knowledge of them, refer to them, and so on … If moral facts are identical with – or otherwise reducible to – natural facts, then cognitivism may be possible without worrisome ontological expansion' ('What the Non-cognitivist Helps Us to See the Naturalist Must Help Us to Explain', in John Haldane and Crispin Wright (eds), *Reality, Representation, and Projection* (Oxford: Oxford University Press, 1993), 280). See chapter 2 of my *God, Value, and Nature* for a more detailed and not entirely unsympathetic discussion of Railton's position.

26 Compare Karl Rahner: '*That* God really does not exist who operates and functions as an individual existent alongside other existents, and who would thus as it were be a member of the larger household of all reality. Anyone in search of such a God is searching for a false God. Both atheism and a more naïve form of theism labour under the same false notion of God, only the former denies it while the latter believes it can make sense of it' (*Foundations of Christian Faith: An Introduction to the Idea of Christianity*, trans. William V. Dych (London: Darton, Longman & Todd, 1978), 63).

27 Hence Herbert McCabe: 'If God is whatever answers our question, how come everything? Then evidently he is not to be included amongst everything. God cannot be a thing, an existent among others. It is not possible that God and the universe should add up to two' ('Creation', in *God Matters* (London: Continuum Press, 1987), 6).

28 Hence we are told that to know God is to know what is to be done (Emmanuel Levinas, 'A Religion for Adults', in *Difficult Freedom: Essays on Judaism*, trans. Seán Hand (Baltimore, MD: Johns Hopkins University Press, 1990), 17), and that 'there can be no "knowledge" of God separated from the relationship with men' (Emmanuel Levinas, *Totality and Infinity*, trans. Alphonso Lingis (Pittsburgh, PA: Duquesne University Press, 1969), 78).

29 See, for example, Alvin Plantinga, *Where the Conflict Really Lies: Science, Religion, and Naturalism* (Oxford: Oxford University Press, 2011).

30 Robert S. Corrington is a contemporary exception, although he comes from a very different perspective from that of the naturalists with which I am concerned. See his *Nature and Spirit: An Essay in Ecstatic Naturalism* (New York: Fordham University Press, 1992). The ecstatic naturalist, we are told, 'has a special kind of openness to what can never be circumscribed. In addition, an ecstatic naturalist recognizes that almost all philosophical theology has taken the wrong tack towards the nature/divine correlation' ('An Introduction to Ecstatic Naturalism: Interview with Robert S. Corrington', *Kinesis* 36, no. 1 (2009), 28). I would be happy to describe myself as an ecstatic naturalist according to the first criterion, but it is no part of my position that almost all philosophical theology has taken the wrong tack in this context.

31 And so I argue, at considerable length, in my *God, Value, and Nature.*

32 This is clearly spelled out in the essays Emmanuel Levinas, 'Loving the Torah More than God' and 'A Religion for Adults', both of which are to be found in the collection *Difficult Freedom: Essays on Judaism*, trans. Seán Hand (Baltimore, MD: Johns Hopkins University Press, 1990).

33 Levinas, 'Loving the Torah More than God', 143.
34 Levinas, 'Religion for Adults', 17.
35 Emmanuel Levinas, 'God and Philosophy', in *Of God Who Comes to Mind*, trans. Bettina Bergo (Stanford, CA: Stanford University Press, 1998), 75.
36 See chapters 5 and 6 of my *God, Value, and Nature* for details of these criticisms.

7   The compatibility of science and religion?

Fern Elsdon-Baker

Over the past few decades, representations of atheistic worldviews have become, to a degree, synonymous with a scientific worldview. This is not entirely surprising given the rhetoric of high-profile 'new atheist' commentators and science communicators like Richard Dawkins, who professedly have a foot in both camps. However, while it is one thing to represent atheists as seeking to adopt a scientific way of thinking about the world as part of their broader worldview, it is an entirely different proposition to represent a scientific worldview as being in and of itself a necessarily atheistic position. Unfortunately, this important distinction has become increasingly blurred in public debate, with these two different, but historically dispersed, intellectual traditions becoming inextricably linked in some aspects of recent public commentary. As a result, one could be forgiven for expecting that science must be in some kind of inevitable and ongoing conflict with religion.

Therefore, the very proposition that science and religion could be seen as compatible is fraught with difficulties. Often, people feel those proposing any kind of compatibility have some kind of religious agenda; the argument being that to do so is to either suggest that we should be importing religious thinking into scientific reasoning, or conversely, that we should be utilising scientific evidence to uphold religious doctrinal stances. Both of these positions are rightly criticised, but they are not the only ways in which science and religion could be seen to be compatible. Nevertheless, this overly simplistic model of how we might think about the relationship between science and religion has unfortunately tended to dominate the mainstream representation of any sorts of discussion about compatibility between science and religion. In part this springs from the way in which people tend to discuss 'science' and 'religion' as rather abstract concepts that are seemingly detached from our day-to-day lives, almost like two external sources of knowledge that are warring away on a latter-day Mount Olympus. This reduces both science and religion to distant, untouchable and equally dogmatic authorities in a battle to the death in which the winning combatant can take the ultimate prize – a claim to enlighten us of that equally abstract concept the Truth. This is, of course, nonsense, as the social world in which we live is far more complex and does not operate like this. It doesn't take much to realise that aspects of scientific and/or religious worldviews can, and do, similarly inform our day-to-day decisions – both large and small – at the level of individuals, community and society. Clearly, if science and religion were so wholly incompatible as some of religion's stauncher critics might have us believe, we as a society and as species would have probably ground to a halt some time ago.

Before I expand what I mean any further I think it is vitally important to make clear my own position and agendas in this debate. My primary concern when it comes to the relationship between science and religion is to build a better understanding of what might act as a barrier to dialogue or conversations between the two. This is in part because I am concerned about what hidden barriers may be in place that act to exclude people from a diversity of backgrounds and worldviews from engaging with contemporary scientific or medical research. Related to this, I am also concerned about prejudice towards those of faith in the name of science. I am myself a lifelong atheist, who grew up in a household of scientists, but I am not anti-religious. I have, perhaps unusually, worked in roles seeking to communicate evolutionary science internationally and in other roles seeking to build interfaith dialogue between all faiths and none. And it is that diversity of personal experience alongside my own philosophical and empirical research in this area that I am reflecting on in this chapter.

To tackle this thorny notion of compatibility between science and religion, I think we first need to go back to basics and ask: what do we mean by 'science', what do we mean by 'religion' and what do we mean by 'compatibility'.

Firstly, let's unpack a little what we mean when we use the term 'religion' both in everyday discussions and scholarly research.

It has been recognised for a long time by sociologists of religion that we cannot simply reduce religion or religious identity to adherence to a doctrinal or scriptural position. Religion and religious identities serve lots of different functions in society that don't simply boil down to the application of scripture to everyday lives. There are far more multifaceted ways in which religious beliefs play out in the lives of believers, or as we might think of it the 'lived experience' of religion. Religious identity can often have more to do with religious practices – diet, prayer, meditation, festivals or fasts – or the sense of belonging to a wider community that these practices also bring, than with specific scriptural or doctrinal positions.

There is also another problem with reducing religion to scripture. Not all of the worldviews we might seek to categorise as religion have scriptures, doctrine or systems of authority that are available to interpret texts – Buddhism is a classic example that is often used here.

Furthermore, when we talk about religion in society we might also be thinking about any form of spiritual belief or supernatural way of thinking about the universe that informs an individual's day-to-day life or the way they make meaning of their life, society and the world around us. This would include any people who might identify as non-religious but still incorporate a belief in things that may be seen to be beyond the realm of what we can empirically test in the natural world, e.g. ghosts, a human soul or life after death.[1]

A religious or spiritual identity can be involved in a whole range of different processes that relate to beliefs, belonging and meaning-making. Religious or spiritual identity can often be part of performative practice, or act as part of a national identity. Alternatively, it can be a more fuzzy notion of a sense of purpose or meaning to the universe and life, or an internal individual spiritual notion of gods, deities or organising structure.

While an individual's religious or spiritual identity can be an important, or even primary, aspect in the way they represent themselves to the world or make decisions on a daily basis, it is important to remember that it is not the only identity individuals have. We all have a mixture of different identities that come to the fore depending on our context or who we are with. I will variably and in multiple ways see myself as a woman, a manager, a friend, a daughter, an academic, a sister, British, a sci-fi geek, an atheist etcetera – all dependent upon where I am and my relationship with, or self-comparison to, others who may be with me. So a religious, spiritual or non-religious identity can be just another worldview or characteristic among many that inform our day-to-day decision-making or the way in which we represent ourselves to others or indeed to ourselves. However, this is not to downplay that these kinds of religious or spiritual worldviews or identities are, and continue to be, significant – if not primary – for the majority of the world's population.

Therefore, the term 'religion' can be used to represent many different things in our day-to-day lives beyond just scriptural or doctrinal positions. It also encompasses social and political identities, practices, a sense of community or belonging, meaning-making and beliefs. It can also include what we might think of as spiritual and non-religious beliefs.

Surely how we think about science is a lot less complicated. It is after all just simply a methodology, a process of empirical observation and experimentation that can help us make predictions about the world around us? Clearly, scientific research is a very useful tool for helping us to understand the nature of things and can tell us something about natural and social phenomena. However, there is a perhaps rather outdated notion, that science is in some way entirely and inexplicably separate from society, that tends to pervade the way we think about scientific knowledge and the scientist's role as part of our culture. Scientific knowledge is not just an abstract idea – a way of knowing about the universe – but it is also applied by us to the way we make meaning of our lives, the universe and everything. Over the years scientific research has been used to support various notions about societal and political progress, how we should live our lives, how we should make decisions about matters of life and death and how societies should function. These questions have in turn informed the direction of scientific funding, what are seen as the most relevant or most pressing avenues of research and of course by proxy the very nature of the kind of scientific knowledge that we generate. So the role science plays in society and culture is clearly not just as a set of untouchable objective theories.

It is also of course a practice, with a growing and increasingly diverse global workforce. It is and has been an important facet of industry and is arguably a driver of GDP. A very significant proportion of what we might think of as scientific research happens outside of the ivory towers of academia and actually takes place in non-academic business research settings. So we need to ditch these notions of glorious and sanctified lone geniuses selflessly striving for knowledge and truth. Scientists are real people too, with a whole array of multiple identities of which being a scientist is only one.

When we use the term 'science' it tends to refer to a big fuzzy mass of activities that include physical and natural sciences, social sciences, mathematics, engineering, technology, medicine, science communication, science PR and advocacy, science education and science policy. Arguably science has come to be seen as one of the foundations of modern society and it is increasingly, though perhaps misleadingly, being painted as the foundation of Western societies' worldview or culture.

Which brings me to my last point about how we might use the term 'science' as part of culture. It is not just a way of thinking or knowing about the universe, but it is not just a practice either. When we talk about science as culture we shouldn't just be thinking about how scientists behave in the lab or the field, or how networks of scientists form consensus and resolve disagreements, or how peer review decisions are made for research publication. We also need to recognise that science is a part of the very fabric of our society and our day-to-day decision-making. This might range from the mundane (e.g. whether to eat the out-of-date chicken in the fridge) to more important decisions about our health and well-being (e.g. whether we should vaccinate our children or whether we should smoke) to decisions about societal and environmental well-being (e.g. should we drive or walk to work, should we support wind farms and stem cell research, who should we vote for?) to our consumer decisions (e.g. should we consume genetically modified or organic foods, should we switch energy supplier?). Our stances or points of view on these issues also relate to how we may perceive others and how they, in turn, may perceive us. If you doubt this assertion, I challenge you to try questioning the audience at a public science lecture as to whether it is always safe to vaccinate children or if GM crops are a good solution to food security problems. Science and the way we engage (or conversely don't engage) with scientific knowledge can also act as an identity. Some of us even feel so passionate about these different scientific issues that we create or participate in activities within communities of like-minded people – I include myself here. Science has become a social way of being and identifying oneself, even for those who are not in any way directly or indirectly involved in scientific research or education to any degree. This can be attested by the ever increasing number of science festivals, science clubs, science comedy nights, science debates, science museums, science discussion groups, etc. This is not some new phenomenon of course – this is a process that has been going on since at least the nineteenth century when there was a rise in public interest in the spectacle and promise of science.

In much the same way that religion is recognised to be about meaning, decision-making, community, belonging and identity, science can also, as part of our day-to-day lived experience, serve the same functions. Thus, when we talk about the compatibility of science and religion, we are not necessarily just talking about whether science or religion can answer certain questions about the nature of the universe, but we are also talking about whether these two cultural perspectives or worldviews can be compatible at an individual level in our day-to-day lived experience of the world. To which the answer has to be, well for many people ... ... yes, as this is something many people of differing faiths do on a day-to-day basis.

But what does this really tell us about the relationship between science and religion? One could argue I have picked examples that are not necessarily the primary issue of conflict between the two worldviews so far (though I might beg to differ on climate change and health). Obviously, where these broad categories of 'science' and 'religion' most interact with each other is when we encounter or think about issues relating to us – humans. We are after all a navel-gazing species. Questions of why we are here, where are we going as a species, are we alone in the universe, are we the pinnacle of development of the universe and the evolution of species are of significance to many of us.

Surely on these subjects people see an intractable and ongoing conflict between science and religion? Isn't it particularly hard for members of certain faith communities to accept aspects of modern biological science like evolutionary theory? There is often an assumption in some media narratives that creationism is a big issue and that you naturally have to be an atheist to accept evolutionary science. This binary perception of a link between being pro-evolution and anti-religious (or at the very least atheistic or agnostic) has of course been reinforced by facets of 'new atheism', particularly in the work of Richard Dawkins. You might be forgiven then for thinking that members of the public would also see the relationship between science and religion in this way, but of the little polling or surveying of public perceptions in this area the results (although only ever indicative) are perhaps a little surprising.

In 2009 a poll undertaken as part of the Darwin Now project was conducted in ten countries worldwide[2] to ascertain public perceptions of evolution, Charles Darwin and the relationship between acceptance of evolutionary science and religion. In one of the questions we asked: 'To what extent do you agree or disagree that it is possible to believe in a God and still hold the view that life on earth, including human life, evolved over time as a result of natural selection?' In all of the ten countries we polled, more people agreed than disagreed that it is possible both to believe in the existence of a God and accept that evolution occurs through a process of natural selection. And overall the majority of people (55 per cent worldwide) felt that it was possible to believe in God and think that evolution occurs through a process of natural selection regardless of their own view on this debate. Perhaps surprisingly, only 19.5 per cent of those polled worldwide felt there was a clash between evolutionary worldviews and belief in a God.[3] So this would suggest that in the public's mind the two positions of 'evolutionary science' and 'religion' are not always intrinsically at war.

Given that this is an area of much public debate, there has been very little scholarly research done to actually ascertain levels of acceptance of evolutionary science outside of the US, let alone research that begins to address the more complex question of what members of the public actually think about the relationship between science and religion. Indeed, the Darwin Now poll was one of the first to look at public perceptions of evolution internationally. Only now are researchers in the US, UK and Canada[4] slowly beginning to piece together a more refined picture of what people really think about these issues in light of the more nuanced understanding of the way in which religion and science can act as identity markers. One aspect of this new research which will provide us with some no doubt interesting data is that which examines whether it is those who are religious who are more likely to see conflict between science and religion. We might expect that it is those who are struggling to balance both worldviews who are most likely to see a clash between them. However, as a survey of US public in 2015 by Pew shows, there might be some more complicated processes at play in these debates:

> [M]ost Americans (59%) say, in general, that science often is in conflict with religion, although a sizeable minority of adults (38%) consider science and religion to be mostly compatible. Those most inclined to see religion and science as generally in conflict are those who, themselves, have no particular religious affiliation or are not religiously observant. At the same time, however, most adults (68%) say there is no conflict between their personal religious beliefs and science.[5]

The wording in this kind of research can play a key role here, with outright incompatibility potentially being seen as less of a concern than issue-specific conflict between these two worldviews (for example concerns over moral or political positions). For example, a survey undertaken in the US in 2007 by the Baylor Institute for Studies of Religion had significantly different findings from the Pew survey. The Baylor survey asked if people agreed or disagreed with the statement that 'Science and religion are incompatible' and found that only 16.8 per cent agreed with the statement with just 6.1 per cent strongly agreeing.[6]

Obviously we need to be really careful about extrapolating from this kind of polling data from the US, which has an idiosyncratic and highly politicised history when it comes to debates over evolutionary science and religion. But what is very interesting is that, even in this more highly charged context, while people may feel there is potential for conflict between science and religion in an abstract sense, a proportion of those who state this clearly feel no conflict between the two worldviews at a personal level in their day-to-day lives.

It is interesting that both the Pew and the Darwin Now surveys also seemed to suggest that in some contexts it might be those with no beliefs or religious affiliations that are most likely to see the strongest conflict between the two worldviews. This is not really that surprising when you think about it – those who reject a worldview (in this case religion) are more likely to see it as being incompatible with their own.

While these surveys can be very blunt tools and there is a lot more work that needs to be done, they do raise some interesting questions. Primarily, these survey results lead us to ask two key questions. Firstly, is this notion of a clash between science and religion really something that is important to people on a day-to-day personal level? Secondly, why, if a significant number of people appear to feel that there does not have to be a conflict between science and religion, is this clash narrative so persistent?

To explore why this might be the case I want to go back to the notion of science as synonymous with atheism. Debates about the role and authority of religion and science in society do not happen in a vacuum. These are not, nor have they ever been, debates purely about appealing to the supernatural or conversely the inexorable rise of an empirical worldview. Both of these worldviews have been active in a range of societal, political and cultural questions and have crossed over into more philosophical domains with regards to questions surrounding morality, and the meaning or purpose of life. So we cannot divorce these debates from those broader contexts. A significant driver then to the idea that science is at its very core atheistic has been the wider debate surrounding the 'secularisation thesis', which in turn has its roots in nineteenth-century narratives around societal progress. The 'secularisation thesis' is basically the view that as society modernises and moves towards more pluralist models based on science, capitalism and democracy, religion will inevitably decline and wither. The increasingly secular worldview that predominates in Europe is held as the archetypal example of this process. However, in recent years sociologists of religion have begun to increasingly voice doubt about the validity of this argument and the secularisation thesis is becoming more widely criticised. In part this is because this thesis doesn't match what we are seeing on the ground in terms of people's lived experience of their own religious or spiritual worldviews. There may be in some places fewer bums on pews, but we need to be cautious of seeing this as an overall decline in religiosity or spirituality, as it may actually be a signifier of a fuzzier type of religious or spiritual identity that is more individualist in nature. And on an international scale it is increasingly clear that reports of the demise of religious and spiritual worldviews have been greatly exaggerated.

Science has been seen by some to play an integral role in this process of secularisation. However, the study of the history of science does not necessarily support this view. For a start, a lot of what we might now characterise as 'science' developed in periods when the relationship between religion and the study of the natural world were seen for the most part as harmonious or at least not in any form of direct contradiction. There are many pervading myths about this relationship – the most well known examples being debates surrounding the work of Galileo and Darwin. Common myths include the idea that Galileo went to jail or was even tortured by the Pope and the Catholic Church for his work – this has now been widely shown to be incorrect by historians.[7] Common myths surrounding Darwin are that he lost his faith due to the publication of his most famous work *On the Origin of Species* or even that he delayed the publication by over twenty years as he was so concerned about the public and religious outcry about his theories. Again, this is an oversimplification and does not relate to what really occurred. Darwin for example was also concerned about the response of his 'scientific' peers as much as he was about censure from the church or theologians. Conversely, he was also perhaps equally concerned about being seen to be associated with the more disreputable aspects of atheism and materialism as well. Nor indeed was he the first or only person to come up with theories that suggested species change over time or, as we might now think of it, 'evolve'. Indeed, work by others such as Lamarck and Chambers had been around for some fifty years prior to the publication of *Origin of Species* in 1859. Chambers' book *Vestiges of Creation* (albeit published anonymously) outsold *Origin of Species* right up to the end of the nineteenth century. Famous debates of the period that are often characterised as clashes between science and religion are now understood to have been related much more closely to wider concerns over the professionalisation of science.[8] It is also important to note that many of those who have in the past championed science or whom we latterly treat as scientific 'heroes' would have been astonished to see themselves as flag-wavers for political secularisation. We must remember that science has developed through different processes and in response to different concerns from these wider political movements. Clearly, what we think of as modern science has developed within these broader societal and cultural contexts, but that is not to say that it has either been driven solely by these political concerns or, conversely, acted as a principal driver for political secularisation. Therefore, we need to be very wary of utilising historical debates out of context to support contemporary concerns relating to the secularisation of society.

Against the backdrop of debates surrounding the secularisation of society, 'science' has been used as a proxy for reason, rationalism and even, to a degree, intelligence. Grand claims from those who would argue that it is not a worldview or ideology but merely a methodological approach to understanding the world. Another worrying dimension of this political narrative is the utilisation of 'science' as a facet of geopolitical narratives – including 'clash of civilisations' positions that pitch the 'West' versus 'the rest' or more increasingly a problematic conception of a 'Western worldview' against an equally problematic concept of an 'Islamic worldview'. Unfortunately, while there is very little comprehensive, representative or in-depth research data about public perceptions of evolution or the relationship between science and religion, this is doubly the case for the 'Muslim world'. Unfortunately, into this research lacuna step anecdote and prejudice and there are those who are beginning to argue that to be 'Muslim' is to be 'anti-scientific' or 'anti-evolution' based on scant evidence. To reduce the notion of Islam as anti-scientific is to buy in to the tide of prejudice that seeks to racialise an entire religion. Clearly it is entirely unscientific to lump a diverse array of ethnicities together as one single-faceted monolithic and fundamentalist whole. And if we want to understand why this is problematic we need not look to either science or religion for answers but only to history.

So can there be compatibility between science and religion? Well, without wanting to sound like a stereotypical philosopher it really does depend on what you mean by 'science' and 'religion'. If we view them as competing truth claims, then there are clearly going to be areas where there might be localised and in some case vociferous debates. It is important to remember that this does not necessarily mean that to be religious is to be anti-science or vice versa. This holds true with other critiques of scientific research – one could plausibly be accepting of modern medicine, have a keen interest in particle physics, but be concerned over the geopolitical or environmental impacts of GM food production. Equally to reject one aspect of scientific research and its application on spiritual or religious grounds clearly does not mean to reject science in its entirety. Similarly, one could be a human exceptionalist – i.e. someone who thinks that humans are the result of some form of special creation – and still accept most aspects of the contemporary biological sciences, scientific knowledge per se and its array of methodologies.

However, when we talk about the clash or compatibility between science and religion we are not just talking about truth or knowledge claims – we are talking about a whole host of different social and cultural processes, not just individual perceptions of two abstract philosophical concepts. It is important to note that some (albeit less than sophisticated) international polls indicate that most people do not see a necessary clash between the two worldviews, and that those that choose this position will include a significant number of people who hold a mixture of religious or spiritual beliefs as well as non-believers, atheists and agnostics. So how much the more vocal and polarising aspects of current discourse represent what people think about the relationship between science and religion on a personal level remains to be seen. But research is beginning to suggest that neither end of the spectrum of this particular debate represents the majority viewpoint.

We should remember that to claim science is necessarily atheistic is itself an unscientific claim, not least because this statement is not supported by any empirical evidence. It also leaves us in danger of adopting a rather paradoxical model of science whereby on one hand it stakes a claim to objective truth, but on the other hand it would exclude the work of a great many scientists both past and present because of their worldview. Imagine if we were to suggest that you couldn't be left wing and a scientist and that we now had to reject all 'scientific' research from those holding left-wing political beliefs. One's political views after all clearly have an impact on the way we see the world, our views on morality, what we might think about societal progress, our sense of identity and belonging or indeed what scientific research we think is most pressing. However, it would be nonsense to suggest that properly conducted and to a degree replicable scientific research should be dismissed based on one's political worldview. We need then to recognise more clearly that any claims that you have to be an atheist to be a scientist are not based on any real idea of how science works – as clearly any truth claim it may make has to allow research to be undertaken in different cultural settings without that social or cultural setting impacting on the nature of the data collected. So when people put forward this view they are taking an ideological position, not an empirically informed or scientific one.

So to conclude. If we view science and religion as abstract competing truth claims vastly removed from our day-to-day lives and the rest of society, then there may well be localised points of disagreement between the two. If we view them as two separate ways of seeing the world that should never encroach on each other's territory, then they cannot be compatible, just merely non-antagonistic. If, however, we recognise that they are two worldviews that are not separate from our day-to-day lives but are very much a part of them and that both these systems of knowledge also have cultural and social components in the way that all of us – regardless of our own beliefs – engage with them, then we are entering into slightly different territory.

So in this broader day-to-day and social or cultural identity sense there is, for a great many of us, a compatibility between the two. Clearly if we take this broader view we can begin to see that there must be some pretty interesting and sophisticated ways in which people do integrate or find compatibility between these two worldviews and identities in their day-to-day lives and decision-making, across a range of geographies and cultures. This is something which has to date been surprisingly yet greatly understudied and we are only just beginning to scratch the surface in understanding what people's perceptions of the relationship between science and religion are, let alone how people of all faiths, beliefs or worldviews might negotiate between these two ways of seeing or understanding the world around us.[9]

Notes

1 See Centre for Longitudinal Studies, UCLA Institute for Education, 'More People May Believe in Life after Death than God, Study Finds', press release, 28 November 2012, <http://www.cls.ioe.ac.uk/news.aspx?itemid=2431&itemTitle=More+peopl e+may+believe+in+life+after+death+than+God%2c+study+finds&sitesectionid=9 05&sitesectiontitle=Press+Releases>.
2 The Darwin Now poll was undertaken by Ipsos Mori in the United Kingdom, USA, Mexico, Argentina, Spain, China, Russia, India, Egypt and South Africa.
3 Ipso Mori, 'Darwin Survey Shows International Consensus on Acceptance of Evolution', 3 July 2009, <https://www.ipsos-mori.com/researchpublications/researcharchive/2379/ Darwin-survey-shows-international-consensus-on-acceptance-of-evolution.aspx>. See also Fern Elsdon-Baker, 'Creating Creationists: The Influence of "Issues Framing" on Our Understanding of Public Perceptions of Clash Narratives between Evolutionary Science and Belief', *Public Understanding of Science* 24, no. 4 (May 2015): 422–39.

4 This includes my own research team, details of whose work can be found at the website, *Science and Religion: Exploring the Spectrum*, <http://sciencereligion-spectrum.org>.
5 Cary Funk and Becka A. Alper, 'Perception of Conflict between Science and Religion', report, Science and Religion, Pew Research Center, 22 October 2015, <http://www.pewinternet.org/2015/10/22/perception-of-conflict-between-science-and-religion/>.
6 Association of Religion Data Archives, 'Baylor Religion Survey, Wave II (2007)', <http://www.thearda.com/archive/files/Descriptions/BAYLORW2.asp>.
7 For an excellent rebutting of this myth and others, read the book, Ronald L. Numbers (ed.), *Galileo Goes to Jail and Other Myths about Science and Religion* (Cambridge, MA: Harvard University Press, 2010).
8 The most famous of these debates is the Huxley/Wilberforce debate which happened in Oxford in 1860.
9 With thanks to Dr James Thompson, Dr Stephen Jones, Dr Thomas Kaden and Prof. Bernard Lightman for their comments and input into this chapter.

Part III
Ethics and values

The chapters in this section look at the practical and existential dimensions of the differences between the religious and the non-religious. How do these differences affect the ways in which religious and non-religious people live their lives, and the values they hold? Are there values which they can share in common?

Anthony Carroll (Chapter 8) argues that religion is not properly understood if it is seen simply as a set of theoretical beliefs, and that we need to pay more attention to the lived experience of religious faith in order to understand how believers see the relationship between God, the world and themselves.

Richard Norman (Chapter 9) suggests that religious believers and atheists can find common ground by recognising moral values as the necessary conditions for human flourishing.

Robin Gill (Chapter 10) largely agrees, but points also to distinctive features of a religious approach, located especially in the mimetic and mythic elements of human culture.

John Cottingham (Chapter 11) asks what scope there might be for convergence in the area of spiritual practices and numinous experiences, but emphasises that what may appear to be experiences shared by religious believers and atheists will have a different meaning and significance for them.

Anna Strhan (Chapter 12) identifies affinities in the ways in which an evangelical church and various atheist communities engage with existential concerns about life and death.

Michael McGhee (Chapter 13) suggests that the attempt to make sense of the contrast between 'good' and 'bad' religion points to enduring moral struggles between conflicting values which are 'contrary states of the human soul'.

Part II

Ethics and values

8   Beyond theism and atheism
The search for truth

Anthony Carroll

In this chapter, I develop the idea that arguments between theists and atheists about the existence of God have played too much of a role in the quest to find the truth which they aim to discover. I am not suggesting that these exchanges are unimportant. They have yielded all sorts of fascinating claims for and against God's existence. Yet, while these arguments are interesting and yield intellectual insights, they provide a very limited account of the lived experience of religious belief and atheism. I argue, by contrast, that a better approach to the question of God's existence is provided by concentrating on the actual experiences of believing in God and of living life as an atheist. Recognising differences that these experiences make to human life identifies the question of God in a much sharper and more relevant focus.

In order to move beyond the classical positions of both theism and atheism, I employ a panentheistic conception of God in which God is understood to be both within and beyond human experience. In being within human experience, I argue that we *can* come to awareness of God through examining our beliefs and practices. However, for this awareness to take the form of a religious faith, I hold that an act of trust in God is indispensable. That God is *also* beyond human experience, I take to be a necessary entailment of the concept of God shared by both theists and atheists. While theists acknowledge the transcendence of God and investigate the predicates that follow from this, atheists often use these predicates as arguments against the compatibility of human experience and the actual existence of God.

A panentheistic conception of God has important implications for how we view the human person. I argue that God's presence in human experience potentially opens us to depths of experience that transcend our ordinary everyday awareness of reality. These experiences are expressed in a variety of ways by religious and non-religious traditions and point in the direction of layers of transcendence which expand a narrow materialistic and reductionist conception of the self. Such an expanded humanism, something I call 'panentheistic humanism', does not oppose God and humanity but rather sees both as intimately related to each other. Neither reducing God to human experience nor removing God to exclusively outside of the boundaries of human experience, 'panentheistic humanism' provides a way to understand this relational nature of God as providing a dimension of transcendence to the human person.

Objections, propositions and relations

Concentrating on the lived experiences of belief and unbelief in God as a way to approach the God question inevitably raises the objection that the way that one experiences something does not determine whether or not that something or someone in whom one believes actually exists. For example, I may not like the fact that someone close to me has died and I may not be able to accept the tragic truth of this, but that does not alter the fact that this is the case and any denial of it, though understandable, is ultimately false. Denying something to be the case can result in the invention of creative illusions which can furnish an imaginative but ultimately untrue world. And protecting ourselves from a cold hard truth can serve the useful function of mitigating the effects of corrosive forces from grinding us down. I may experience the death of a loved one as having more meaning if I believe that they live on in some form than if I have recourse only to the meaning that their life once had. But the extra meaning provided by belief in an afterlife, for example, though real to the one who experiences it, may itself be predicated on a false premise despite the fact that it offers greater consolation.

Consequently, whether or not we feel better in believing or indeed not believing does not decide the truth of the matter. Truth seems to be independent of how it affects us. Our commitment to scientific impartiality and objectivity relies upon this fact, otherwise scientists would be unable to disprove cherished hypotheses. Allowing the facts to speak for themselves seems to carry a noble and heroic truth, namely, that truth is not determined by how we relate to it. It imposes itself on us without concern for us. Therefore, even if it were possible to demonstrate that believing in God provides positive effects, we could not simply generate these if we did not consider this belief to be true.

But this way of understanding truth in the religious realm is problematic. It presupposes the 'object' of truth to be an *extra* something or someone to be *objectively* believed prior to a personal commitment. It assumes the '$n + 1$' model of religious belief. That is to say, that God is another being, albeit transcendent, to add to the set of beings that we call immanent beings. If one holds to the '$n + 1$' set, then one is a believer. If one holds to the 'n' set, then one is not. This way of categorising believers and unbelievers reduces faith to simply differences of propositional assent. But faith is something more than this as it involves someone in a personal commitment. It is by nature a relational concept that means *having a loving trust in* rather than simply believing *that* X. Religious faith is trust *in* God and out of this trust one searches for understanding: *fides quaerens intellectum* (faith seeking understanding).

As an experience of trust, religious faith is not adequately depicted as simply assenting to the belief *that* an object exists. Religious faith, and here

I am speaking as a practising Christian, is a relationship and not simply the affirmation of a set of propositional beliefs. These propositional beliefs follow on from the initial act of trust *in*, they do not precede it. In this sense, religious truth is not 'objective' because it is essentially relationship involving. If this relationship is denied, then the propositional account of religious faith can simply deem there to be no existing state of affairs to correspond to the set of truths that constitute the faith of a religious believer. And, it is plausible that affirmation of this relationship might simply be fictional. Relationships with fictional characters can be extremely powerful and even move us to tears and so on, but they are ultimately not relationships with real beings. So, despite the evidential support for religious experience of the effects of this relationship, the belief which it implies may actually turn out to be false. That some people are inspired by their religious faith to heroically give their lives for the poor and dispossessed and engage in generous acts of selflessness, though praiseworthy, is not in itself proof that what they believe in is actually true. It is possible that it could all be a consequence of belief in a very powerful fiction that is motivating this behaviour.

This impasse in the relational understanding of religious belief seems to lead us to a dilemma. Either one suspends doubt in order to believe or one doubts and so does not believe. Faith without doubt or doubt without faith seems to be the choice facing the person of faith and the non-believer. However, putting the choice in this way fails to recognise that the opposite of faith is certainty and not doubt. In fact, faith can include doubt that is based on the absence of empirical verification as St Thomas famously demonstrated. In this case, doubting in God does not necessarily mean having no relation to God. Rather, it means that this relation is critical, and it is questioning. The doubting that is a part of faith is done in the form of dialogue with God and not as refusing to speak with a non-existent God.

This is a difference between belief understood as faith *in* God and unbelief understood as not believing *that* God exists. Trusting in God is a condition of entering into this relationship. It simply cannot get started without the initial step being taken. And, this dilemma is not unusual in situations involving a trusting and loving relationship. Analogously, making a personal and intimate commitment to someone also has a similar structure. While the existence of the other is not usually in doubt, it is the case that the love may be. Whether someone really loves me is sometimes uncertain and the experience of taking the risk of loving them is similar to the experience of risking faith in God. I may find my love rejected by another, and in the case of God, I may find that my initial faith collapses and I am left only with doubt.

Nevertheless, despite these difficulties, it is usually the case that by the fruits of these relationships one comes if not to certainty then at least to a greater degree of confidence in one's initial decision. On the one hand, this can lead to a continuation of faith in God or to a continuation of belief that the other person really does reciprocate the love that one has for them.

And, on the other hand, it can lead to a rejection of one's initial decision to believe in God or to face the fact that the other person does not really love one. Common to both situations is the need for an initial act of trust in order for the process to actually begin. There is no certainty prior to taking this risk and things can go wrong in both faith journeys and in loving human relationships. In fact, there is no certainty after taking this risk since faith, like love, is by its nature an uncertain business and there is no guarantee that it will work out. But what is certain is that unless such an act is made then the journey cannot begin. A free decision on our part seems to be a condition of both faith and of a loving relationship.

Moving beyond theism and atheism

Exchanges between theists and atheists seem to be stuck in this dilemma. Both seem to adopt defensive attitudes or even proselytising ones which serve to secure each of the parties in their own positions. And, it is not difficult to see reasons for this. Risking living without a faith in God is very difficult for a believer. It may well involve letting go of their upbringing and of a range of commitments and this requires a great deal of courage. Similarly, risking entering into a relationship with God for an atheist is also possibly frightening and life-changing. Given these difficulties, it is no wonder that positions become entrenched and an open enquiring attitude is difficult to cultivate.

As a result, a mutually patronising attitude can easily develop in these exchanges. Such an attitude presupposes that all relationships should proceed along the same pathway. However, it is undeniable that people of faith and those of none seem to live happy and fulfilled lives. Both find ways of flourishing that suggest that the journeys of religious faith and unbelief are not necessary ones for happiness. Living a fulfilled life seems to be dependent on the way that a person actually lives out these positions. The common ground here is that of authenticity. If a person is honest in their search for truth and lives out the existential truth found in an authentic life, then what right has anyone else to judge them?

However, what can be helpful in such exchanges is to develop a clearer understanding of what is at stake in taking a position. For example, having a religious faith does not mean that questions disappear. Rather, the actual lack of certainty characteristic of religious faith points to some inadequacies with the too-affirmative style of declarations about God that are made in both theism and atheism. The notion that faith in God is defined by affirming a set of divine predicates, such as the claims that God is omnipotent and omniscient, for example, has led to a great deal of philosophical speculation on religious belief, and characterises religious faith as if it were like a crossword puzzle which tries to solve the logical entailments that follow on from affirming or denying these propositions. But the actual experience of religious faith is much richer and more dynamic than engaging in a problem-solving exercise and is much more akin to falling in love with someone. However, in the case of falling in love with God there is a crucial difference. God is both within oneself and transcendent of oneself.

This understanding of the self and God's presence within it is something that religious traditions speak of in terms of 'God being nearer to us than we are to ourselves'. This is an experiential dimension that a person of faith discovers in a range of ways such as in intercessory prayer, in praise, and in contemplation. The distant God of theism, based on the affirmation of a set of propositional characteristics, inadequately captures this dimension of religious faith as it tends to focus on the transcendent characteristics of God, rather than on the *transcending* presence of God in our experience. And, this *transcending* presence of God in experience is what one would expect in a relational understanding of God. God so conceived is not simply distant from us but also with us and in us.

The focus on a distant conception of God emerges out of theism's tendency to concentrate on the abstract-predicate model of faith which places God outside of this experience of the human self. This way of conceiving of God takes on a particular importance in the early modern period as the Christian religion begins to come under attack due to the rise of atheism and materialistic conceptions of natural science. Seen as a way to uphold the metaphysical foundations of reality in the face of these critiques, Christian apologists used the methods of philosophical argumentation to counter these positions. However, as a consequence of this approach, the arena for debate between religious belief and atheism was set by a philosophical theism which debated the abstract truths of the Christian religion in a language far removed from that of lived human experience. This style of debate became embodied in an apologetics of rationally justifying the essential truths of the Christian religion using highly abstract theoretical reasoning. As a type of discourse which removed consideration of God from the ordinary realm of life, it was further reinforced by the fear of condemnation for professing heretical doctrines. In the face of heresies such as pantheism, theism could safely abstract God from the natural world of human experience and focus on the divine attributes which had fewer resonances in the changing world of space and time.

Yet, in a relational understanding of God, a fusional notion like pantheism is rejected. The term 'pan*en*theism' describes this relational conception of God in which all things are in God and God is transcendent of all things. We can become aware of dwelling in God through cultivating various forms of spiritual practices. Sometimes these practices will be part of a religious tradition and sometimes, and perhaps increasingly so today, these practices will be detached from specific religious traditions and structures. The degree to which the grounding in a particular religious tradition structures these experiences of God and shapes the language used to express them is a matter of much scholarly debate. However, less controversial is the view that such experiences share characteristic family resemblances that occur across religious and non-religious boundaries and in all cultures. They open out the self to broader horizons and often with a depth of intensity that leaves a lasting effect on the person and indeed at times a whole community.

Such a panentheistic way of talking about God provides a language to articulate forms of religious experience that are present in many different traditions and individual experiences. The example of offering reverence to God and to others is an illustration of this. In the reverential act of bowing, for example, the submission of oneself to God and to others in the humble act of lowering one's head is not an act of humiliation but, done with the right attitude, it is actually experienced as a deep respect for God and for other people. This experience of offering reverence to another is one of liberation of the egocentric self. And this freedom of self is not an enslavement to God or to another. Rather, in the experience of bowing, our self transcends itself, it breaks out of the confines of the narrow egocentric self. Bowing, understood in this way, is a self-emptying gesture in which the self is filled with the presence of another in relational exchange. Just as we bow to others, others bow to us in this process of mutual liberation from egocentric grasping. In so doing, we cultivate a larger self which is not our own possession but rather a shared space of encounter. In this space a meeting takes place between persons, between God and an individual, and also between communities.

Of course, different acts of reverence manifest and express different relations. For example, in a Christian religious ceremony, such as that which takes place when a thurifer incenses a congregation during a liturgy, the thurifer first bows to the assembled congregation as a recognition that the people are offering themselves with the bread and the wine as gifts to God. This is a gesture of thanksgiving, of gratitude, and of reverence for the receipt of the gift of all the activities, intentions, and prayers that, like the incense itself, rise up to God in the liturgy. This symbolic gesture enacts and represents the Christian belief that the goal of all human existence is to praise, worship, and to serve God. In bowing to the congregation the thurifer acknowledges this with deep respect to all those who are gathered. In their turn, the congregation bows to the thurifer who incenses them. The thurifer here represents to the congregation the one who brings the offerings of the people to the altar, the symbolic place of transformation and communion between God and humanity. This moment of communication in the Christian liturgy takes place in silence. It is a wordless encounter that is symbolically mediated through the various gestures, objects, and people involved in this part of liturgy. And, in being wordless it is no less communicative. Rather, the absence of words makes the necessary space for these symbolic mediations, which transcend any cognitive and propositional accounts of the religiously understood transaction which is being enacted, to be effective.

This shared space of encounter connects all those involved in the liturgy to one another in a spirit of reverence and solidarity. The experience of offering oneself to God in this manner induces this reverence and solidarity in those sincerely involved in the practice of liturgy, and such moments as these offer glimpses of transcendence and of the connectedness which this union with God implies. That these glimpses may be no more than the effect of the *effervescence* of the social group when it assembles is clearly a possibility. However, in order for such experiences of reverence to occur it is necessary to believe in the truth upon which they are founded. Without the initial act of trust that what one is involved in is a real encounter with God and not simply an act of social solidarity, the experiential process of this kind of religious reverence is short-circuited and made inaccessible to the individual and to the community. Such scepticism tends to reduce the experience of a religious liturgy to that of a spectator event and prevents it being experienced as a shared participatory time of transcendence.

Reflections on such experiences as that of reverence are far away from the focus of theism–atheism debates, which appear to trade more upon the assertion of the self, divine or human, rather than on the emptying and filling of self that is at the heart of the religious journey, and I would hold, of an authentic human one too. Part of the problem with this 'assertive model' of the self is the lack of respect for the other which it manifests. It tends to be 'preachy', certain, and self-righteous rather than dialogical, exploratory, and interested in the other's experience. In theism-and-atheism disputes, this assertive model has been little grounded in experience and is rather more based on sparring with propositions from contradictory starting points. Given this, there is little wonder that the exchanges between theists and atheists have been polemical. This basis of encounter between people of faith and those who do not believe poorly accounts for the actual reality of the journey of faith and ends up losing its grounding in human experience.

This is another reason why shifting the focus away from intellectual arguments for and against the existence of God is an important way to begin to take the dialogue forward and perhaps to find some common ground in experiences such as of reverence for others. A more fruitful way forward is to begin to learn how it is that religious people and atheists negotiate life's challenges and opportunities. In exploring these areas of human life, we can become aware of important insights into our capacities to overcome difficulties, to celebrate the beauty of life, and to forge greater respect for and solidarity with one another. The focus in such an encounter is different from trying to trounce one's opponent by the superior argument. It is rather a much more grounded way to engage with others and one which shows a much greater insight into the diversity of paths that we follow, and a much greater openness to acknowledging the variety of ways in which we seek to live an authentic life.

Conclusion

In seeking existential truth people of religious faith and unbelievers may have much more in common than one might be led to believe from listening to some recent polemical exchanges. I have argued that both unhelpful attitudes and inadequate characterisations of faith have contributed to a situation in which the exchange between people of religious faith and unbelievers tends to be more polemical than open and exploratory. Often based on a propositional-assent understanding of faith, this theistic conception has set the exchange with atheism in terms of an intellectual martial arts combat. Polemics between believers and unbelievers have tended to get trapped in the heat of the emotion of this intellectual sparring, rather than focusing on the light that these positions shed on living an authentic human life. One of the hopes of this article, and indeed of this collection as a whole, is that in fostering a more creative exchange between these different positions both sides may learn things that alone it would have been difficult to discover.

For example, in denying idolatrous images of God, atheism may well take religious thought beyond its sometimes anti-humanistic tendencies that have been fuelled by a whole host of taboos and have inhibited human flourishing for many. In expanding atheistic humanism to larger horizons of relationality, a panentheistic understanding of humanism may enable atheism to broaden its conception of the self and so to deepen its understanding of what it is to be truly human. Both positions clearly seek to provide ever more adequate accounts of what it is to live a fully human life. A panentheistic humanist account of this, as I have sketched above, intends to shift the focus of this account of fullness from the transcendental realm closed off to human life, to the *transcending* presence of God in human experience. This provides a way to conceive of the God–human relation not as one of opposition, a conception that often motivates the charge against religious belief as being anti-humanist, but rather, as one of participation. Such a relation of participation is spoken of as a process of 'divinisation' in the Christian tradition and is meant to indicate that this relation is constitutive of our very being. The human self in this understanding has access to dimensions of fullness that do not negate human freedom but rather accomplish it. Learning more about these experiences of fullness within human life in a range of religious and non-religious traditions can serve the common good through enabling possibilities of access which may at present be unnecessarily closed for some people. Moreover, in better understanding what contributes to such experiences of fullness we are in a better position to develop criteria of discernment for judging when exchanges between believers and unbelievers are really focused on promoting human well-being or not. But whatever the outcomes of the dialogue between believers and unbelievers in the time ahead, one should hope that it will lead to a greater insight into the experience and understanding of the human condition and to a greater respect between believers and unbelievers for the singularity of the path through life that each person makes.

Fostering such a dialogical approach to the exchange between people of religious faith and unbelievers is an important corrective to the often overly dominant oppositional approach. And, while the oppositional approach of recent times may well have been necessary for something positive to now take place, it is important that more balanced encounters develop if we are to grow in mutual understanding. At a time when there is a real danger that advances in toleration and the respect for plural worldviews can no longer be taken for granted, the need to develop peaceful and creative ways of different positions encountering one another is ever more urgent. Limited though the dialogue between people of faith and unbelievers is, it nevertheless plays an important role in both embodying respectful encounter between people of different convictions and also in sending out a message about the kind of values that we hold in common. Such encounters also help to generate bonds of solidarity that can break down unhelpful stereotypes that necessarily get generated when one is simply conducting a series of monologues. Learning *about* one another makes possible the potential for learning *from* one another and this can lead to new directions both for atheism and for religious faith.

Of course, none of this can happen without innovation. Repetition of former patterns of engagement and approach merely duplicates what is already known and provides little of real value and interest for moving things forward. And, if we are to better understand the human condition in a deeper way, we will need to be open to the experimentation with styles of life and belief that is currently common in many societies. The example of interreligious dialogue may be instructive here. While there have been setbacks in this area there have also been very important insights that have fundamentally changed religious traditions in many parts of the world, making them more open and inclusive of other paths. Fascinating learning processes which have taken place into methods of prayer and contemplation, for example, demonstrate that such exchanges can be fruitful. Identifying and encouraging equivalent learning processes between religious traditions and atheism may well also provide important developments in our understanding of the human condition and of God.

And, in order for such innovations to occur, there is a need to create new spaces of encounter between people of differing worldviews where open, free, and respectful exchanges can take place and are fostered. Religious institutions such as churches often tend to focus on their own faithful who are either assumed to already accept the tenets of the faith or who are in formation in this faith. There is little room for people who are not of that faith to engage in open enquiry about a religious faith without feeling the social pressure to either conform to the beliefs of that faith or to leave the community. Atheist organisations can also share this sense of catering to their own faithful without fostering this kind of open enquiry that can lead to innovations. Moreover, while these issues can be dealt with in the often more neutral environments of higher education establishments, in these contexts they tend to be treated as merely intellectual issues to be debated at a theoretical level without any real grounding in the existential search for truth which they involve.

Shifting the basis of encounter between believers and unbelievers from theoretical argumentation over abstract truths to the experiential exploration of different positions will require courage to move beyond tried and tested formulas. Experimenting in this area is something few organisations, whether religious or atheist, seem particularly well equipped for at present. Often more concerned to defend our own positions and to look after our own adherents rather than those outside of these groups, there is much work to do for us to cultivate such open communities of enquiry. However, if we really want to foster the well-being and flourishing of people and to promote a serious search for truth today, then such innovation will be necessary if we are to move beyond theist–atheist polemics. Rather than repeat the oppositional approach to these engagements inherited from early modern times we now have the possibility to explore new ways forward for understanding both the depths of human experience and the ways in which these are open to transcendence. In this contemporary search for truth neither side should consider itself to have a monopoly on the answers. In fact, the openness required to engage in these new approaches may well privilege those who have the better questions rather than those who seem to have all the answers to questions that many on both sides of the divide are no longer asking.

9 Ethics and values
How much common ground?

Richard Norman

Over the past 200 years, as traditional religious belief has declined, many people have said that although they are not Christian and not religious, they retain the same values as religious believers. George Eliot, as reported by the Cambridge don Frederic Myers,

> taking as her text the three words which have been used so often as the inspiring trumpet-calls of men – the words God, Immortality, Duty – pronounced, with terrible earnestness, how inconceivable was the first, how unbelievable the second, and yet how peremptory and absolute the third.[1]

That idea has been attacked from two directions. There are religious believers who object that moral values lack a firm foundation unless they are grounded in something external to human beings, such as the will of a divine creator. From the opposite direction, essentially the same view was taken by Nietzsche:

> They are rid of the Christian God and now believe all the more firmly that they must cling to Christian morality. That is an English consistency; we do not wish to hold it against little moralistic females à la Eliot. In England one must rehabilitate oneself after every little emancipation from theology by showing in a veritably awe-inspiring manner what a moral fanatic one is ... We others hold otherwise. When one gives up the Christian faith, one pulls the right to Christian morality out from under one's feet.[2]

Where does the truth lie? Can there be common ground between religious believers and non-believers on moral values – not only on what they are, but on why they matter? That is the question I want to address. I am pleased to be doing so in company with my former colleague Robin Gill. Robin and I co-chaired a Centre for Applied Ethics at the University of Kent, and the experience confirmed for me the scope for people from religious and secular backgrounds to work together fruitfully on moral and ethical issues while honestly acknowledging the differences.

Divine commands

I begin by looking at two distinctively religious positions which appear to offer little scope for common ground: divine command ethics, and natural law ethics. Robin has discussed both of these in his work, and recognises their weaknesses but believes that they both still have something to offer.[3]

Few theologians or philosophers would now maintain that moral questions can be settled simply by an appeal to supposed divine commands. They would defend a 'divine command' theory of morality only in a highly modified and qualified form. The fact remains that in practice the moral thinking of a great many religious believers very often takes the form of an appeal to authority – typically, in the monotheistic religions, an appeal to the authority of a sacred text, which is equated with the moral authority of the deity. There are large numbers of Christians who continue to invoke Leviticus 18:22 as their definitive ground for regarding gay sex as morally inadmissible, just as there are many Muslims who point to comparable texts in the Qur'an. Thoughtful Christians and Muslims of course recognise that it does not settle the matter, but the fact remains that countless numbers of religious believers, throughout history, have thought and acted as though it did, just as they have assumed that any number of other moral questions are appropriately settled in the same way. If we are to do justice to the range of religious approaches, we cannot avoid saying something about this one.

Why does the appeal to textual authority not settle moral questions? Because of the inescapable need for selection and interpretation. To take another example, the commandment 'Thou shalt not kill' is thought by some to settle contentious questions about voluntary euthanasia and abortion. There is, however, no universally accepted interpretation of that commandment. Some Christians take it as support for absolute pacifism, and link it with other texts which point to the rejection of violence. Others insist on a distinction between killing in civil life and killing in war, and take the commandment to be entirely consistent with military action on behalf of the state.

The point here is not just an ad hominem one, about the failure to agree. It is a deeper point about the relation between moral values and any appeal to authority. Which text you select, and how you interpret it, will always be determined by prior moral assumptions. The selecting and the interpreting are done by drawing on moral values which are already taken for granted. Hence the appeal to authority cannot itself be the source of those values. Those who interpret in different ways the commandment not to kill do so because of their *prior* views about the wrongness of killing, and about whether killing in war is significantly different from killing in civil life. Likewise those who appeal to the Bible for their moral judgements on gay sex already assume that who you have sexual relations with is a matter of deep moral significance, unlike judgement about how to cut your hair and whether to eat fish which have scales and fins. We should perhaps be grateful if the text which they invoke is the one in Leviticus 18 rather than the one in Leviticus 20 which says that men who engage in homosexual acts should be put to death. If they refrain from applying the latter text literally, why is that? Because, clearly, they recognise that it would be wrong. Again, the moral assumption precedes the choice and interpretation of the text.

Serious philosophical defenders of a divine command theory of morality recognise that it cannot be the whole story. Values, they acknowledge, are not simply and solely the product of divine commands. What they tend to say is that our relation to the authority of a divinity is an important part of the explanation of why values should *matter* to us. It explains why *moral* values are not simply values we would *like* to live by, but are requirements which we have an *obligation* to live by. Without the recognition of moral values as backed by a divine will, as part of the creator's design for the universe and our place in it, there is, they say, a 'motivational gap' – a gap in our account of the binding force of morality.[4] I shall return to this idea of a motivational gap and how it might be filled.

Natural purposes

A second exclusively religious position which rules out the scope for common ground is the version of the natural law tradition which appeals to the concept of 'natural purposes'. This too has popular currency in the area of sexual morality, and especially in the religious denunciation of gay sex. Homosexual activity is described as a misuse of human sexuality because it is contrary to its natural purpose. The Catholic Church in particular has traditionally maintained, and still does, that homosexual acts are 'intrinsically disordered' because they are 'contrary to the natural law' insofar as they 'close the sexual act to the gift of life' which is its proper purpose. Many Protestant Christians maintain a similar position on similar grounds, and for the Catholic Church this has also of course been the basis for the moral condemnation of contraception.

Like the appeal to sacred texts, such a position is arbitrarily selective. On the wide range of human capacities it imposes an arbitrary restriction. Why should it be assumed that the use of human sexual organs for non-procreative pleasure is contrary to the intentions of the creator? Ironically, what seems to be doing the work here is a biological reductionism of a kind which secular humanists are often accused of espousing. Granted, ecclesiastical teaching allows for a dimension of sexuality as the emotional union of two people, but it also maintains that this cannot and must not be detached from the biological purposes for which it is intended. Biology is paramount.

Both the positions which I have considered so far are exclusively religious in a way which rules out the prospect of common ground with the non-religious. They rule it out not because they assume the existence of a deity, but because they claim a privileged access to the divine will and employ this as the sole criterion of right and wrong. As such they are, I suggest, problematic even from a theistic perspective. They presuppose the ability of human beings to attain a clear and unequivocal insight into the intentions of the deity, and their confidence in that ability sits uneasily with any acknowledgement of the mystery or inscrutability of the divine.

Evolutionary biology

The tendency to biological reductionism is paralleled by a prominent strand in some humanist ethical thinking: the attempt to base ethics on evolution. I want to suggest that secular appeals to biology, when they take this form, are in the end unsatisfactory in much the same way as religious appeals to biological purposes are. The facts of our evolutionary origins do have a limited role to play in thinking about ethics, but this line of thought does not take us very far, and is less illuminating than is often supposed.

It is often argued by religious critics that if the evolutionary account of our origins were the whole story, morality would be impossible. We would have to accept that human beings are nothing more than survival machines which have evolved to compete successfully in the struggle for existence. The phenomena of moral conscience, of concern for others, of obligations and duties imposed by moral values and principles not of our making are, it is said, impossible to explain in purely naturalistic terms. Therefore, the argument goes, we must either accept that they are all an illusion, or recognise that our moral capacities have to be accounted for in other terms, as an endowment conferred on us by a divine creator in whose image we are made.

In response to such criticisms it is important to point out, as humanist thinkers regularly do, that our moral capacities can perfectly well be explained from an evolutionary perspective. The genetic predispositions of human beings to care for and sacrifice themselves for their young, and to cooperate with one another in organised groups, clearly have a survival value for the species in the struggle for existence. They explain in turn why the capacity for empathetic identification with others, the ability to be moved by the feelings of other human beings, is a deep feature of our biological nature, and is the foundation on which moral awareness is built. Equally explicable in evolutionary terms is the survival advantage conferred by our employment of a complex language. It enables humans to cooperate in organised ways, to foresee the further consequences of their actions, to weigh up reasons and deliberate about what to do. When these abilities are brought to bear on our instinctive capacity for empathy, they can extend our human concern for others in ways which go beyond our immediate biological kin. They enable us to think rationally about the impact of our actions on different people, and to raise questions of consistency and fairness.

The proper attention to the evolutionary facts does, then, have a role to play in the understanding of our moral capacities. It shows that they are not an illusion. It shows how morality is possible. Our moral capacities are entirely explicable as features of a species which is the product of the evolutionary process, and they do not stand in need of some other, non-natural explanation.

But that is all. Evolutionary theory removes any suspicion of mystery. It does not, however, have positive ethical implications – it does not tell us how to live. As in the religious case, so here, we need to be wary of appeals to biological purposes – to the suggestion, for instance, that we are 'designed for social cooperation'. If we are looking for answers to ethical questions, evolutionary theory can take us no further. If our moral capacities are explicable in evolutionary terms, so too are other features of our biological nature, and that includes our moral limitations. It includes our tendency to identify with our immediate group and to exclude strangers. It includes our tendencies to react impulsively when under pressure, and to respond aggressively to a perceived or imagined threat. These are the familiar stuff of moral conflicts and dilemmas and temptations. Evolutionary theory cannot tell us how we should resolve the conflicts or resist the temptations. It can explain why they arise, but it leaves everything as it is.

Human flourishing

The religious appeal to natural purposes, and the secular appeal to evolutionary theory, are both too restrictive. They both pick out too limited a range of the features of our biological nature as having moral significance. I now want to put forward a broader version of the idea that ethics is grounded in human nature, one which is built on a more expansive vision of what it is to be human, and I want to suggest that this is the best place to look for common ground. It could be seen as drawing on the 'natural law' tradition in a broader sense. It is a way of thinking about ethics which goes back to Aristotle, and which has been developed in recent years by the philosopher Philippa Foot.[5] The core idea is that to understand how we are to live, we should look at what makes us human. It is the idea that a good human life is one which develops and uses to the full our distinctively human faculties and capacities. The things which we need for a good life are those things which enable us to flourish as human beings.

This, I am proposing, is our best bet for finding a way of grounding shared values which are common to religious and non-religious perspectives. Theists will see our distinctively human faculties as qualities with which we are endowed by a divine creator who intends that we should use them to the full. Secular humanists will see our possession of these faculties as a brute fact about what it is to be human, but one with implications for what it is to flourish and to live a fully human life.

The key concept here is that of 'flourishing'. The word is deliberately chosen to refer to something more than 'happiness'. Flourishing is not just a psychological state, it is not just a maximum of felt pleasurable experiences. In that case, it may be asked, what does it consist in? How do we know what it is? The danger is that, because of its vagueness, it may lend itself to being used not just as an empirical description but as a term which has evaluative judgements built into it. It would then be a mere truism to say that a good human life is one which enables a person to flourish. What we counted as a 'flourishing' life would become question-begging, dependent on prior values.

I do, however, want to argue that the concept of 'flourishing' can be empirically grounded in facts about our human nature. We can take our cue here from the facts about other species. We know what it is for a dog to flourish. It cannot flourish if it is kept indoors or kept on a leash. A dog needs to go for walks. And when we see a dog let off its lead and immediately racing around, following scents, and bounding up to other dogs to sniff them and play with them, we can recognise that this is what it is for a dog to flourish. No doubt there are felt experiences involved. Clearly it gets pleasure from running around. But it enjoys those activities because they are essential to being a dog, exercising its canine faculties.

So it is with humans. As with dogs, we can bring this into perspective by looking first at the negative case, at what it is for humans to be prevented from flourishing. Most fundamentally, humans cannot flourish if their basic physical needs are not met – if they lack food and shelter, if they are sick or physically maimed. But there is more to it than that. Humans also fail to flourish if they are bored, lonely, frustrated, constricted, disabled by fears and obsessions. These are familiar ways in which human lives can go wrong. Conversely we can see, as a matter of fact, that humans are flourishing when they are able to lead lives which are active, confident, creative and emotionally rich. Our needs for lives and activities of these kinds are, just as much as our physical needs, shared human needs grounded in our shared human nature.

The concept of 'flourishing', then, is one which we can use to throw light on the idea of a good life. But what has this to do with morality, with specifically *moral* values? A strength of this approach, I suggest, is that it does not draw a sharp distinction between the idea of a good human life and the idea of a *morally* good way of life. Nevertheless, the questioner may insist, is there not an inevitable tension between the pursuit of a flourishing life and the altruistic demands of morality – the moral obligations to show concern for others and, sometimes at least, to sacrifice our own needs in order to meet the needs of others? Yes, of course, such conflicts do arise in particular cases, but this is where our understanding of what it is for human beings to flourish has to take into account also our nature as *social* beings. As Aristotle famously put it, we are 'political animals' or, to translate it more accurately, 'social animals', and as he went on to say, this is true of humans in a stronger sense than it is of other gregarious species such as ants or bees. Humans use language. Other species make sounds to express pain and pleasure, but language serves to indicate what is beneficial and harmful for us, and therefore also what is right and wrong; for what is distinctive of human beings, in contrast to other animals, is that they alone have an awareness of good and bad and right and wrong and other values, and it is the sharing of these that constitutes living together in a community.

(Aristotle, *Politics*, bk 1)

Because we share a language with which we make sense of our lives and our purposes, then, questions about what makes a good human life are, from the start, questions about *shared* values, about how *we* ought to live, and how to live *together*. But our nature as social beings involves more than just the use of language, and this is where the facts noted briefly in connection with evolutionary theory come into play. The human capacity for empathy is more than merely a biological necessity for child-rearing. The infectiousness of other people's joys and sufferings enlarges our lives, and becomes a condition of human flourishing. In order to live full lives we need qualities of kindness and compassion which will lead us to foster in others the joys which we can share with them, and to combat the sufferings of others which would sadden us and diminish our own lives. Cooperation with others is more than a mere necessity for survival. We flourish by taking pleasure in shared tasks and achievements, and therefore we need the qualities of trust and loyalty which are integral features of genuine cooperation. Because we find fulfilment in communities which shape our identity and help to make us who we are, we need shared commitments to fairness and justice.

We need these qualities – the traditional virtues of kindness and compassion, trust and loyalty, fairness and justice – in a strong sense. They are not merely instrumental needs. They are not merely *means to an end*, ways of inducing others to get along with us so that we can each satisfy our own individual desires. It is not that there is some independently identifiable condition of individual happiness, and that these virtues are instrumentally useful as means of achieving it. Rather, the virtues are (again as Aristotle would say) *components* of a flourishing life. They are integral to a fulfilled human existence, because such an existence is, in its essential nature, an existence shared with others and enjoyed in common.

What this approach has going for it is, first and foremost, that it is the right way of thinking about ethics. But also, importantly, it offers the best prospect for convergence between religious and non-religious perspectives. Humanists will see ethical values as grounded in our shared human nature. Religious believers will see that shared human nature as the gift of a divine creator who offers us the potential for richly fulfilled lives. That is not to say, of course, that such an approach holds out any prospect of a universal consensus. I have already indicated that it is directly at odds with a religious morality which claims to base itself on divine authority and to derive that authority from sacred texts and religious institutions. It is at odds, also, with that strand in the Christian tradition which emphasises the fallen state of human beings, in a condition of original sin from which they can be redeemed not by the exercise of any human capacities but only by divine grace. It is at odds with a version of Islam which sees the only good as unconditional submission to the revealed will of Allah. My hope that it can offer a common ground is nevertheless bolstered by the fact that this tradition of what we can call 'humanistic naturalism' has been influential in both Christianity and Islam. A theoretically developed version of it is a major strand in Aquinas's moral philosophy, and there is a strong Aristotelian influence also in the thought of Averroës (Ibn Rushd), including his ethical thinking.

Of course I am not suggesting that anyone seeking such common ground has to be a student of Aristotle and Aquinas and Averroës. The existence of common ground is most obviously apparent in the availability of a shared moral language of specific values – concern for others, mutual respect, honesty, fairness and justice. It is almost a commonplace that these are 'shared human values' and that religious and non-religious people can engage in fruitful moral debate on this terrain. But there are good reasons for digging deeper. First, by showing how these shared values are grounded in human needs and the facts of the human condition, we can recognise that their availability is not merely an accident, not a mere historical legacy or a pragmatic result of cultural consensus. We can show convincingly *why* they are shared. Second, the ability to do so can furnish an answer to the religious dogmatists who insist that, whatever the moral conclusions to which secular values appear to point, the sacred texts say otherwise. Third, the perspective of humanistic naturalism can provide a framework within which to debate values which appear to be more contestable, including some on which there may be disagreement depending on whether they are considered from a theistic or an atheist perspective.

Robin, in his work on health-care ethics, endorses the widely adopted set of four principles proposed by Tom Beauchamp and James Childress – autonomy, justice, non-maleficence and beneficence – but suggests that they should be complemented with four virtues to which he thinks that a distinctively religious approach can alert us: the virtues of compassion, care, faith and humility.[6] I do not myself see a sharp divide between 'principles' and 'virtues'. To the *principle* of autonomy there corresponds the *virtue* of respect for autonomy. The 'principles' of justice, non-maleficence and beneficence are classic moral *virtues*. The agreement on those four principles is not just a convenient consensus. We can see them as virtues rooted in our shared human needs.

What about Robin's additional four virtues? He is led to them by considering their prominence in the healing stories in the accounts of Jesus' ministry in the Synoptic Gospels, but he also thinks that they should have an appeal to those in other faith traditions and to secular humanists. Should they? The position which I am defending provides us with a framework in which to debate that question. I have already indicated the reasons why compassion and care are essential human virtues. What about faith and humility? These may be more contentious. Faith in the sense of mutual trust is clearly a virtue which human beings need, but how separable is it from faith in the religious sense? Is humility a proper recognition of the limits of human power, or does it presuppose a human subservience to a divine power? There may be no easy answers to such questions, and perhaps in the end no agreement to be reached, but at any rate, within the shared framework which I have been proposing, we can discuss rationally the place which these qualities might have in human life and the ways in which they might or might not contribute to human flourishing.

The 'moral gap'

I turn back now to the idea of a 'moral gap' which, according to some religious thinkers, can be filled only by a modified 'divine command' theory of morality. What exactly is this 'gap' supposed to consist in? It is, I take it, thought to be a motivational gap. We can recognise, without the need for any appeal to specifically religious considerations, that we should act with concern for others, with fairness and honesty, but, it is pointed out, we may fail to do so, through weakness of will. And the suggestion is then that only an understanding of these moral requirements as stemming from the commands of a deity can provide the necessary sense of *obligation* which is a distinctively moral motivation.

There is no denying that, if people see their moral obligations as being commanded by an all-powerful and all-wise supernatural being, this can provide an additional motivation. However, there are two problems here. First, there is no guarantee that anything, including an appeal to divine commands, can close the motivational gap. The classic expression of moral weakness is that of St Paul: 'For the good that I would, I do not; but the evil which I would not, that I do' (Romans 7:19). Paul knows that it is God's law that he disobeys, but he knows also that sometimes 'the law of sin' is stronger than the law of God.

There is also a deeper problem. We may indeed know that we ought to act from compassion or justice or honesty, and we may fail to do so, but if the additional motivation which is then drawn on is obedience to the supposed commands of a deity, it is not intrinsically related to the content of the values on which we know we ought to act. Any additional motivation provided by divine authority could equally well be harnessed to motivate actions of a quite different kind – and, as we well know, it all too often does so. Those who are inclined to torture and kill heretics or infidels, to persecute those whom they see as sinners or outsiders or sexual deviants, and who might otherwise be hesitant to do so, may be enabled to overcome their reluctance if they come to believe that God is telling them to do it. There may be a moral gap there, and an appeal to divine commands may function to close the gap – but it would be much better left unclosed.

My point here is not just a gratuitously opportunistic one. Rather, the point is that if people are not sufficiently motivated by good moral reasons, then the only way to fill the motivational gap is for them to become more deeply aware of the reasons themselves. In the case of other-regarding values such as compassion, justice or honesty, that means becoming more aware of *what it is like* to be the victim of cruelty or injustice, *what it is like* to be cheated or betrayed, exploited or enslaved. This greater awareness is generated most powerfully by *stories* – accounts, whether historical or fictional, of particular individuals, which bring to life the felt experience of suffering and the experience of having that suffering met by good actions.

I want to add, in conclusion, that this is where there may be a role for particular religious traditions. They each have their own repertoire of stories which have a special resonance for the members of that religious community. I have referred to the use which Robin makes of the gospel stories about Jesus' healing of the sick. Other stories in the Christian tradition which can strengthen moral awareness include the gospel parables such as the good Samaritan, and stories of Jesus' own abandonment and suffering and crucifixion. The stories of the captivity of the people of Israel in Egypt and in Babylon are motivating narratives of injustice and resistance. The power of such stories is, in part, their appeal to the sense of belonging to a moral community, a church or whatever, but it is wider than that. What the stories bring out, from their particular perspective, are the facts of shared human experience – what it is like to suffer, to feel lonely or abandoned, to live as a slave or in exile from your homeland. These sensitivities can be enhanced by stories from a particular religious tradition, just as they can be enhanced by stories which are not specifically religious, by historical narratives, biographies, novels and poems which belong to a wider shared culture.

I am suggesting, then, that insofar as there is a motivational gap between on the one hand the facts of human suffering and human flourishing and, on the other hand, our willingness to act on those facts, the gap is most effectively closed by stories, religious or non-religious, which make the facts of experience more vivid to us. It is not, however, the role of such stories to provide the basic grounding of our shared moral values. That is done, I have argued, by our understanding of what is needed for a flourishing human life. Because our human nature is as it is, we need supportive and emotionally satisfying relationships of mutual recognition, mutual loyalties and mutual sympathies, and we therefore need the moral virtues, the qualities which enable us to foster and sustain such relationships. I have argued that this grounding for shared values can be recognised equally by those who are religious and by those who are not. This grounding is not universally recognised. Those who share the values will not necessarily arrive at the same moral conclusions, and the divisions will sometimes be along the religious/non-religious fault-line. But at a time when fundamentalism and fanaticism can lead some people to do terrible things, it is vitally important that we cultivate the common ground we have.

Notes

1 Frederic Myers, 'George Eliot', in the *Century Magazine* (November 1881), quoted in Marghanita Laski, *George Eliot and Her World* (London: Thames & Hudson, 1973).
2 Friedrich Nietzsche, 'Skirmishes of an Untimely Man', *Twilight of the Idols* (1889), in *The Portable Nietzsche*, ed. and trans. Walter Kaufmann (New York: Viking, 1954), §5.
3 Robin Gill, 'Faith and Truth in Public Ethics', in *Theology* 117, no. 5 (September 2014): 334–41.
4 John Hare, *The Moral Gap* (Oxford: Clarendon Press, 1997), cited in Robin Gill, *Health Care and Christian Ethics* (Cambridge: Cambridge University Press, 2006), 25–7; also John Hare, 'Is There an Evolutionary Foundation for Human Morality?', in Phillip Clayton and Jeffrey Schloss (eds), *Evolution and Ethics: Human Morality in Biological and Religious Perspective* (Grand Rapids, MI: William B. Eerdmans Publishing Co., 2004), 187–203.
5 See especially Philippa Foot, *Natural Goodness* (Oxford: Oxford University Press, 2001).
6 Gill, *Health Care and Christian Ethics* (see above, note 4), chs 4 to 7, respectively.

10 Faith, ethics and values

Robin Gill

Let me say at the outset that I agree with the central positive points, if not all of the details, that my colleague Richard Norman makes. This is not entirely unexpected since we have worked together over many years to promote ethical discussion and debate within our own university. As someone clearly identifiable as a theologian and Anglican priest within a pluralistic university, it has been immensely helpful to me to have a thoughtful and morally sensitive colleague who is explicitly a secular humanist. This is particularly important because I want all academics, students and administrators within the university to think and act ethically whether they see themselves as religious or not. Any belief that only the religious (or, equally, only the secular) can be ethical runs directly counter to this shared aspiration.

We also share a conviction that neither divine commands nor natural purposes can 'be the whole story' in religious ethics. Some forms of traditionalist Jewish ethics based upon the Torah have claimed that the whole of Jewish ethics is based upon divine law. However, even within the Torah itself virtues seem to abound alongside divine laws, together with examples of good and bad moral behaviour. To take a single instance, the opening verses of Deuteronomy do appear as straightforward divine commands: 'Moses spoke to the Israelites just as the Lord had commanded him to speak to them' (1:3). However it very quickly appears that leaders are also expected to make their own moral judgements:

> I took the leaders of your tribe, wise and reputable individuals, and installed them as leaders over you ... I charged your judges at that time: 'Give the members of your community a fair hearing, and judge rightly between one person and another, whether citizen or resident alien.'
>
> (1:15–16)

It might also be noted that in the much contested, and for me deeply theological rather than scientific, first chapter of Genesis, there is a repeated phrase 'and God saw that it was good.' The Hebrew word for 'good' here apparently means good and not perfect (a crucial point in theodicy), but also note that here 'God saw', not 'God commanded' (crucial to the Euthyphro objection).

Within Christian ethics it is even more difficult to sustain an exclusively divine command understanding of ethics. As Richard points out there clearly are a couple of commands in Leviticus against homosexuality, but in the New Testament it is only Paul and not Jesus who repeats them. And even Paul does not recommend stoning to death as the required punishment for homosexual activity – any more than do present-day Christian traditionalists in North or Central Africa. It is not just pro-gay theologians such as me who engage in scriptural hermeneutics. The Jewish Bible was already engaged in internal scriptural hermeneutics (for example on the propriety of sacrifices) long before Christians continued this process within the New Testament (as competing statements in the latter on divorce show) and then beyond the New Testament with serious thinkers such as Augustine. It is quite possible that *any* intelligent moral appropriation of ancient texts (even from secular sources such as Aristotle) in the modern world (and even texts from, say, Kant, Marx or Nietzsche) requires the use of hermeneutics and thus selectivity or, as I would prefer to call it, discernment.

The same, I believe, is also the case with natural purposes and (ironically) evolutionary biology. Trying to read ethical principles straightforwardly off observations of 'nature' (as in natural law ethics) or off the blind forces of evolution (as in evolutionary ethics) faces very obvious problems and ambiguities. Some, especially in earlier generations, have argued that homosexuality is 'unnatural', but others point out that it is to be found within nature among a number of species. Again, a desire to survive and flourish for self, kith and kin can be seen as a by-product of evolution, but so (in various species including some humans) can an urge for dominant males to rape females and kill their offspring from another male (facilely excused as genes just being 'selfish'). This is not to claim that either nature or evolution is wholly irrelevant to ethical decision-making. But it is to claim that neither can be the whole story.

On this we agree. However, Richard goes further than me when he asserts: 'Our moral capacities are *entirely* explicable as features of a species which is the product of the evolutionary process, and they do not stand in need of some other, non-natural explanation' (Chapter 9, p. 109; emphasis added). The word 'entirely' in this sentence is troublesome. It is not simply conventional religious believers who are cautious here. Anthony Kenny, in his 2007 Royal Institute of Philosophy Annual Lecture, argued that 'it is difficult to see how language could originate by natural selection':

> It is not easy to see how the human race may have begun to use language because language-using individuals outbred the non-language users. This is not a difficulty in seeing how spontaneous mutation could produce a language-user; it is the difficulty of seeing how anyone could be described

as a language-using individual at all before there was a community of language-users. Of course, there are animal systems of communication that have some similarity with human language ... But human language is separated by a gulf from the communicative abilities of other animals.
(Kenny 2015, 262)

And Roger Scruton has argued that sociobiological 'explanations' of human altruism only work if they employ 'a minimalist concept of altruism', equating, say, the behaviour of an ant instinctively marching into the flames that threaten its anthill with that of an officer who intentionally 'lays down his life for his friends' (Scruton 2012, 26; and 2014, 55–7). Both Kenny and Scruton see such evolutionary explanations as remarkably thin.

On this last point Richard and I might agree, especially if it is related specifically to ethics. After all we share a strong interest in virtue ethics and in our practical work together we have both found this to be a good meeting point for those coming from differing religious and secular perspectives. In my own wider work in public bioethics I have also found the framework of virtue ethics to be especially helpful in establishing common ground *and* in attempting to locate how a theologian might be able to expand and enrich this common ground.

In his 2003 Royal Institute of Philosophy Annual Lecture Jürgen Habermas, not usually renowned for his theological sympathies, expounded the theme that in Europe religious tolerance has been the pacemaker for cultural rights. And at the end of his lecture he reminded the audience that even secular cultural groups 'are equally expected to adapt their internal ethos to the egalitarian standards of the community at large'. To this he immediately added the interesting warning that: 'Some of them may find this even tougher than do those communities who are able to resort to the highly developed conceptual resources of one or the other of the great world religions' (Habermas 2015, 323).

Only those religious or secular groups that are convinced that they can learn nothing of importance from anyone who is not of their group can afford to ignore this search for common ground. In contrast, those of us who do not start from this exclusive conviction, and hope instead to learn from others, need to be attentive and polite to each other. For me as a Christian that means, amongst other things, that in public ethics I must never use Jesus as a weapon. Very specifically I have tried, over the last sixteen years of my engagement in bioethics, to bring to public discussions values or virtues that I previously found to be largely absent from the secular bioethics lexicon. They are values or virtues that I personally (Gill 2006) derive from Jesus' healing ministry – namely, compassionate care, faithfulness and humility – but they also have resonance within other forms of faith including secular humanism, as Richard demonstrates. They do not contradict secular bioethical values such as non-maleficence, beneficence, autonomy and justice, but they might enrich and deepen them.

In what follows this article will point to areas where religious faith (admittedly filtered through my own engagement in Christian ethics) can enrich and deepen purely secular ethics. It will argue, rather circuitously, that a strong sense of moral obligation, moral formation embedded in liturgy, and moral concepts going well beyond self- or kin-interest, are especially characteristic of religious faith and can be quite thin outside that faith. I am going to draw on points that I will develop and defend in more detail in my next monograph, *Moral Passion and Christian Ethics* (Gill, forthcoming).

Flourishing

I will illustrate this last claim by looking at Richard's use of the concept of human flourishing – as it happens, a key concept also used by a theologian currently working in bioethics (Messer 2013). Richard's argument might be summarised as follows:

Human flourishing *is not*:

- just a psychological state;
- just happiness.

Human flourishing *is*:

- empirically grounded;
- derived from human needs/nature;
- dependent upon physical needs being met;
- dependent upon personal/emotional needs being met;
- dependent upon social needs being met;
- enlarged by the infectiousness of other people's joys and sufferings;
- enlarged by the pleasure in shared tasks and achievements;
- enlarged by compassion and kindness;
- fulfilled in community.

The first two points differ radically from some forms of utilitarianism. The central points envisage an empirically based assessment of human needs. The final points are very much those of a virtue ethicist. Each in turn needs to be considered.

Utilitarianism

Neither Richard nor I are card-carrying utilitarians. From the points that he makes I would imagine that he does not think that utilitarianism on its own adequately addresses the complexity and subtlety of ethics in the manner that virtue ethics does. However there is a recent group of Christian ethicists who take a quite different stance.

The American Catholic theologian Charles Camosy was instrumental in starting a dialogue with Peter Singer in his 2012 book *Peter Singer and Christian Ethics: Beyond Polarization*. John Perry, then working for the McDonald Centre for Theology, Ethics and Public Life, Oxford, organised a conference that resulted in a book that included a contribution from Singer. Perry argued that utilitarianism has Christian roots and ongoing affinities with versions of Christian ethics based upon 'well-being' or 'eudaimonia'. He maintained that – shorn of its single-mindedness, quasi-mathematical certainty and proposals such as infanticide – what is left of Singer's utilitarianism *is* compatible with Christian ethics. However the liberal Catholic theologian Lisa Sowle Cahill argued, in contrast, that Catholic social ethics and utilitarianism 'alike require expanded notions and practices of moral discourse' to address global problems effectively (Perry 2014, 123). Recalling the battles between double-effect and proportionalist styles of Catholic ethical reasoning, she finally judged both to be too individualistic to address global issues. John Hare's father supervised Peter Singer's doctorate, so he brought unique insights, concluding that Singer's atheism presents him with a problem:

> My suggestion is that by thinking of ourselves as following a God who sustains the moral order of the world, we gain resources for actually living in a way that fits that order. By taking theism out of the picture, we lose those resources, and the attempt to live that way becomes unstable in a way it was not before.
>
> (Perry 2014, 103)

Sadly this was a one-sided dialogue. Singer made few concessions in his contribution, repeating some of his most naive criticisms of Christianity and even when he detected points of contact – on say addressing world poverty – he disparaged Christians for not living up to their own teaching. For a long time he was a moral relativist (despite his strong moral criticisms of others). He is now more tempted by secular forms of moral objectivism and is moving away from making personal preferences his ethical basis, but he still makes little or no concession to theism. At best other contributors report that in conversation Singer agreed that his ethical task would be easier if he were a theist. But this may be little more, say, than my admitting that Jehovah's Witnesses have a very clear eschatology while not remotely accepting their eschatology as true.

Empirical assessment

One obvious way to make an empirical assessment of human needs is to use the developing work of moral psychology (see Tiberius 2015). I am not aware of theologians making much use of this literature yet and not all philosophers have noted it either. However an important exception is Lorraine Besser-Jones, in her 2014 book, *Eudaimonic Ethics: The Philosophy and Psychology of Living Well*.

At every stage Besser-Jones systematically lets empirical data from moral psychology control her philosophical thesis on eudaimonic ethics. She also distances herself from much of the philosophical literature on virtue ethics and wholly ignores any version of theological virtue ethics. Her topics range from sociability, autonomy and character to virtuous fulfilment and agency. The guiding principle is that a naturalistic account of innate psychological needs can supply the main framework of a virtue ethic that aims to promote functional 'eudaimonia' or well-being. Using psychological self-determination theory, derived from observing how children interact, she argues that:

> We seek out behaviors that allow us to feel competent; we gravitate toward engaging in meaningful interactions with others that allow us to feel connected to them; we make efforts to engage in those actions that are of our own choosing and ... with which we identify.
>
> (Besser-Jones 2014, 17–18)

She admits that this is a pragmatic approach to ethics and does not cover the full range of our moral obligations to others. Disarmingly she concludes that:

> Gone are discrete character traits, such as justice and compassion.
>
> (Besser-Jones 2014, 2)

Personal well-being is all. Clearly this does not address Richard's final points. Perhaps quantifiable experiments within moral psychology are just too prosaic to allow anything more. After all, how does one test or quantify the agonising moral decisions about life and death that we occasionally face?

However before responding to Richard's final points it is worth noting a theologian who has recently turned to empirical evidence beyond the prosaic, namely Michael Banner in his 2014 book *The Ethics of Everyday Life: Moral Theology, Social Anthropology, and the Imagination of the Human*.

This book represents a fascinating departure for Banner. Fifteen years earlier he rejected his youthful 'liberal' engagement with religion and science and championed instead 'dogmatic Christian ethics', quoting Karl Barth extensively when discussing – stridently and in detail – the moral problems of euthanasia, abortion, health-care rationing, the environment, biotechnology and sexuality (Banner 1999). But his focus now is upon what he terms the ethics of 'everyday life' rather than upon specific moral problems. Barth is mentioned in passing only twice and his new dialogue partner is social anthropology. He argues throughout that the detailed ethnographic studies of social anthropologists – with their concepts such as 'kinship' – have more to inform theologians than do either moral philosophers or bioethicists. For example, he argues that it is social anthropologists who can best untangle the complex kinship relationships that result from IVF (*in vitro* fertilisation) and surrogacy (and even heart-transplant patients who befriend their donor's family) or who can identify changing forms of private mourning ritual within apparently secularised societies. The picture of 'everyday ethics' that emerges from this, he argues, is very different from, and richer than, that envisaged by bioethicists.

Perhaps it is not too surprising that a theologian finds affinity with social anthropologists. The latter have never lost sight of the complex role that religious rituals, artefacts, buildings and stories still have in many societies and cultures around the world. And some of the leading social anthropologists – such as Evans-Pritchard and Mary Douglas – were themselves deeply religious. Social anthropology may point to an empirical dimension of human flourishing that Richard only touches upon at the end of his article.

The religious option in virtue ethics

My own interest in empirical data over many years has largely focused upon the sociology of religion, attempting to develop what I term 'sociological theology' (Gill 2012–13). Since this is already in the public domain, I will not repeat material from that venture here. Instead I will focus upon the recent work of the German sociologist Hans Joas. There are two important features of this work: first identifying religious faith and secularism as 'options' in the modern world and second setting these options into a fresh cultural evolutionary framework, now known as the 'Axial Age' framework.

In his 2012 book *Glaube als Option*, translated in 2014 as *Faith as an Option*, Joas follows Charles Taylor (2007) in arguing that the secular intellectual option, developed so strongly in the eighteenth century, is still viable today and is not likely to disappear – even though it is a position that is itself imbued with faith-type virtues and narratives. Secularism does not need to be adopted in the strident and frequently crude form of the so-called new atheists or even, one might add, in the more sophisticated but blunt form of A. J. Ayer's 'verification principle' – now largely discredited because it could not defend itself as being empirically verifiable. Nor can the secular option be dismissed cogently by people of faith claiming, for example, that 'without God there can be no morality'. Instead Joas proposes that religious people (across faiths and denominations) and non-religious people – committed neither to the stridency of the new atheists nor to the sectarianism of religious moral exclusivity – should dialogue together on a mutual understanding that their respective positions are both 'options', albeit different options. Joas summarises his argument as follows:

> The rise of this secular option [especially in the eighteenth century] entails a fundamental shift in the preconditions for faith ... Of course, the rise of the secular option should not be understood as the cause of secularization; but it does establish it as a possibility. In the first instance, then, the optionality of faith arises from the fact that it has in principle become possible not to believe, and subsequently from the

condition of religious pluralism as well ... the unavoidable decision to embrace either faith or nonfaith or to take up one of the various religious options is not a choice as understood by economists.

(Joas 2014, xii)

Focusing upon the faith option for the moment, what does the term 'option' here entail? Joas clearly distinguishes it from the term 'choice' used by those economists who have championed rational choice theory. He has long argued that most people do not 'choose' a particular faith, say, for its health benefits (which can be considerable), for its ability to enable social cohesion, or for its power to generate moral values. He rejects such 'benefits' as extraneous to religious faith as such. He might have added that adopting a religious faith on such grounds is, in economic and social terms, excessively burdensome. So, to return to my earlier example, if I were tempted to convert to the Jehovah's Witness faith solely because it generates a dedicated and tightly formed moral community (as millennial movements characteristically do), I might think twice, on purely economic grounds, about the cost in terms of both time and money, as well as the social isolation and public ridicule that a commitment to this particular faith would also involve.

Pausing for a moment of introspection, it seems to me that religious faith is more likely to be generated by largely non-cognitive attractions to sacred spaces, buildings, artefacts or rituals, or to holy lives, rather than by cognitive arguments justifying faith. Active secularism, in contrast, is more likely to be generated by aversion to such 'attractions'. Mild scepticism – whether non-active religious or secular – might be distinguished from both of these options by its focus upon cognitive arguments that are typically, and unsurprisingly, found to be inconclusive. They are inconclusive because they typically founder upon the initial arbitrary decision about whether the starting point of such arguments should be a presumption of faith or secularism. So, Western atheists, claiming that it is for theists to prove their case, typically conclude that classic arguments for the existence of God never amount to proof (Aquinas' proofs were never actually intended to be proofs against that presumption). In contrast Western theists, claiming that it is for atheists to prove their case, have tended recently to claim that the latter cannot disprove the existence of God irrefutably (how do you 'prove' a non-existence?) and that, while no single argument is 'proof' of God's existence (how could it be if God is transcendent?), some or all of the main arguments for the existence of God are cumulatively persuasive.

Anthony Kenny, again, concluded similarly that: 'Often, both theist and atheist philosophers, instead of offering arguments, adopt a strategy that might be called grabbing the default position – that is, a tactic of throwing the burden of proof on the opponents' (Kenny 2015, 265). Instead he suggested that 'agnosticism' should be the default position – a position that rejects a claim to certain knowledge or irrevocable faith either way, but still allowed him to say in the same lecture both 'I am not myself a believer' *and* 'I think belief in God can be reasonable' (Kenny 2015, 259 and 269).

In the conclusion to a recent study of the philosophical and theological implications of the cognitive science of religion, Roger Trigg has introduced a new twist to the default position dilemma. He uses a combination, of anthropological observations about the ubiquity of religion in some form or another even within previously isolated human societies, together with cognitive science observations of the religious responses of very small children, to argue that: 'We are not natural atheists ... Our uninformed reactions to the world are much less skeptical and are inclined to entertain minds apart from bodies, post-mortem survival, [and] disembodied agency' (Trigg and Barrett 2014, 218). Manifestly both of these contexts involve the study of people who have no access to Western philosophical discussions about the existence or non-existence of God. In that sense theirs are 'uninformed reactions' and largely non-cognitive in philosophical terms. Perhaps there is a clue here.

As an actively religious person I have always found my own lifelong religiosity (or indeed other people's lifelong irreligiosity) to be cognitively puzzling. The language of pre-cognitive attraction or aversion seems to me to be more compelling. Nor am I particularly convinced by the cognitive accounts of converts (to or from faith). As Charles Taylor (2007, 563f.) again observes, even the new atheists tend to offer conversion narratives about sudden cognitive (atheistic) illumination, when the reality is that conversion is typically extended over time and multifactorial or even that many conversion narratives are just grossly exaggerated. So in Christianity the formative conversion narratives of St Paul, Augustine and Luther are presented as moments of sudden cognitive illumination, yet behind each are hints of long-held attractions and aversions.

So where does this leave the person of faith today? I would tentatively suggest that it leaves her in good company. She is surrounded by people of religious and secular faiths who have opted for, remained in, or defaulted to, positions that are finally explicable only in the most personal and non-cognitive terms. This does not, of course, mean that rational cognition has no place or that values cannot be agreed across different religious and secular faiths. On the contrary, rational cognition is an essential guardian against totalitarian claims (sometimes dangerously linked to violence in the modern world as Richard notes) made by proponents of any particular faith option (whether religious or secular). But it does mean that rational cognition is unlikely to be able to generate the moral obligation and commitment typical of faith options. Indeed those traditions in moral philosophy, such as act-utilitarianism, that explicitly try to avoid the obvious faith element of, say, Marxism or even principled Kantianism, tend to struggle to generate moral obligation and commitment. Here, at least, there does appear to be a 'moral gap'.

The Axial Age framework

In *Faith as an Option* Joas also alludes to his wider work on religious universalism with the late Robert Bellah, notably in their 2012 edited book *The Axial Age and Its Consequences* and in Bellah's own 2011 book *Religion in Human Evolution: From the Paleolithic to the Axial Age*. The Axial Age – a term devised by the philosopher Karl Jaspers in 1949 – refers to the middle centuries of the first millennium BCE when there was an extraordinary flourishing of texts articulating universal human concerns in different parts of the world: the Hebrew prophets, Greek philosophy, Chinese thought and Indian Hindu and Buddhist texts. Joas summarises the achievements of these Axial Age texts, suggested by some (but not all) of the contributors to *The Axial Age and Its Consequences*, as follows:

> Self-sacrifice rather than the heroic use of violence, universalism rather than blood-brotherhood against enemies, the transcendence of the 'source of all holiness' against sacralization of the earthly ruler or earthly political orders – these are the key Axial Age achievements.
>
> (Bellah and Joas 2012, 108)

It is clear that Joas is making a normative and not simply a descriptive claim here, since these characteristics are depicted as 'achievements'. However the Axial Age texts do at least encompass both theistic and non-theistic options and still have the power to inspire non-theistic humanists or Buddhists and theists alike. They are texts that together and separately inspire people across different cultures and faith options. In that sense at least they might be regarded as 'universal'. For Joas and Bellah (the first is a liberal Catholic and the second an Episcopalian) they offer humanity a normative perspective that is not tied too closely to the particularities of any single faith tradition – a perspective that then shaped later faith traditions such as Christianity and Islam and, more recently, secular humanism.

Whatever the merits of this claim about the Axial Age, there is one framework that shaped Bellah's thinking and that is especially relevant to my suggestion that faith is more likely to be generated by largely non-cognitive attractions to sacred spaces, buildings, artefacts or rituals, or to holy lives, rather than by cognitive arguments justifying faith. This framework is provided by the veteran evolutionary psychologist Merlin Donald who also contributes to *The Axial Age and Its Consequences*. He distinguishes between four successive stages, or 'layers', in the evolution of primate/hominid culture, using a cognitive criterion for classification. The first stage is the episodic. Here prehominids do not differ from other primates. These primates have greater self-awareness and event-sensitivity than other mammals but their cognition is episodic and reactive. The second stage is mimetic. Here early hominids do differ profoundly from other primates. While they still lack language they have developed skills, gestures and forms of non-verbal communication well beyond other primates as well as showing variability of custom and culture. The third stage is mythic. Sapient humans now have language and thus the capacity to form oral social records. They have developed narrative thought and share oral collective myths. The fourth stage is theoretic and is represented especially by the Axial Age. Humans now develop extensive verbal and non-verbal symbolisation, massive external memory storage (for example written texts and now virtual texts) and have institutionalised thought and invention.

Donald argues that these four stages or 'layers' are still present in the modern mind and inform the way that we think and act:

> The modern mind ... is a complex mix of mimetic, mythic, and theoretic elements. Art, ritual, and music reflect the continuation of the mimetic dimension of culture in modern life. The narratives of the great religious books reflect the mythic dimension, as do the many secular myths of modern society. These two great domains – the mimetic and the mythic – are mandatory, hard-wired, and extremely subtle and powerful ways of thinking. They cannot be matched by analytic thought for intuitive speed, complexity, and shrewdness. They will continue to be crucially important in the future, because they reside in innate capacities without which human beings could not function.
>
> (Bellah and Joas 2012, 72)

Perhaps he ought to have added that the episodic layer is also still part of the modern human mind, evident, for example, in our intuitive spatial and eidetic awareness – albeit an awareness that seems to be more developed in some other primates. The episodic also still shapes our sexual attractions.

If this framework is adopted it offers important clues about religious faith as an option. Perhaps an initial attraction to sacred spaces, buildings, artefacts or rituals, or to holy lives, belongs mostly to the mimetic layer. It has often been noted that religious attraction has many affinities with musical attraction. It is mysterious in both to the theoretic mind as is the fact that some people experience the attraction but others not. Max Weber's celebrated observation that he was 'religiously unmusical' captures this affinity and quirkiness. The mythic level is almost as imponderable to the theoretic mind. Narratology theories are famously contradictory. Trying to capture in analytic terms the mechanisms, meaning and significance of myths, grand narratives and parables always seems finally to fail. After all myths, grand narratives and parables might not actually be needed if they could be captured in analytic terms. Reducing poetry to prose – or, indeed, music or art to words – has a similar problem. Academic theologians, like philosophers, are typically drawn to the theoretic layer when discussing religion. Theoretical analysis is, after all, our job. It helps us to write articles like the present one.

But, if my argument holds any water, theoretical analysis ends in distortion if it concludes that this is the only layer that is needed adequately to discuss religious faith or, indeed, human flourishing. Like many of the most fulfilling features of human life – love, friendship, aesthetics, morality – faith attraction may initially be generated by the mimetic layer and then sustained by the mythic layer.

By placing this mimetic layer in an evolutionary context, as Bellah does following Donald, there is an obvious danger. Older theories of social evolution tended to consider it to be 'primitive' and thus 'inferior' to the subsequent mythic and theoretic layers. This danger is not entirely absent from the project, since it does, in Donald's words, tend to regard the Axial Age as 'the absolute cutting edge of human experience at the time' (Bellah and Joas 2012, 74). In addition, as the sociologist José Casanova (ibid., 200) points out, if ritual is basically seen as a product of the mimetic layer, then is all ritual in subsequent layers to be seen as 'religious', or just some 'ritual', and if the latter, how do we distinguish between the two?

There is another problem that ought to be mentioned. In such an evolutionary framework there is inevitably some unverifiable speculation. For instance, it is posited that early hominids in the mimetic layer lacked language. That might seem plausible but it is still a speculation. Suppose instead that early hominids always did have language and when 'they' did not then they are not considered to be hominids. In contrast, a framework that is not tied to successive layers of evolution might simply distinguish between specifically hominid activities that do require the use of language (mythic and axial activities) and those that do not of necessity (mimetic and eidetic activities). It remains the case that even usually wordy forms of mimetic activity can still function powerfully without language, as can be seen in mime within theatre and ballet, scat within jazz singing, and in both liturgical silence and more noisy, but often wordless, 'speaking' in tongues within corporate worship. The 'acting out' of the Eucharist (with deep roots in the Passover meal) is also mimetic, sustained by mythic narrative, and is a crucial part of moral formation for many practising Christians. It embeds values shared with secular humanism, but it also provides a profound and repeated communal process of repentance, forgiveness and grace (Waters 2014).

My suggestion is more modest and less evolutionary than Bellah. I am happy to go with Donald's observation that 'mimetic culture still forms the underpinning of human culture' and to worry less about when it first emerged. He sees it as closely related to the development of hominid skills (well beyond that of other primates) in a prelinguistic age. Yet, much more importantly, he sees mimetic culture as persisting throughout distinctly hominid existence:

> It persists in numerous cultural variations in expression, body language, and expressive custom (most of which people are unaware of and cannot describe verbally), as well as in elementary craft and tool

use, pantomime, dance, athletic skill, and prosodic vocalization, including group displays ... imagination – mimetic imagination – recreates an experience in time. It survives in the performing arts and in the essentially theatrical nature of human relationships and living patterns. Most visibly, it is the basis of role-playing, fantasy, and self-identification with various roles.

(Bellah and Joas 2012, 58)

In the modern world it is now obviously possible to live without a religious faith option, or, I suppose, without any of the features of mimetic culture. But we might conclude that if people really have no 'faith' whatsoever, whether religious or not, and no other expression of mimetic culture – including the virtuous aspects of human flourishing that Richard outlines – then their lives will be considerably impoverished. Something like that may indeed be the fate of those with very severe forms of autism. But as a liberal democrat I believe that no one should properly be coerced into faith, or into the requirements of a particular faith, any more than they should, or seriously can, be coerced into love, friendship, aesthetics, performing arts or even personal morality. But equally people of faith should not be excluded from the public forum, especially if they can resonate with, and perhaps enrich, communal and social values shared with other faith options, whether religious or secular.

Bibliography

Banner, Michael (1999) *Christian Ethics and Contemporary Moral Problems*. Cambridge: Cambridge University Press.

Banner, Michael (2014) *The Ethics of Everyday Life: Moral Theology, Social Anthropology, and the Imagination of the Human*. Oxford: Oxford University Press.

Bellah, Robert N. (2011) *Religion in Human Evolution: From the Paleolithic to the Axial Age*. Cambridge, MA: Belknap Press of Harvard University Press.

Bellah, Robert N. and Hans Joas (eds) (2012) *The Axial Age and Its Consequences*. Cambridge, MA: Belknap Press of Harvard University Press.

Besser-Jones, Lorraine (2014) *Eudaimonic Ethics: The Philosophy and Psychology of Living Well*. New York and London: Routledge.

Camosy, Charles (2012) *Peter Singer and Christian Ethics: Beyond Polarization*. Cambridge: Cambridge University Press.

Gill, Robin (2006) *Health Care and Christian Ethics*. Cambridge: Cambridge University Press.

Gill, Robin (2012–13) *Sociological Theology*, vol. 1: *Theology in a Social Context*; vol. 2: *Theology Shaped by Society*; vol. 3: *Society Shaped by Theology*. Farnham, UK: Ashgate.

Gill, Robin (forthcoming) *Moral Passion and Christian Ethics*. Cambridge: Cambridge University Press.

Habermas, Jürgen (2015) 'Religious Tolerance – The Pacemaker for Cultural Rights', in Ted Honderich (ed.), *Philosophers of Our Times*. Oxford: Oxford University Press.

Joas, Hans (2014) *Faith as an Option: Possible Futures for Christianity*. Stanford, CA: Stanford University Press.

Kenny, Anthony (2015) 'Knowledge, Belief, and Faith', in Ted Honderich (ed.), *Philosophers of Our Times*. Oxford: Oxford University Press.

Messer, Neil (2013) *Flourishing: Health, Disease, and Bioethics in Theological Perspective*. Grand Rapids, MI: William B. Eerdmans Publishing Co.

Perry, John (ed.) (2014) *God, the Good, and Utilitarianism: Perspectives on Peter Singer*. Cambridge: Cambridge University Press.

Scruton, Roger (2012) *The Face of God*. London: Continuum.

Scruton, Roger (2014) *The Soul of the World*. Princeton, NJ, and Oxford: Princeton University Press.

Taylor, Charles (2007) *A Secular* Age. Cambridge, MA: Belknap Press of Harvard University Press.

Tiberius, Valerie (2015) *Moral Psychology: A Contemporary Introduction*. New York and London: Routledge.

Trigg, Roger and Justin L. Barrett (eds) (2014) *The Roots of Religion: Exploring the Cognitive Science of Religion*. Farnham, UK: Ashgate.

Waters, Brent (2014) *Christian Moral Theology in the Emerging Technoculture: From Posthuman Back to Human*. Farnham, UK, and Burlington, VT: Ashgate.

11 The spiritual and the sacred

Prospects for convergence between religious and non-religious outlooks

John Cottingham

> Two roads diverged in a yellow wood
> And sorry I could not travel both
> And be one traveller, long I stood
> And looked down one as far as I could ...
> Then took the other ...
> Robert Frost[1]

Divergence, convergence and objectivity

People take different roads through life, not just in publicly visible ways, such as in their choice of occupations or partners, but also in respect of what might be called the interior tone of their lives. So two people with outwardly similar levels of achievement, health and material goods may lead very different lives, the one seeing his or her existence as full of meaning and value, the other plagued by a sense of futility and purposelessness. Indeed, one and the same individual, as she or he goes through life, may switch from one state to the other, as reported by the protagonist at the start of Dante's *La divina comedia*: 'Halfway along the road that is our life/ I found myself inside a murky wood/ where the straight path ahead was all confused'.[2]

If the road ahead was always clear, with no existential crises of the kind Dante describes, and no crucial decision points such as Robert Frost refers to, the life in question would not be a recognisably human life – or at least it would be a very untypical one. Unlike the other animals, whose lives follow a set pattern determined by environmental conditions and their inbuilt drives and goals, each of us to a great extent maps out his or her own distinctive pathway, as we struggle to see the right way forward. Hence, while the life of any given cow or horse will not significantly diverge from that of any other in similar circumstances, the life of a human being, however much it may have in common with that of a similarly placed neighbour, always has its own unique trajectory.

We would not want it to be otherwise. The varied and diverging forms of human activity, and the hard choices each of us faces about which path to follow, are a sign of humanity's greatness.[3] Even though our freedom is not always comfortable, and its attendant dilemmas and doubts and mistakes can cause anguish, few of us would relish an existence in which all the available roads were made to converge into just one approved route.

Nevertheless, though divergence may in certain respects be something to be celebrated, there are other respects in which its opposite, convergence, is to be welcomed. In the domain of scientific inquiry, for example, it seems evident that a plethora of competing explanations for a given phenomenon is a sign that something is amiss. To be sure, different teams of scientists may pursue different hunches and different lines of inquiry, but the expectation is that ultimately our scientific theories will converge, or at least show a tendency to converge, as they get closer to the truth. As Bernard Williams once observed, in science 'there should ideally be convergence on an answer, where the best explanation of the convergence involves the idea that the answer represents how things are'. The very notion of objectivity in the sciences seems to presuppose that our theories and explanations should in principle be constrained by the way the world is, so that there will, or should ideally, be a convergence which is, as Williams went on to put it, 'guided ... by how things actually are'. [4]

In the domain of ethics, in contrast to that of scientific inquiry, Williams himself was very sceptical about the possibility of convergence: he saw no prospect of a 'convincing theory of knowledge for the convergence of reflective ethical thought on ethical reality in even a distant analogy to the scientific case'.[5] His attitude here partly reflected the influence upon him of Nietzsche's deflationary view of the status of morality, that 'peculiar institution', as Williams called it, based on the (supposedly dubious) idea of binding and inescapable obligations.[6] The current philosophical consensus, however, has emerged as very much more sympathetic to the idea of objective and authoritative moral requirements than was common among Williams' generation; and it is probably fair to say that the majority of moral philosophers working today hold that there are objectively right answers to ethical and moral questions. Such answers may of course be very difficult to establish (requiring complex investigation and careful debate), and there may also be hard cases where we are forced to choose between competing goods, but in principle, so runs the prevailing contemporary view, genuine objective ethical truth about what is good and right is, as it were, already there waiting to be investigated, just as scientific truth is. And this gives grounds for thinking that, although it may take a long time to achieve, we may in principle expect an ultimate convergence in ethical thought, just as in science.

In the case of religious thought, by contrast, things look very different. For here what is at stake is not just the acceptance of a theory in physics (for example about the nature of gravity) or in ethics (for example about the relation between justice and utility), but the adoption of an outlook concerning the ultimate significance of the entire universe and our place within it. Thus the theist, who holds that the meaning of each individual's existence lies in his or her relationship to a loving personal creator, will presumably see the whole of reality in a completely different light from the Buddhist who maintains that the very idea of an individual self is an illusion, or from the contemporary scientific naturalist who holds that our existence is a pure accident generated by forces that manifest only 'blind, pitiless indifference'.[7] The prospect for convergence between such radically distinct and incommensurable worldviews appears, to say the least, to be remote.

Yet the advocates of the various theistic or non-theistic outlooks just mentioned all typically maintain that their own respective worldviews are *objectively correct*, representing the true, the enlightened, answer as to the ultimate nature of reality. And to espouse an objectivist view of truth, as our earlier discussion has indicated, is to hold that differing views ought ultimately to converge. Hence, if one maintains that, for example, the Islamic, or the Christian, or the scientific naturalist worldview is objectively correct, this seems to carry with it a presumption that ultimately, given enough time, everyone on the planet should come to acknowledge the truth of the worldview in question. Certainly many religious believers have indeed displayed just such a confident expectation of eventual convergence – a notable example being the attitude of many Christians in the imperialistic climate of nineteenth-century England, as seen in a verse from the once popular hymn 'From Greenland's Icy Mountains':

> Shall we, whose souls are lighted
> with wisdom from on high,
> Shall we to those benighted
> the lamp of life deny?
> Salvation! O salvation!
> The joyful sound proclaim,
> Till earth's remotest nation
> has learned Messiah's Name.[8]

The attitude persists. In our own time we find militant fundamentalists of various creeds, secular as well as religious, who apparently envisage a world in which their own chosen form of orthodoxy will reign supreme over all the planet. But (no doubt as a result of many factors, including rapidly widening travel and communication) there has also arisen, in many quarters, a more reflective 'globalist' outlook that inclines towards tolerance for, and even welcoming of, diversity in religious belief, even on the part of those who are themselves devoutly committed to a particular creed or faith. Those attracted to this more tolerant stance may be prepared to put on indefinite hold, as it were, the theoretical requirement that competing worldviews should ultimately converge on the truth, constrained by the reality of 'how things actually are', and substitute instead the more modest hope of finding some convergence at the level not of doctrine and theory, but of practice and behaviour. For as Rudyard Kipling so eloquently observed over a century ago, it is at the practical level of human need, the universal longing for solace and comfort amid the inevitable pains of human life, that common ground is likely to be found, irrespective of differences of doctrine and ideology:

> My brother kneels, so saith Kabir,
> To stone and brass in heathen-wise,
> But in my brother's voice I hear
> My own unanswered agonies.
> His God is as his fates assign;
> His prayer is all the world's – and mine.[9]

Spiritual praxis as common ground

The Buddhist tradition speaks of *dukkha* (suffering, anxiety, difficulty) as one of the fundamental features of human existence, and there is no doubt that many people turn to religion partly for urgent practical reasons, as a means of finding some way to cope with the suffering that is our human lot. Our modern technological age has tended to prioritise cost-effective quick-fix solutions for our plight, such as tranquillisers and behaviour therapy, but the great religions, whether of the non-theistic variety (such as mainstream Buddhism) or the theistic kind (both polytheistic, as in Hinduism, and monotheistic, as in the Abrahamic faiths), have all evolved complex spiritual practices, including prayer, fasting, meditation, chanting and various prescribed movements and rituals, part of whose purpose is evidently related to dealing with suffering; the goal is either eventually to escape from the world of suffering altogether, or else perhaps to reconfigure it within a framework of significance that alleviates it or helps us to bear it. In a more positive vein, such spiritual praxis also seems aimed at cultivating calmness of mind – what the Stoics called *ataraxia* (tranquillity) – together with an attitude of joyful openness and attentiveness to the good or the divine, or to reality as a whole.

These are complex notions whose diverse metaphysical implications would require much time and effort to explore; but when we look at the varying religious traditions at the level of praxis rather than of theory, we do seem to find a considerable degree of convergence. If we observe a line of monks, clad in habits of uniform cut and colour, all with heads bowed in a posture of attentive submission and concentration, all joining in unison in a repeated chant or hymn, our strong impression is likely to be that despite all the variations in culture and tradition that have shaped these differing sects and groups, there is in the end a single underlying religious impulse, perhaps as old as humanity itself, which is manifesting itself here. And as we watch the monks completing their meditation and liturgical observance and turning towards the more active part of their daily routine – which will almost certainly include acts of compassion towards others, or service to those in need or distress – we are likely to be struck again with the *overlap* between these different ways of life, rather than by the metaphysical doctrines that may divide them.

One could of course argue that the above similarities apply only to rather special groups of people – those who have chosen a monastic style of existence that sets them apart from the occupations and involvements of ordinary human life. But the broad category of spiritual praxis is certainly not confined to those with priestly or monastic vocations, nor indeed is it even necessarily restricted to those who would describe themselves as religious – as witnessed in our own time by the apparently growing numbers who classify themselves as 'spiritual but not religious'. It is striking that this latter group includes many of the so-called 'new atheists', some of whom have underlined the importance in their lives of certain heightened forms of spiritual experience, the significance of which, they argue, does not depend in any way on theistic or other metaphysical beliefs. Thus Christopher Hitchens, towards the end of his life, declared in a debate:

> I'm a materialist ... yet there is something beyond the material, or not entirely consistent with it, what you could call the Numinous, the Transcendent ... It's in certain music, landscape, certain creative work, and without this we really would merely be primates. It's important to appreciate [this] and religion has done a very good job of enshrining it in music and architecture. [10]

Similarly, Sam Harris, another prominent spokesman for the new atheism, has observed that 'spiritual experiences often constitute the most important and transformative moments in a person's life. Not recognizing that such experiences are possible or important can make us appear less wise even than our craziest religious opponents.' [11]

Once again, then, we seem to come up against the fact of convergence not at the theoretical or doxastic level (for what wider gulf in belief systems could there be than that which divides the theist from the typical secularist critic of religion?), but at the level of praxis and experience. Believers and non-believers alike may be moved to tears by the beauties of nature, or by a masterwork such as Bach's *St Matthew Passion*, or by those moments in our relations with others when we lay aside our demanding and egoistical selves and feel filled with outgoing impulses of tenderness and love. The labels used may be different – religious people may speak of 'sacred' moments, while humanist and atheists may, like Hitchens, prefer terms such as 'numinous' – but the specially charged nature of the experiences themselves cannot be denied. They take us beyond the routine world of useful toil and pleasant recreation, important and valuable though those things are, towards a domain of value and meaning that is not obviously manifest in the material structures that compose our bodies and our environment, nor derived merely from our biologically inherited drives, but which seems to reflect something richer, deeper and more awe-inspiring.[12]

How are we to interpret these 'sacred' or 'numinous' experiences, which seem to be a part of our universal human birthright, and whose special resonance is likely to be acknowledged by anyone who 'wears a human heart', [13] irrespective of religious allegiance or its lack? The very fact of their universality is, for those who hope for better things for mankind, encouraging. They are of a different order from our desire for progress in science or technology (urgently though we need the latter in order to address the dangers that threaten both our own species and perhaps all living forms on the planet), but relate instead to our need to transcend our nature, reaching beyond the given to something finer. This 'reaching forward' is not merely a matter of intellectual inquiry, but involves deep emotional and imaginative sensibility, together with what can only be described as moral yearnings, for self-improvement and for deeper awareness of the demands and mysteries of love and compassion; and to this should be added 'aesthetic' yearnings (for want of a better term) – impulses to struggle upwards and attune ourselves to what is beautiful, not just passively but also actively, by creating shapes, words, colours and sounds that resonate with our sensibilities and give expression to our longings.

If there is indeed a convergence here at the level of lived human experience, there will of course nevertheless be wide differences in how religious and non-religious people respectively understand and interpret what is going on. For the theist, the very universality of spiritual impulses and experiences of the sacred may be adduced as evidence for a *sensus divinitatis*,[14] a capacity to apprehend the divine that in some form or other is shared by all humankind, even though it may not necessarily be recognised under that description. The secularist, by contrast, is likely to favour a 'naturalistic' interpretation – perhaps that these impulses and experiences derive from biologically explicable capacities and dispositions inherited from our evolutionary past. It is not perhaps obvious how a capacity for so-called 'spiritual experience' might confer a selective advantage, but there is great deal of speculation in the contemporary literature on how religious and quasi-religious impulses might have played a useful role (e.g. in promoting social solidarity), or else been a by-product of other traits whose presence was beneficial in evolutionary terms.[15] Except for the crudest reductionists, however, the question of the social and biological origins of these phenomena does not affect the question of their value and importance for us here and now; and that value and importance, as we have seen, is something on which religious and non-religious thinkers seem happy to agree, notwithstanding the radical divergence in their respective worldviews.

Reconciliation and its limits

Those who, like the present writer, are by nature reconciliationists, wanting to reach out to those of different belief systems in the hope of finding common ground, will no doubt welcome the signs of convergence at the level of human praxis and experience that have so far been sketched out. But it is important that our search for what is shared does not lead us to gloss over crucial differences, or to assimilate outlooks that are ultimately incommensurable. Convergence in behaviour is, notoriously, not an infallible indicator of 'what lies beneath', in the thoughts and feelings of the subjects in question. Three people might witness a public execution with identical composure and stillness of posture, yet the first be wracked with sympathy for the victim, the second be bursting with sadistic delight at the demise of his enemy, while the third is simply blankly indifferent. And even were it to be the case, as some devotees of so-called 'neurophilosophy'[16] suppose, that we could 'read off' the mental states of the subjects from a scan of their brain activity, so that we could tell whether the attitudes were ones of distress or exultation or neutrality, there may still be significant divergences in how each of the three subjects interprets the *meaning* of what is going on – divergences which could not be identified even through the most exhaustive printout of the respective bodily states, including the electrochemistry of the brain.

The reason for this limitation in what scientific investigation could even in principle establish is, to put it crudely, that 'meanings ain't in the head', as the American philosopher Hilary Putnam once trenchantly observed.[17] To understand the meaning of what someone is thinking about and experiencing we need to look not just at the physically investigable processes going on inside the body, brain and nervous system, but *outwards*, to the complex social network of human interaction that generates all our conceptual resources and allows us to describe and interpret our experience.

Reflecting on the implications of this should raise serious doubts about the claim that there is one single phenomenon, called 'spiritual experience' or 'experience of the sacred or the numinous' that is common currency irrespective of the religious or non-religious outlooks of the practitioners. So although a reconciliationist may initially be hospitable to the idea that one can cultivate spiritual awareness without religion, and in particular without theistic religion, we need to pause and ask exactly what *kind* of awareness is in question. It is certainly a welcome development to find secularists such as Sam Harris paying attention to the phenomenon of spiritual experience (the 'great hole in secularism, humanism, rationalism, atheism …'),[18] and acknowledging that there is more to understanding reality than many scientistically oriented philosophers are commonly prepared to allow. But spiritual experience cannot be considered in isolation, as a kind of 'self-standing' phenomenon, as it were. We always need to ask about what the experience is an experience *of*. And it is significant that the reality that is disclosed by spiritual experience according to naturalists such as Harris (who in this area is strongly influenced by Buddhism and kindred creeds) turns out to be a wholly impersonal one. It is not one that addresses us personally with a call to change, or requires anything of us, but is a blank and impersonal flux.[19]

This is not to deny that the spiritual mindfulness that growing numbers of contemporary secularists advocate may be cultivated in ways that do not require subscribing to any of the theistic doctrines that they deplore. And many of the resulting states mentioned by Harris, and familiar from many types of Eastern religion, turn out to have very considerable appeal: a sense of 'selfless well-being', 'self-transcendence', 'paying attention to the present moment', a feeling of 'boundless love' (albeit of a fundamentally impersonal kind), a sense of being 'at one with the cosmos', and 'bringing stress to an end'.[20] Nothing said in the present essay is intended to deny the value of such goals. But we need to recognise how far they diverge from the religious encounters with the sacred described in many of the texts of classical theism – those intensely *personal* encounters, infused with awe and charged with moral significance, where the individual feels him- or herself to be checked, to be scrutinised, and to be called upon to respond and to change.

This electrifying charge of moral significance is vividly apparent in many, much admired passages in the Hebrew Bible, that most seminal source for classical Western theism, as in the following psalm:

> Let the heavens be glad, and let the earth rejoice: let the sea roar, and all it contains.
> Let the field exult, and all that is in it: then all the trees of the forest will sing for joy
> Before the LORD, for he comes, he comes to judge the earth: he will judge the world in righteousness, and the peoples in his faithfulness. [21]

The language of such texts may be uncongenial to contemporary scientific naturalists, who pride themselves on having totally rejected the notion of any supernatural being (the 'God hypothesis', as Richard Dawkins disparagingly calls it).[22] But reading such passages in context makes it clear that God is not introduced as an immaterial force that is supposed to *explain* the behaviour of the oceans and fields and the woods; rather the vivid beauty and splendour of the natural world is that which *makes manifest* the divine. The world is understood *religiously* – not as a blank impersonal process, not as A. E. Housman's 'heartless witless nature',[23] not as a manifestation of 'blind, pitiless indifference', as Richard Dawkins characterises it, [24] but as 'charged with the grandeur of God'. This is the vision powerfully expressed by Gerard Manley Hopkins when he speaks of all things as being 'charged with love ... charged with God, [so that] if we know how to touch them [they] give off sparks and take fire, yield drops and flow, ring and tell of him'. [25]

The feebleness of modern labels like 'aesthetic' for the type of language found in the psalm just quoted is even more apparent in an earlier psalm, where God is described as the one who 'breaks the cedars of Lebanon and makes Lebanon skip like a calf', who 'shakes the wilderness and strips the forests bare, while all in the temple cry "Glory"'.[26] The cry of 'Glory' (in Hebrew *kavod*, כָּבוֹד) signifies something weighty with significance, sacred, mysterious, a manifestation of the divine, as conveyed in the description of the pillar of fire and cloud which led the Israelites out of Egypt, or the cloud atop Mount Sinai where God's law was manifest to Moses.[27] We are not talking of 'natural beauty' in the attenuated modern sense, but of something fearful that calls forth reverence and awe, like the burning bush, flaming but never consumed, where Moses was told to keep his distance.[28] These are not 'impressive sights', of the kind familiar from television nature programmes, but events pregnant with moral significance, as is clear from the lines in the earlier psalm quoted, where the forests 'sing for joy' not just in pantheistic exuberance, as it were, but rather because *the world is to be judged*. In psychological or phenomenological terms, what is happening here is an experience where the subject is overwhelmed by the power and beauty of nature in a way that is somehow intertwined with awareness of one's own weakness and imperfection, and a sense of confrontation with the inexorable demands of justice and righteousness. The 'religious understanding' involved here is, in short, the kind of awareness which enables one to see the world transfigured, so that it is irradiated with meaning and value, and the human subject, caught up in that mystery, is unmistakeably called on to be no longer a spectator, a mere 'tourist', but to *respond*, to be a morally responsive agent, part of a cosmos that is *diaphanous*, transparent to the divine.

Set against this, the meditative goals of impersonal and boundless oceanic well-being have an essentially quietist character. They stem from a long Eastern tradition of spirituality in which the paramount objective is achieving bliss by detaching oneself from the stressful world of struggle, commitment and dependency. It is of course true that many Eastern sages advocate a path of virtue and right conduct (and indeed the compassionate outlook of many practitioners of Eastern spirituality is greatly to be respected and admired); so in this sense there is an ethical component involved. But it is not a component that is intrinsically connected to any underlying vision of moral goodness at the heart of reality; for the Eastern vision is one in which personal commitments and demands are based on an illusion, and ultimate reality is simply an impersonal continuum of conditions that arise and pass away.

Although constraints of space require us to bring to a close this brief survey of the content of spiritual experience across the theistic, non-theistic and secularist outlooks, enough has perhaps been said to indicate that the initially promising idea of convergence at the level of spiritual praxis and experience is not in all respects well founded. For the reconciliationist, concerned about the evident dangers of religious confrontation in today's world, this is no doubt a disappointing result. But if the frameworks and worldviews we have been discussing turn out in the end to be radically and irreconcilably distinct, it does not follow that this need necessarily lead to an angry stand-off between those of different outlooks. The religious bigotry and oppression that blighted our history in past centuries has largely faded in much of the developed world (though significant swathes of fundamentalist intolerance still remain even in supposedly 'advanced' Western countries, not to mention other parts of the world). But when all that is said, it cannot be denied that we find at the heart of the theistic vision at its best, together with the secular liberalism and humanism that are its offspring, and also running through much Eastern religious thought, a precious thread of compassion and respect for our fellow human beings, which no divergences of doctrine and belief, however radical, ought to undermine.

Notes

1 Robert Frost, 'The Road Not Taken', from *Mountain Interval* (New York: Holt, 1920).
2 *Nel mezzo del cammin di nostra vita/ mi ritrovai per una selva oscura/ che la diritta via era smarrita.* Dante Alighieri, *La divina comedia: Inferno* (*c.*1310), canto 1, opening lines, trans. JC.
3 Compare René Descartes, *Meditations* [*Meditationes de prima philosophia*, 1641]: our will or freedom of choice is the one human faculty that is perfect of its kind, so that it is 'above all in virtue of the will that I understand myself to bear in some way the image and likeness of God'; Fourth Meditation, trans. JC. (Descartes goes on to point out, however, that this quasi-divine power of free choice can nevertheless be a source of error and sin, when we exercise it in the wrong direction.)
4 Bernard Williams, *Ethics and the Limits of Philosophy* (London: Collins, 1985), ch. 8, 136.
5 Williams, *Ethics and the Limits*, 152.
6 Ibid., ch. 10.
7 Richard Dawkins, *Rivers Out of Eden* (New York: Basic Books, 1995), 133.
8 'From Greenland's Icy Mountains' (1819), by the Anglican parson Reginald Heber, who became Bishop of Calcutta in 1823.
9 Rudyard Kipling, *Kim* (1901), ch. 14.
10 Christopher Hitchens, in debate with Tony Blair (2010), quoted in Jules Evans, 'The New Atheists Are Actually Transcendentalists', *Philosophy for Life and Other Dangerous Situations* (Jules Evans' blog), posted 24 January 2014, <http://philosophyforlife.org/the-new-atheists-are-actually-transcendentalists/>.
11 Sam Harris, *Waking Up: A Guide to Spirituality without Religion* (New York: Simon & Schuster, 2014), cited in Evans, 'New Atheists'.
12 See John Cottingham, *How to Believe* (London: Bloomsbury, 2015), ch. 2.1.
13 The phrase is David Hume's, speaking of our universal moral impulses of benevolence, in his *Enquiry concerning the Principles of Morals* (1751), 5.2.
14 '[A] tacit confession of a sense of deity inscribed in the hearts of all'. John Calvin, *Institutes* [*Christianae religionis institutio*, 1536], 1.3.1.
15 See further Joseph A. Bulbulia, 'The Evolution of Religion', in R. I. Dunbar and L. Barrett (eds), *The Oxford Handbook of Evolutionary Psychology* (Oxford: Oxford University Press, 2007), ch. 44.
16 For this term, see for example Patricia S. Churchland, *Neurophilosophy: Toward a Unified Science of the Mind–Brain* (Cambridge, MA: MIT Press, 1989).

17 Hilary Putnam, 'The Meaning of Meaning' (1975), in *Philosophical Papers,* vol. 2 (Cambridge: Cambridge University Press, 1985).
18 Harris, *Waking Up,* 202.
19 The argument of the next few paragraphs draws on material from chapter 5 of Cottingham, *How to Believe.*
20 Harris, *Waking Up,* 17, 18, 3, 5, 43, 48.
21 Psalm 96 [95]: 11–13.
22 Richard Dawkins, *The God Delusion* (London: Bantam Press, 2006), ch. 2.
23 In 'Tell me not here, it needs not saying', *Last Poems* (1922).
24 Dawkins, *Rivers Out of Eden,* 133.
25 G. M. Hopkins, *Note-Books and Papers,* ed. H. House (Oxford: Oxford University Press, 1937), 342, cited in W. H. Gardner (ed.), *The Poems and Prose of Gerard Manley Hopkins* (Harmondsworth: Penguin, 1953), 231. Compare Hopkins's famous poem, which begins: 'The world is charged with the grandeur of God', from *Poems (1876–1889).*
26 Psalm 29 [28]: 5–9.
27 Exodus 13:21, 16:10, 24:16.
28 Exodus 3:5.

12 Matters of life and death

Anna Strhan

In his 1909 essay 'Bridge and Door', the sociologist Georg Simmel describes the human being 'as the connecting creature who must always separate and cannot connect without separating ... And the human being is likewise the bordering creature who has no border' (1994, 174). We are beings who make sense of the world through our capacity to connect and to separate things, and Simmel argues that this guides all human activity, shaping our physical, symbolic, emotional and imagined spaces and leaving material marks in the world around us. Exploring the nature of modes of connection and separation is perhaps particularly pertinent to understanding the relations between 'atheism' and 'religion', or between 'non-religion' and 'religion', as it is indexed in the very act of naming these as fields of exploration. In my writing 'non-religion', for example, what modes of uniting and disuniting shape my instinct to hyphenate the word (or not)? As the prefix 'non-' carves out a space of separation from religion, it also draws attention to the doubled nature of lines of division: 'the separation of objects, people or places is always shadowed by the idea – the "fantasy" or the danger – of their connection' (Tonkiss 2005, 31). Drawing out a deeper understanding of the (simultaneous) practices of connection and separation between religious and non-religious cultures can enable us to develop more nuanced understandings of the everyday realities of members of these groups, which move beyond common assumptions that their interrelations are necessarily antagonistic, and instead open up common grounds of human experience, as well as the lived experience of modes of difference.

Matters of life and death have often loomed large in oppositional modes of relationship between the religious and the non-religious. Religions are often stereotypically characterised by their critics as immortality cults, attempting to escape or deny the inevitability of death through focusing on a putative transcendent realm that is perceived to diminish the fullness of this life. The question of life is also a key source of tension, for example, in the culture-wars clashes, as life has become caught between technocratic explorations (for example, of the human genome) and religious oppositions to abortion and stem cell research on the basis of the 'sanctity of life' (Bennett 2010; Pyyhtinen 2012; Thacker 2010). Concepts of life reverberate throughout religious traditions. In Christianity, this is expressed in Jesus' telling his followers, 'I am the way, the truth and the life' (John 14:6) and 'I came that they may have life, and have it abundantly' (John 10:10), while in Hinduism, Shakti represents the creative, all-pervading life force. The idea of life also resonates throughout non-religious cultures. Olli Pyyhtinen suggests that if, in the Renaissance, the decisive form of reality was 'mechanism', for the modern era it has been the category 'life' (2012, 79). He notes that French vitalism, under the influence of Bergson, and German *Lebensphilosophie* were among the most influential philosophies in Europe in the early twentieth century, to the extent that Simmel wrote in 1916 that 'the concept of life now seems to permeate a multitude of spheres and has begun to give, as it were, a more unified rhythm to their heartbeat' (cited in Pyyhtinen 2012, 79). While these ideas languished under the taint of Nazism for much of the latter twentieth century, ideas of vitalism and philosophies of becoming, emphasising the vibrancy of life, are firmly back, under the influence of Deleuze, and permeating a wide variety of disciplines (ibid.).[1] At the same time, a different inflection of life is given in the form of Michel Foucault's concept of 'bio-politics' (1990) together with Giorgio Agamben's (1998) concept of 'bare life'. Agamben deployed the concept of 'bare life' to address the fact that bio-political states can strip someone to bare or naked life, which produces bodies that can be killed with impunity. This approach to life has expressed (and perhaps intensified) the gloomy spirit of political diagnoses in the 'post-9/11 era' (Singh 2015, 55), as Agamben's analysis has been used to try to articulate that which in life is irreducible to either social processes or living biological organisms.

The concept of life – and life's interrelation with death – is of course implicated both in metaphysical orientations and in existential and ethical questions about what it means to live a good life, or a life filled with meaning, as opposed to bare life, and it is beyond the scope of this chapter to provide an exhaustive survey of how these ideas figure across religious and non-religious traditions. While questions of life and death might appear perennial concerns for religion, in what follows, I explore the particular contemporary significance of ideas of life and death within the moral landscapes of different religious and non-religious groups. I draw here on qualitative sociological research I have conducted, which is largely in the field of contemporary Christianities, with the hope that these ideas might find resonances beyond the contexts I address here. The chapter considers the significance of the idea of 'life' for an 'open' evangelical church, the Sunday Assembly, and the School of Life, and practices of reflecting on 'death' in Death Cafés, drawing this together with Simmel's writing on life and its interrelations with death. I conclude by suggesting that attending to modes of practical engagement with ideas of 'life' and 'death' across these different religious and non-religious groups, rather than focusing solely on the propositional content of beliefs about life and death, opens up opportunities for reflection on common existential grounds of experience, moving beyond assumptions that relations between these groups are necessarily antagonistic.

What do we do when we 'do life'?

I have been conducting ethnographic fieldwork with different kinds of evangelical[2] church in London since 2009, and through this, I have often been struck by both particular affinities and acts of distancing from non-religious and other religious groups that members of these churches engage in across different contexts. At an open evangelical[3] church where I carried out fieldwork in 2013–14, which I call 'Riverside', for example, one Sunday morning the minister said to the congregation that some of them may have heard about 'atheist churches that have started meeting to celebrate life together'. He said that one of these was having a harvest festival, and would be giving the food they collect to Riverside's food bank, and so a member of the Riverside staff was visiting them that morning to collect the food 'and to build links with them'. This incident not only reveals the friendly institutional relationships between atheist and open evangelical churches; the description of the atheist congregation as gathering together 'to celebrate life' also opens up a wider point of connection to the contemporary significance of life for both.

The Sunday Assembly is perhaps the most notable contemporary example of a network of 'atheist churches', which seeks to 'replicate the "positive" aspects of regular churches' – such as the sense of community belonging and rituals – but without the belief in God (Alexander 2014). The Sunday Assembly describes itself as 'a secular congregation that celebrates life' and as having 'a mission to help everyone live life as fully as possible'. Its website sets out its 'charter', stating 'We're not here to tell you how to live your life – we're here to help you be the best version of you you can be', and its charter includes the ideas that: it is a '100% celebration of life. We are born from nothing and go to nothing. Let's enjoy it together'; it 'has no doctrine'; it 'is radically inclusive – this is a place of love that is open and accepting'; it 'has a community mission. Through our Action Heroes (you!), we will be a force for good'; and 'we won't tell you how to live, but will try to help you do it as well as you can'.

The ways in which 'life' figures here in many ways mirror how members of both Riverside and the charismatic evangelical churches I have studied in London talk about life. These different congregations name their small group study and discussion meetings 'life courses', and 'life groups' is commonly used as a title for small group meetings across global evangelicalism. The leaders of Riverside describe the materials developed for use within the life courses, 'Life Resources', as intended 'to enable you to become the best possible version of yourself', resonating with the Sunday Assembly's aims.[4] The Riverside leader who developed these resources introduced them to the congregation one Sunday morning. Her first slide posed the question, 'How do I become the best version of me I can be?', and she asked the congregation to consider who it was who looked at them in the mirror that morning, adding that when she looked in the mirror that morning, she had thought 'when did I become so old?' She repeated the question from the slide, and added 'how do you become the best version of who you are and who you are created to be?' She said that this question was what they were going to be focusing on that year in their services and small groups, and said 'it's something we need to be *intentional* about'. She said that when you learn to drive or swim, you initially have to be 'really intentional about what you're doing, and then it becomes second nature … It's the same with being the best we can be. We need to *practise* it for it to become second nature to us.' She said that we become like the people we follow, and added that when she was young, she had wanted to be like Kevin Keegan, and said that as a church community, 'our intention is that we become like Jesus, so that the loving our enemies, forgiveness, love, joy and tenderness that Jesus displayed become second nature to us'. She said that over the coming year, 'we're going to take time to focus on being like Jesus. I've called it LIFE.' Her next slide had LIFE in bright yellow letters in the centre against a black background, together with other concepts that would form their focus over the course of the year. These concepts included: following, rhythm, belonging, giftedness, resources, ritual, wholeness, transform, image, inclusion, connection. She said that they were going to begin with the question of 'following', and asked everyone to turn to the person next to them to ask 'what footprints are you leaving behind you at the moment?', and allowed some time for everyone to chat about that, before the service moved onto the Bible reading, and then the sermon that morning, which was on the theme of 'bringing hope to local children and young people … so that they live well in this journey of life'.

Riverside's elaboration of 'becoming the best possible version of yourself' as a central aim of LIFE includes, as with the Sunday Assembly, a strong focus on 'inclusivity' and 'community'. There is a particular emphasis on the inclusion within the church of those who have been socially excluded through categories such as race, sexuality, disability or social class, and Riverside repeatedly emphasises that their vision is to 'build inclusive communities', where 'everyone has hope, feels they matter, and is given the opportunity to achieve their potential'. Members of both Riverside and charismatic evangelical churches I studied also frequently spoke about 'doing life' with each other. When I asked my informants what 'doing life' meant, they said it was about seeing faith as not just about being in church, or reading the Bible, but as something found in everyday moments of relationality, just hanging out with each other and doing very mundane things together, and implying a sense of 'building community' through these interactions.

The idea of 'doing life', 'life courses' and 'life resources' that we see in these churches resonates not only with the Sunday Assembly, but also with another non-religious organisation, the School of Life. This was set up in 2008 by the philosopher Alain de Botton and others with the aim of 'putting learning and ideas back to where they should always have been – right in the middle of our lives', and 'runs courses in the important questions of everyday life'.[5] The School of Life runs a shop selling books, clothes, e.g. the Philosopher's Shoe and the Philosopher's Jumper, and a range of other items, such as Philosophical Honey (priced at £20, which the website tells us 'is food for the soul – connecting us with history and culture', and is 'sourced from the birthplaces of great Greek philosophers'[6]), a Comfort Blanket and a Writing as Therapy Journal.

The School runs courses (with costs from £20 for Secular Sermons to £700 for week-long intensive courses) about 'things we all care about: careers, relationships, politics, travels, families', and describes itself as

> a place to step back and think intelligently about central emotional con-
> cerns. You will never be cornered by dogma, but we will direct you
> towards a variety of ideas from the humanities ... that will exercise,
> stimulate and expand your mind.[7]

Riverside, the School of Life and the Sunday Assembly all present themselves as concerned primarily with a way of life, not *the* way of life or *the* meaning of life: they offer a way of 'doing life' that seeks to find and acknowledge meaning *in* life. While religious groups are often presented by those outside them as offering authoritative moral teachings about life and death, at Riverside we can see a more subjunctive mode of address that resonates with the turn away from 'dogma' that we see at the School of Life and the Sunday Assembly. There is little stated emphasis on 'inclusion' at the School of Life (and the costs of their courses and products would be prohibitive for many, with the Comfort Blanket, for example, priced at £170), yet we can see the focus on reflexive self-awareness and intentionality that permeated Riverside's life courses as also present in these School of Life courses. The promotional material on the class on 'How to Manage Stress', for example, states that through participating, 'You'll become accurate in pinpointing the causes of your anxiety. You'll tame your unhelpful inner voices – and internalize better alternatives. And you'll discover how to spend time worrying about the things that really matter, rather than those that don't.'[8]

We might interpret the emphasis on reflexive self-awareness permeating these ideas of life as bound up with wider social processes of individualisation.

While both Riverside and the School of Life emphasise the communal nature of their life courses and classes, there is also an emphasis on the individual's responsibility to shape herself or himself in order to 'become the best possible version' of themselves. While Riverside does also place an emphasis on forms of political and civic engagement in order to 'build more inclusive communities', such that this individual responsibility for transformation is also bound up with the communal and political, at the School of Life, the focus is much more squarely on learning individual techniques to 'manage stress' or to deal with 'imposter syndrome'.

Sociologist Zygmunt Bauman argues that with the retreat of formerly dominant 'heteronomous' modes of addressing suffering and mortality, there has been a rise of 'autonomous' means, which are self-contained and self-directed, and aim to engage resources within the self's actual or potential possession (Bauman 1999, 42). We are unable to manage our recalcitrant existential fears in their 'pure and unprocessed form', and so we

> slice the great, overwhelming fear into smaller and manageable bits – recast the big issue we can do nothing about into a set of little 'practical' tasks we can hope to be able to fulfil. Nothing calms better the dread one cannot eradicate than worrying and 'doing something' about the trouble one can fight.
>
> (Ibid., 44)

While the School of Life is not necessarily focused on either ignoring or staving off existential angst, there is nevertheless a sense that individuals should seek to manage themselves better to deal with the struggles they face in life. While people have always faced struggles and problems in life, these, as Ian Craib (1994) notes, might once have been seen as moral choices in the context of a larger community or as religious struggles with the forces of destiny, or as political problems to be solved through collective action. The cultural shift, Craib argues, was to start 'seeing them in terms of individual morality with individual solutions', as the modern person as an autonomous individual became perceived and experienced as increasingly isolated from wider society (ibid., 98–9). In many ways, the idea of 'life' across these groups is inflected with this sense of individuals managing themselves better to deal with the struggles and disappointments of life, although we also see at the Sunday Assembly and Riverside a sense that this is inextricably bound up with a desire to work to help others also live flourishing lives, and Riverside encourages and enables different kinds of civic and political activism to these ends.

These connections across religious and non-religious organisations are in many ways not surprising, as both the Sunday Assembly and the School of Life situate themselves as drawing on aspects of religious traditions while 'free from dogma'. But what might lie behind the specific contemporary prominence being accorded to 'life'? We might interpret the pervasiveness of concepts of life as a strategy of differentiation from religious – and especially other Christian – cultures that place significant theological emphasis on life after death. Thus, in many ways, the identities of the open evangelical and non-religious organisations are both shaped through their acts of distancing from other, more conservative, religious traditions. The celebration of life and idea of 'doing life' can be seen as a means of finding modes of transcendence, enchantment and wonder in everyday, immanent life, rather than locating transcendence in some other-worldly realm. Simmel's writings also capture this sensibility, presenting transcendence as immanent within life, as he describes life as 'that which at all points wants to go beyond itself, reaching out beyond itself', a form of pure potentiality, that is always *not yet*, being made and remade (cited in Pyyhtinen 2012, 84). This dynamic sense of life-as-becoming is emphasised across Riverside, the Sunday Assembly and the School of Life. At the same time, Simmel also argues (1997) that the experience of fragmentation in modernity intensifies a desire for coherence across all spheres of social interaction. We could perhaps thus locate this sacralisation of 'life' as also bound up with an existential desire to see all – even the most mundane, everyday details of our lives – as ultimately connected as part of 'life'. This is not so much about finding a transcendent vantage point from which to understand life and death, but about finding the transcendent within the ordinary. Simmel describes how Rembrandt's paintings vividly evoke this illumination of everyday life: 'Light does not come from outside (such light would inevitably fall unevenly); rather, in order to illuminate its ordinariness, from within, shining through equally in each path that leads from the core of life to life's appearances' (2005, 116).

Remembering death as a way of life

While the School of Life focuses on finding techniques to deal with the struggles of life, at the same time there is also an acknowledgement of both the ultimate recalcitrance of life, and of the importance of reflecting on death as an everyday practice of life. The School of Life's promotional blurb about its Memento Mori paperweight states that '[m]any of the obstacles we face in our lives are rather like the waves of the sea: relentless, bleak, repetitive and, ultimately, not responsive to our wishes or longings.' It notes that this is 'a basic premise of the human condition' and we should not

> be continually shocked and dismayed when life does not answer to our demands. We should learn to accept all we cannot change and face it

with a degree of heroism and Stoic strength, as a sailor battling the waves might.

The Memento Mori paperweights are designed to be 'vivid reminders of mortality and the transient nature of life' and to 'put our prosaic obsessions into question' by measuring them 'against the finality of death'.[9] Practices of *memento mori* – reflecting on the condition of mortality – were developed in Stoic philosophy, and were taken up in Christian Europe, circulating throughout the visual arts, for example, as symbols of death in still-life paintings. Acknowledgement of mortality is likewise inextricably interwoven throughout contemporary Christian practices, such as in the Ash Wednesday liturgy, when priests sign a cross with ashes on the foreheads of those attending Mass or Eucharist with the words 'from dust you came, to dust you will return', or in the celebrations of the Mexican Day of the Dead festival, which draws on pre-Columbian as well as Catholic rituals of remembrance.

This idea of consciously reflecting on death is also found beyond the School of Life in other non-religious cultures, such as the Death Cafés movement, which was started in 2011 by Hackney-based former council worker Jon Underwood, inspired by the *Café mortel* pioneered by Swiss sociologist Bernard Crettaz.[10] Death Cafés are largely pop-up meetings, run as a social franchise rather than for profit, and have spread across Europe, North America and Australasia, with meetings having been held in twenty-nine countries. 'At a Death Café people, often strangers, gather to eat cake, drink tea and discuss death', the Death Café website states.[11] When I interviewed Jon Underwood, he described their shared objective as 'to increase awareness of death with a view to helping people make the most of their finite lives'. He said that some of the people who attend the Cafés do have a belief in life after death, but that the groups didn't tend to focus on discussing that, as 'generally, it's fairly unproductive territory, because people have their view, it's quite strongly held, and that's that'. Resonating with the avoidance of 'dogma' in the approaches taken to life at Riverside, the Sunday Assembly and the School of Life, Underwood said that they don't seek to offer one way of dealing with death: 'We don't have any answers ... We might suggest some things, and we might know of resources, but the only answers are people's own.'

The popularity of Death Cafés might be seen as in one sense a response to a widespread cultural denial or avoidance of death in contemporary secular societies. Ernest Becker argued in *The Denial of Death* that death is so terrifying that we don't want to think about it:

the idea of death, the fear of it, haunts the human animal like nothing else; it is a mainspring of human activity – activity designed largely to avoid the fatality of death, to overcome it by denying in some way that it is the final destiny for man.

(1973, xvii)

Simmel likewise suggests that much of life might be defined as *Todesflucht*, a 'fleeing from death' (cited in Pyyhtinen 2012, 94). While religions have often been seen as denials of death, the acknowledgement of death – and of the fear of death – that animates many religious practices and the Death Cafés might perhaps also be seen as often bound up with the desire to become oriented towards the fullness of life, an inhabiting of and affirming of life in the present. Indeed, awareness of life perhaps requires, as Simmel argues, 'death as its opposite, its "other"' (cited in Pyyhtinen 2012, 87). While conflicting beliefs about death and teachings on the potential horrors or blessings of an afterlife tend to figure prominently in oppositional relations between the religious and the non-religious, practices of attending to the fact of mortality across religious and non-religious cultures provide an alternative mode of connection and a means of acknowledging shared existential grounds of what it is to be human.

Conclusion

In this brief sketch of modes of engaging with ideas of life and death, we can see that although the terms may carry different resonances in particular contexts, attending closely to concepts such as these that are prominent across religious and non-religious cultures may help deepen the understanding of affinities between groups that we are often tempted to treat as separate. Although the discursive strategies of particular religious and non-religious groups are often acts of distancing from another culture, in each act of 'othering' there is also, as Simmel highlights, a haunting by the possibility of connection, and these modalities of otherness, separation and desire raise important questions about the kinds of subjectivity and experience these relations enable and foreclose. Studying these modes of interrelationality can help us draw more precisely into focus the question of what is delimited as 'the religious' in everyday social life, in which engagement with ideas of life and death figure prominently, for example, and thus often continue to permeate non-religious cultures.

Theologian Philip Goodchild argues that the 'death of God' in contemporary society and culture affects the believer and unbeliever alike, and that the philosopher of religion therefore has to be concerned with the conditions under which the mind is set in motion. He questions whether the concept of life might set the mind in motion, and suggests that this would require 'an attention to life ... and the thinking of life would also be the life that thinks, the awakening thought that arises from the swirling depths of consciousness and expresses its vital power in thought itself' (Goodchild 2012, 174). He goes on to question whether the concept of life might perhaps today fulfil functions formerly attributed to God:

> it replaces God, or rather, as a biblical and philosophical name for God, the concept is one of the few acceptable names under which God can be thought outside of the confines of institutional religion, in all God's transcendence, immanence and inspiration. If life does play such a role, then perhaps our sharpest divisions are not between theists or atheists, nor between participants and non-participants in religious practice, but would arise from the thinking that undergirds our ways of life. For the substitution[s] of concepts such as 'God' and 'life' are less significant than our frameworks of thinking insofar as these constrain or enable us to perceive reality, to touch it, participate in it and live it.
>
> (Goodchild 2012, 174)

Following Goodchild, attending to different ways of engaging with life and death, and the existential and ethical effects of these, cuts across the religious/non-religious and theistic/non-theistic/atheistic divides that have so often focused on the propositional contents of beliefs about life, death and im/mortality.

Attending to practical, lived engagements with concepts of life and death might open up not only modes of connection between the religious and the non-religious, but also a more nuanced understanding of common human concerns with what it means to live a good life within the limits of human finitude, and of what it means to be human. The concept of 'natality' might here also provide a useful further point of connection. Hannah Arendt argues that it is natality, rather than mortality, which reorients our social imaginaries to fully perceive our human interconnectedness, as our being born means being welcomed into a whole 'web of human relationships which is, as it were, woven by the deeds and words of innumerable persons, by the living as well as the dead' (Arendt, cited in Jantzen 1998, 149).

Exploring engagements with life and death might also entail, following Foucault and Agamben, examining the ways in which some lives come to count for more or less in specific contexts. As the anthropologist Veena Das describes, we can see the dangers of modes of dehumanisation 'as if stitched into everyday life when one withholds recognition from the other, not simply on the grounds that she is not part of one's community but that she is not part of life itself' (2007, 16). In Europe, this is a question of particular contemporary relevance as we witness a proliferation of dehumanising framings of migrant lives associated with the swelling of far-right political movements in Europe and elsewhere. And we can also see how the concept of 'life' can provide a means of resistance to such discourses, for example, in the Migrant Lives Matter movement. Further reflection on the varieties of ways in which people engage with 'life' and its interrelations with mortality thus has the potential to help us understand better the kinds of practices and orientations that unite (as well as divide) us from each other across religious and non-religious cultures, and might encourage a deeper affirmation of, appreciation of and attentiveness to life and its wonders, as well as acknowledgement of its struggles and tragedies. As Mary Oliver expresses this in *Red Bird*:

> Instructions for living a life:
> Pay attention.
> Be astonished.
> Tell about it.
> (Cited in Moody and
> Shakespeare 2012, 176)[12]

Notes

1 Examples of work in this turn include: Deleuze and Guattari 1987; Deleuze 2001; Bennett 2010; Connolly 2011, 2013; Lash 2006.

2 I use the term 'evangelical' here, following David Bebbington, to refer to the tradition existing in Britain since the 1730s, marked by the characteristics of *conversionism, activism, biblicism* and *crucicentrism* (1989, 3).

3 I use the term 'open evangelical' to characterise a movement dissatisfied with dominant evangelical understandings of faith, in whose view 'evangelicalism has suffocated itself through a tight hold on propositional belief, personal salvation, and overheated conviction' (Engelke 2013, 20).

4 This language pervades contemporary evangelical cultures, with US pastor Joel Osteen's book *Your Best Life Now: Seven Steps to Living at Your Full Potential* (2004) having sold over 4 million copies. It should be noted, however, that not all evangelicals agree with Osteen's theology (see e.g. Strhan 2015, 127).

5 From the home page of the School of Life website, <http://alaindebotton.com/the-school-of-life/> (accessed 22 December 2015).

6 From 'Philosophical Honey', Gifts for a Thoughtful Life, the School of Life website, <http://www.theschooloflife.com/shop/philosophical-honey/> (accessed 23 December 2015).

7 From the home page of the School of Life website, <http://alaindebotton.com/the-school-of-life/> (accessed 23 December 2015).

8 From 'How to Manage Stress', course description, the School of Life website, <http://www.theschooloflife.com/london/shop/how-to-manage-stress/> (accessed 23 December 2015).

9 From 'Memento Mori Paperweight', Gifts for a Thoughtful Life, the School of Life website, http://www.theschooloflife.com/shop/memento-mori-paperweight-sea/ (accessed 23 December 2015).

10 See Sophie Elmhirst, 'Take Me to the Death Cafe', *Prospect* [online magazine], 22 January 2015, <http://www.prospectmagazine.co.uk/features/take-me-to-the-death-cafe> (accessed 23 December 2015).

11 From 'What Is Death Cafe?', the *Death Cafe* website, <http://deathcafe.com/what/> (accessed 23 December 2015).

12 The research presented in this chapter was supported by the Leverhulme Trust, under the Early Career Fellowship Award Scheme (ECF-2012-605).

The chapter expands on themes which formed the basis of a post at the Nonreligion and Secularity Research Network blog, available at <http://blog.nsrn.net/2014/02/26/launch-series-what-do-we-do-when-we-do-life-studying-relations-between-religious-and-non-religious-cultures/#more-332> (accessed 22 December 2015).

Bibliography

Agamben, Giorgio (1998) Homo Sacer: *Sovereign Power and Bare Life*, trans. Daniel Heller-Roazen. Stanford, CA: Stanford University Press.

Alexander, Nathan (2014) '"Atheist Churches" Aren't New', *Nonreligion and Secularity Network* [blog], 23 May 2014, <http://blog.nsrn.net/2014/05/23/atheist-churches-arent-new/>.

Bauman, Zygmunt (1999) *In Search of Politics*. Cambridge: Polity Press.

Bebbington, David (1989) *Evangelicalism in Modern Britain*. London: Routledge.

Becker, Ernest (1973) *The Denial of Death*. New York: Free Press.

Bennett, Jane (2010) *Vibrant Matter: A Political Ecology of Things*. Durham, NC: Duke University Press.

Connolly, William (2011) *A World of Becoming*. Durham, NC: Duke University Press.

Connolly, William (2013) *The Fragility of Things*. Durham, NC: Duke University Press.

Craib, Ian (1994) *The Importance of Disappointment*. London: Routledge.

Das, Veena (2007) *Life and Words*. Berkeley: University of California Press.

Deleuze, Gilles (2001) *Pure Immanence: Essays on a Life*, trans. A. Boyman. New York: Zone Books.

Deleuze, Gilles and Félix Guattari (1987) *A Thousand Plateaus: Capitalism and Schizophrenia*, trans. Brian Massumi. London: University of Minnesota Press.

Engelke, Matthew (2013) *God's Agents: Biblical Publicity in Contemporary England*. Berkeley: University of California Press.

Foucault, Michel (1990) *The History of Sexuality*, vol. 1: *An Introduction*, trans. R. Hurley. New York: Vintage Books.

Goodchild, Philip (2012) 'Thinking and Life: On Philosophy as a Spiritual Exercise', in Katharine Sarah Moody and Steven Shakespeare (eds), *Intensities: Philosophy, Religion and the Affirmation of Life*. Farnham, UK: Ashgate, 165–76.

Jantzen, Grace (1998) *Becoming Divine: Towards a Feminist Philosophy of Religion*. Manchester: Manchester University Press.

Lash, Scott (2006) 'Life (Vitalism)', *Theory, Culture & Society* 23, nos. 2–3: 323–9.

Moody, Katharine Sarah and Steven Shakespeare (2012) 'Afterword', in Katharine Sarah Moody and Steven Shakespeare (eds), *Intensities: Philosophy, Religion and the Affirmation of Life*. Farnham, UK: Ashgate, 177–8.

Osteen, Joel (2014) *Your Best Life Now: Seven Steps to Living at Your Full Potential*. New York: Faith Words.

Pyyhtinen, Olli (2012) 'Life, Death and Individuation: Simmel on the Problem of Life Itself', *Theory, Culture & Society* 29, nos. 7–8: 78–100.

Simmel, Georg (1994) 'Bridge and Door', in *Simmel on Culture*, ed. David Frisby and Mike Featherstone. London: Sage, 170–4.

Simmel, Georg (1997) 'Religion and the Contradictions of Life', in *Essays on Religion*, ed. Horst Jürgen Helle. New Haven, CT: Yale University Press, 36–44.

Simmel, Georg (2005) *Rembrandt: An Essay in the Philosophy of Art*, trans. Alan Scott and Helmut Staubman. New York: Routledge.

Singh, Bhrigupati (2015) *Poverty and the Quest for Life: Spiritual and Material Striving in Rural India*. Chicago: University of Chicago Press.

Strhan, Anna (2015) *Aliens and Strangers: The Struggle for Coherence in the Everyday Lives of Evangelicals*. Oxford: Oxford University Press.

Thacker, Eugene (2010) *After Life*. Chicago: University of Chicago Press.

Tonkiss, Fran (2005) *Space, the City and Social Theory: Social Relations and Urban Forms*. Cambridge: Polity Press.

13 Our proud and angry dust
Secular and religious continuities

Michael McGhee

Reactivity and renunciation

As we struggle in the West to accommodate ourselves to the murderous realities of jihadism and what we call Islamism or Islamo-fascism, and as Muslims suffer the ugliness and paranoia of the distinction-crushing 'Islamophobia', it is timely to reflect again on those immediate, instinctive reactions to recent atrocities that blame 'religion' for our troubles, and to reflect precisely on human *reactivity* as a vengeful escalator of violence. Whatever else we think of religion, it is an arena – a cauldron, perhaps – both of human reactivity, our instinct to lash out, and its determined and passionate disavowal and renunciation.

But these are opposing human tendencies which persist whether or not they are given religious expression. The formation, the development, the appropriation of the religious traditions depend upon states of human subjectivity and these states persist beyond the widespread loss of religious belief in a secular age. The problem of human subjectivity is shared alike by the religious and the secular. Freedom from *belief* is not freedom from the (inner) struggle between violence and justice, and if one were to introduce the term 'spirituality' into this discussion at all – and I would do so warily because it has so many vapid connotations – it would be to refer to the arena within the individual and within the community in which this struggle is played out. It is a convenient distraction to blame religion for the current atrocities, and people fall for it, 'even' intellectuals blame the Muslims and their religion, or just religion itself, playing into the hands of scurvy politicians who have an interest in concealing the political realities that prompt, are the object of, 'radicalisation'. As for religion, it's good and it's bad ...

The problem is well summed up by William Blake, who talks of 'the two contrary states of the human soul' and delineates them thus in these contrasting quatrains:

Cruelty has a Human Heart
And jealousy a Human Face

Terror the Human Form Divine
And Secrecy, the Human Dress ...
    ('A Divine Image', in *Songs of Experience*)

For Mercy has a human heart,
Pity a human face,
And Love, the human form divine,
And Peace, the human dress.
    ('The Divine Image', in *Songs of Innocence*)

Blake here gives poetic expression to the idea of the moral struggle reflected in our traditions. The conflicted and contentious appropriation of a religious tradition, what we appeal to and select, what we reject and disregard, notice or pass over, reflects the subjectivity of our cultural formation, the state of our collective 'soul'. Our propensity towards violence may be *reinforced* by the traditional narratives that valorise it – and, it has to be said, our horror and despair at violence may be stifled and overcome – but those narratives already reflect and give voice to, already reject and challenge, the innate and sensual attractiveness of violence. The ways in which we appropriate the tradition that confronts us depend upon a common subjective formation, a formation which the *agon* of our conflicted traditions either favours or challenges.

Humanists used to acknowledge, even express respect for, a fairly bland version of New Testament ethics, an effete benevolence that they might extend to passages in the Jewish and in the Islamic scriptures, without, however, engaging with the *particularity* of a language of moral psychology, subjectivity or the inner life that dramatically delineated the turmoil and desperation of the human scene, the tumultuous oscillation between self-sacrifice and self-aggrandisement, the graphic portrayal of human needs and desires, hubris and betrayal, revenge and love. It left out the experiential notions of redemptive love, the struggles with our demons, the psychic realities of torture and death, of self-deception, pharisaism, double-mindedness, sanctimony, hypocrisy – the stuff, indeed, of all great literature, but stuff nevertheless whose content *saturated* the projected formation of belief itself. Part of the problem with this humanist approach was that it abstracted from but made assumptions about what the *theology* must be, generally that of a frowning Jehovah whose arbitrary and contradictory will had to be obeyed by believers. Notice the centrality of this reference to believers, as though the dramatic role of being a believer was the only religious role available, as though there were not also seekers, disciples, practitioners and renunciants.

Readers of Kierkegaard will be aware of his distinction between Christendom and Christianity, and the corresponding distinction between objective and subjective thinking and the necessity for a transformative subjective appropriation of Christianity. The 'objective thinker' is left unaffected by, even if strongly attached to, doctrines and general truths about the human condition, while the 'subjective thinker' is precisely *affected*, realising the truth, as we say, coming to terms with mortality, for instance, rather than simply agreeing as one indifferent fact among others that all men are mortal. Other religious traditions can make similar distinctions, between what we might call lip service and authenticity, but *pace* Kierkegaard, we have to acknowledge a darker side to religious authenticity; in other words, and to echo the polemicists, there is 'good' religion as well as 'bad' to stand over against lip service, and the lukewarmness of conventional religious adherence is as much a problem for the jihadist recruiter as for the most humane evangelist. If someone is a nominal Christian or Muslim or Jew we need to know what their nominal allegiance is *to*, since it is this which is likely to be awakened in times of crisis: it determines the form and direction of human indignation in the face of injustice, oppression, atrocity.

Blaming religion is a distraction from, even a deliberate evasion of, the realpolitik that has given rise to retaliatory terrorist attacks on the streets of Europe in revenge for 'Crusader aggression against Islam'. There is an ancient sophistical move that conflates explanation with justification, as though what is explained is thereby justified. But explaining that some atrocity is a retaliation does not justify it, nor does it, as some MPs aver, absolve the perpetrators from responsibility for their actions. But reactive retaliation and escalation are precisely what are *renounced* in humane discourse, whether religious or secular. Propaganda always seeks to strengthen a case by the dark arts if necessary, and ideological manipulation and misrepresentation (not to mention the discreet use of secrecy and misdirection) are manifestly part of the scene, as here, when the Western powers are described as Crusaders (reviving ancestral memories) and their target is said to be Islam itself – a claim which (pressingly) invites indignant solidarity – and when the same Western powers conceal their real geopolitical interests from their own populations. But populations *over there* are, after all, being bombed from a distance by foreign powers, and are part of the collateral *carnage*, and it might escape particular notice that these powers are not bombing Muslims because they are Muslims. It is one thing to make judgments about whose side you are on when the bombs are falling, and quite another to express dissent from the relative safety of the democratic West. But there is still a question about the proper response to political injustice, about when the use of force is necessary, about when the spirit of *ahimsa* or non-violence could prevail, about whether one should be involved in civil disobedience, about whether one should ever seek to match atrocity with atrocity.

The blunt but ambiguous truth, though, is that of course religion is to blame – and of course religion is *not* to blame. And this Janus face is an essential aspect of the phenomena. Those who are driving a political agenda in a war-torn country can easily reinforce the mobilisation of significant population groups (who are mobilised in the first place because they are under attack) by vividly ancestral representations of the Crusader enemy, representations that are embedded in regional and premodern forms of religious imagination, representations matched by virile, charismatic exemplars of happy, holy warriors fighting the enemy on their behalf and calling them to arms, joyfully embracing death. But they *are* representations of a genuine enemy, though the form of the representation naturally reflects the worldview of those to whom the appeal is made. The question is, how does propaganda derived from a barbarous, ancestral worldview, reinforced by obscurantism, brutal patriarchy and intolerance, engage the imaginations of those diaspora children, young men and women who have been raised and educated in the liberal and democratic West, and who have felt inspired to join the fight against the Crusader? One thing to consider is the prior state of the imagination that is thus engaged.

We have to make a distinction here. On the one hand there is the impulse to help to defend others with whom one recognises kinship, and on the other, there is the absorbing of that ancestral, premodern and very particular worldview derived from early Islamic history and early *and* current political ambition. It is easy enough to make sense of and to understand the ambition to overturn a political settlement of border and regime imposed after the First World War by the Great Powers. But it is less easy to see how such idealism can survive the primeval savagery. The reality on the heavily and secretly policed ground, as it were, is likely to be quite different from what is shown in the happy selfies or photo-ops of smiling young warriors fulfilled by their dedication to the work of Allah, but the question of how they are impelled to make the journey, not an easy one, needs some kind of philosophical explanation because it represents an intensely immediate example of what constitutes (religious) conversion, even as we insist that talk of religion *at all* here is a distraction from the politics.

The idea of what goes on behind the propaganda applies as much to the liberal, democratic West, of course, with its manipulated media. 'Liberal' itself is an obscurantist marker that conceals realities that include geopolitical interventionism, the protection of corporate interests that motivates support for brutal and illegitimate regimes, consumerist materialism, sexual licence and promiscuity, as well as conditions of discrimination, unemployment, marginalisation and neglect that breed resentment and despair – and drug- and alcohol-dependence – and a corresponding failure or even absence of *education* in the sense of formation or *Bildung*. To come back to the state of the imagination, it is precisely this which is formed by education – or left undeveloped and ancestral. It is part of the role of education not so much to 'teach British values' as to stir a critical and creative imagination out of the resentful vacuity of unfulfilled and manufactured desire. But now, the notion of conversion does not require a *religious* connotation, and what has been characterised here are the natural objects of the kind of unsatisfactoriness that the Buddhists call *dukkha* which is traditionally said to impel the movement towards liberation from greed, hatred and delusion. A humane education provides the terms within which this sense of unsatisfactoriness can be expressed. In its absence an untrained and adolescent imagination remains with its default archetypal settings and is entirely malleable.

It is not that a humane education of this kind can compensate for these other conditions of alienation. But it does provide the possibility of a counterbalance of critical citizenship that protects against propaganda, though this latter is a minor benefit. It is worth noting here that Johann Wolfgang von Goethe was concerned to emphasise the importance of *expression* or *Äußerung* for the formation or *Bildung* of the human person, but also to balance this with the necessity for *denying* expression, the necessity for *Entsagung* or renunciation, particularly when what is expressed is damaging to others or, more acutely, is the pure reactivity that unleashes fury, escalates violence and perpetuates injustice. Such renunciation requires *grounds*, however; there has to be reason to renounce. *Bildung*, constituted by the moral balance of expression and renunciation in the formation of the human person, is precisely an education into moral life and values. But I should re-emphasise that I do not intend the apparently benign 'British values' that are to be taught in UK schools. These are the values of 'democracy, the rule of law, individual liberty, and mutual respect and tolerance of those with different faiths and beliefs' – benign in principle but in the form of a targeted and antagonising reproach of those who are all too well aware that this message is directed at *them* – but something much more like the values implicit in the works of creative imagination, in music and poetry but also in literature and drama, in comedy and tragedy, in satire, in the notions of human folly and human wisdom.

Alienation is coupled with a sense of injustice intensified by the appeal of a transnational identity, that one's own people, fellow Muslims, are under attack – and here is the credulously absorbed untruth – just because they are Muslim. So, moral indignation by itself is not enough for radicalisation, nor resentful exclusion from a consumerist society, since a person possessed of the world's goods (rich Saudi citizens, for instance) can independently feel the hollowness of a life of consumer acquisitiveness, and solidarity with a population oppressed and under attack. Alienation is from the moral as well as the political culture of a society that one starts to see both as corrupt and as hostile to one's own people. But there has to be more to it than that – the consumerism and the promiscuity and the injustice start to become part of a totalised object of hostile *reaction* which breeds disdain and hatred rather than the more reflective pity for those who are their creatures, precisely those unbelievers whose government and way of life are the enemy that has to be destroyed.

But by contrast, all these things are also the traditional intentional objects of a considered *response*, of conversion, *metanoia*, amendment of life, withdrawal from the fleshpots, transformation and *political activism*. There are strands of the religious traditions that provide a vehicle for strong emotions of indignation and resentment, associated with the perception of gross injustice and oppression. Naturally, one can feel these things in the face of outrages against fellow human beings *simpliciter*, and there are plenty of representations of this in the traditions, though there are also more narrowly conceived representations which run counter to this humanism, and this seems to be the case with radicalised jihadis. Moral feeling can be focused exclusively in favour only of those with whom one has a communal or tribal or sectarian sense of solidarity and shared identity – a self-referential altruism towards kith and kin, benevolence and generosity towards the brothers – a narrowness of focus which casts others coldly, contemptuously and murderously into the exterior darkness. The larger sympathy – to say nothing of compassion – has less initial energy, is both more vulnerable and more difficult to cultivate. These strands of the traditions provide a vehicle because they are already the precipitate and expression of just those kinds of reaction and response; they engage with, because they are themselves an expression of, the natural dispositions of our common human nature – dispositions that inform practice and are reflected and vindicated in sacred texts. These strands engage with the psyche when lived traditions meet what present themselves – or can be presented – as the same kind of violent political realities within which they were originally forged, so that what was quiescent or merely private flares up into collective response and activity informed by the same ancient stories and the practices of retaliation and reprisal that they draw on.

The archetype of the heroic warrior – a wonderful mirror image of an empty and marginal life – is the fulfilment of a dream of brotherhood beyond the petty but touchy narcissism of the local gang, a revelling in a romance of soldiery without experience of the horror and pity of war, fighting injustice, but also fighting demons. But we need to distinguish cases. The grave faces of the Paris terrorists make clear that there is also soldierly idealism here, and resoluteness. But there is something else, and there is evidence in the propaganda and witness reports, that all this may also be cover and permission to give free rein to a sensual, orgasmic appetite for acts of cruelty and arbitrary power, a need to punish, to take revenge; vulnerability to the creed is increased by inner insecurities, anxious repressions, patriarchal attitudes, controlling but hypocritical puritanism, the craving for approval and recognition by manly role models, and so forth.

We are all formed by immediate reactions, cultural prejudices, which we have to *contain and correct* in the light of empirical and moral judgments that are themselves the response – of a horrified compassion – to the world we are making for ourselves. What we find in our religious texts are just these cultural prejudices, reflections of our unregenerate humanity, *and* the effort to contain, overcome and transcend them. In other words, our religious traditions ambivalently reflect a human struggle that continues whether we are religious or secular, and this has a bearing on how we are to understand religion at all, not as the source or ground but as the *expression* of moral struggle. The religious traditions are the ancestral but not the only home of a struggle between violence and compassion, and secularisation seems to change nothing. It is a struggle in which most of our instinctively available energy favours violence rather than the more reflective forgiveness and love, a struggle which gives sense to the idea of 'repentance' and self-overcoming, and this struggle continues whether we think in religious terms or not. However, this 'horrified compassion', as I called it, depends upon the active presence of a countervailing vision, that of the wonder and beauty of humanity and the natural world, compromised though they both are by our disastrous exploitations.

These ideas of love and forgiveness, which may or may not be associated with corresponding *feelings*, are creative, intelligent, strategic and procedural responses to the escalation of violence, as is the resolution not to return evil for evil, and these are *human* resolutions, even if they are formulated in religious forms. The key notion is that of renunciation, *Entsagung* – which is the collective work of *souci de soi* (self-concern) – and there is space within religion precisely for this renunciation, just as there is space outside it. Such renunciation is not motiveless; it is, rather, a response to the consequences, one driven by pity or compassion at the human condition. *Compassion* is a more reflective notion than that of sympathy; it depends upon our seeing ourselves and others in the light of a tragic sense of the folly and frailty, but also the wonder and the beauty, of human life.

It might be said here, as it often is by polemicists, that 'religion', particularly in the form of a confident belief in a glorious afterlife, anaesthetises us from the full horror of those consequences and that it disdains 'pity' as a weak and uninformed response. But this is not 'religion' *tout court* – such beliefs, fully imagined and engaged, are precisely an ideological tool whose function is indeed to anaesthetise those responses just when they are most likely to arise, in the midst of military action. Function is important here. You are with a band of brothers and you are 'believers' incensed by the madness of ancestral belief, and the very act of questioning is protected against by a culture of murderous contempt and hatred towards those who are *not* believers. There is no negative capability allowed or comprehended here, only the absolute conviction of an unconverted subjectivity.

Radicalisation activates these archetypal and emotionally charged self-images, along with their corresponding intentional objects, a representation of the enemy that reinforces and justifies the heroic self-image, which then governs the actions of those under its spell. If you are fighting demons then you have to treat demons as they deserve and action has a mythological content. Something like this, as well as a cultivated transnational solidarity, must be one of the conditions of receptivity or vulnerability, though there must also be others, including the close companionship – the loving eye contact – of like-minded friends, intense discussion with quietly charismatic recruiters. Credulity allows subliminal entry of the ideology on the back of a critique of injustice, materialism, consumerism, the long history of Crusader assaults on Muslims. There is, obviously, some truth in some parts of this critique, it is not wholly fantasy, but captures aspects of the complex reality of political struggle, intervention and ambition in the Middle East, otherwise radicalisation could hardly begin; there needs to be a foothold for indignation, an objective correlative.

The reception of a traditionalist, puritanical and obscurantist Salafism is the regional means of mobilisation which provides the terms of the story of the struggle not just against the Crusaders but also against corrupt local regimes that are in alliance with them. But how, again, does it work among that vulnerable minority of European Muslims? Sometimes, particular versions of a religious tradition simply remain dormant or nominal, as we have noted, so that someone who claims truly not to be religious would, if properly activated or recruited, *become* religious in just these terms. We tend to think of the nominal in terms of *belief*, and thus miss the active and necessary work – the practising – of the *virtues* associated with peace and forgiveness, for instance, but also of protest, and the speaking truth to power, whose real form is that of a vital, imaginative passion, the only antidote to radicalisation.

Radicalisation depends upon the intimacy of the cult and a charismatic leadership that can overwhelm critical judgment, and upon the commonplace that the old narratives – which filter and distort the realities of contemporary conflict – told with the fascinating power of the storyteller, can, to use Wittgenstein's phrase, strike with the force of truth and revelation, particularly if the recipients are disenchanted with the liberal alternative where they perceive very clearly the gap between the reality and the rhetoric.

The background premodern world picture is absorbed in the course of the narrative and the analysis, and its terms recited in the narration, providing a simple discourse and rhetoric. But the *application* of the traditional story trades on systematic misrepresentation, e.g. that the Christian crusaders are fighting a total war against Islam, that Islam and this particular strand of belief and practice are identical, and that other 'so-called' Muslims are heretics and apostates. But there is more to it than that, because as I have said, the representations sanction and justify violence and provide cover not just for intolerance and private sadism but for an innate bloodlust and fascination with and enjoyment of arbitrary power. There is a deep-seated, atavistic satisfaction in beheading the mythological 'enemies of Islam', shedding the blood of the infidels, dragging their corpses through the streets, taking their women as sex slaves, the grotesque emblem of the subjection of women and the imprisonment of the feminine. The emphasis in all this is on belief and ideology, which express but leave unchallenged, even as they manipulate, our cruel and violent nature annexed nevertheless to a justifying idealism and heroism.

Conversion as a moral necessity

Those who wish we could do away with religion altogether on the grounds that religion is 'bad', and those who think that 'genuine' religion is essentially 'good' ... both ignore the possibility that the contested complex of phenomena that we call 'religion' is both 'good' and 'bad', that 'bad' religion is as genuinely 'religious' as 'good' religion, and here I would identify one aspect of the religious with the background world picture within which their virtues and vices are framed. The point is that there is not simply one such world picture: the frame already encapsulates, is saturated by, the moral vision within whose terms the narratives are developed.

The temptation has always been to *define out* the bad, so that genuine religion can only be good. However, when John Donne bleakly responds, 'Oh where?' to the injunction to 'seek true religion', he is deploying an *ethical* criterion:

> ... men do not stand
> In so ill case here that God hath with his hand
> Sign'd kings' blank charters to kill whom they hate,
> Nor are they vicars, but hangmen to fate.
>
> ('Satire III')

There is some good sense in this; like many others Donne was concerned to show that the arbitrary power that presents itself as 'religiously' sanctioned may be corrupt and hypocritical. But it is more plausible to say that the errant, 'cover', behaviours he complains of are to be criticised on the grounds not that they are a corruption or perversion of *religion*, but a corruption or perversion of *particular teachings*; in this case it is the old Divine Right doctrine of the king as a 'vicar' or representative of Christ as a cover for tyranny rather than the just rule implied by the reference to Christ; but there are familiar corruptions and distortions of the doctrine of love, or the spirit of self-sacrifice turned into masochism or passive aggression. If we identify that teaching or set of teachings with 'genuine religion' we have still made a mistake, because the religious traditions are *the arena* within which competing moral visions, competing teachings, work themselves out in tense confrontation with one another. We may justly complain about the misapplication and misquotation of particular religious teachers, but this is part of the whole phenomenon – and 'good' religion may draw on such misquotation too.

There is an ancestral competition between Blake's contrary states of the human soul, an ancestral competition projected into our conception of the divine; and when we look at religion in the round and think of the idea of religious renewal and religious reaction, we are always and necessarily *selective* because the religious traditions, I would prefer to say the cultural traditions as they thus expressed and understood themselves, are in internal conflict. What determines the direction of the 'selection' is the state of the soul, the degree of self-possession and self-knowledge. The Christian Right select what mainstream Christians discard, for instance, taking the killing fields of the Old Testament as divine authority to follow the same path, an authority that follows and justifies prior inclination. Lebanese Christians massacre Palestinians, and could offer similar scriptural justification if they were called upon. When after an atrocity someone declares that these people are not Muslim, we understand the ethical rejection of the conduct ('not in my name'), but they are for all that Muslims, albeit Muslims who favour a patriarchal, obscurantist and punitive vision of the world and the divine – just as the seventeenth-century Covenanters who slaughtered thousands were Christians. It is the *version* of Christianity, of Islam, of Buddhism, of Hinduism that is rejected, and what it reflects of the subjective formation of those who embrace it. If someone says – an Archbishop, perhaps – that it is *blasphemous* to claim that these killings are done in the name of God, the 'blasphemy' is against Blake's apotheosis of mercy, pity, peace and love:

> To Mercy, Pity, Peace, and Love
> All pray in their distress;
> And to these virtues of delight
> Return their thankfulness.
> ('The Divine Image', in *Songs of Innocence*)

'Apotheosis' or 'making divine' is of course tendentious here, but I use it as neutrally as may be for a conversation between the religious and the secular. The relationship of Blake's God to his creatures is precisely mediated by these virtues which it is the task of God's creatures to incarnate or realise in their own lives and it is in this that their beatitude is said to consist. Yahweh is, of course, particularly as he rampages through Deuteronomy, of a less gentle disposition; it is no accident that he is such a good field commander. For classical theism God is beyond the order of all beings and cannot be represented by the human mind; but his relationship to his creation *can* be represented, and different doctrines of that relationship continue to coexist in a tense, disputatious disharmony.

There is one significant point, however, that whereas one pole of the two contrary states of the human soul is human, all too human – and horror builds masterpiece upon masterpiece – the other pole represents the hope of a dawning possibility, an aspiration, a creative response of horrified compassion, and a necessity for conscious *renunciation* of this all too human. Mercy, pity, peace and love represent new possibilities not much explored and not much supported by psychic energies heavily deployed elsewhere: they present themselves as beckoning possibilities, an opening out, the possibility of discovering new meaning. Whether or not one thinks theologically, there is a strand of theology which makes the notion of the divine the vehicle for the *exploration* of these possibilities, and the important human disposition is openness, a sense of a constantly receding horizon of what makes sense and of how it is possible to act and respond.

When Rousseau in his *Social Contract* talks about the advantages of passing from the state of nature to participation in a civil society, he evokes and deploys a secular notion of conversion. We can pass from being 'a narrow stupid animal' with purely private interests and appetites, to being a creature of intelligence, 'a man', as he puts it. However, the transition is to the status of citizen and member of the body politic, and it implies an identification and solidarity with other citizens, and it excludes women and others outside the circle of a particular city state. This conversion of identity, then, remains partisan, is compatible with hatred and violence, and can be manipulated by charismatic and ideological forces. A conversion from the futility of materialism and promiscuity can lead to deadly and intolerant forms of puritan zeal, but it is also possible to realise the folly of intolerance and puritan zeal, of unresolved but refocused hatred.

So where do we locate what is 'good' in good religion? Blake famously offers us a criterion based upon a moral vision that relates itself to the perceived 'other' of his own period:

> And all must love the human form
> In Heathen, Turk, or Jew ...
> ('The Divine Image', in *Songs of*
> *Innocence*)

This imperative appears to be premised upon a conception of what it is to be a human being represented in the *Songs of Innocence and Experience*, that tragic sense of life which gives form and content to compassion. Here we have the idea of a vision, the loving recognition of our common humanity beyond the barriers of race and religion, and over against the contemptuous exclusivity that is hostile to 'Heathen, Turk, or Jew', Crusader, jihadi, heretic, infidel, etc. This is a moral vision, but it is the unexpected and creative outcome of a kind of despair about the terrible futility of cruelty and violence that can irrupt even into a self-confident warrior ethos, after the death of a close companion, for instance. That sense of futility can remain in the form of despair, and the contrary vision, of compassionate solidarity, is a fusion of faith, hope and love – faith and love in the form of that venture of the spirit that conceives the possibility of 'redemption', and hope in the sense that such a possibility can be fulfilled.

Part IV

Diversity and dialogue

The contributors to this section explore the diverse and complex landscape of religion and belief in contemporary societies. They highlight the fact that the significant differences are not only between religious belief and non-belief but also within the two categories of 'religion' and 'non-religion'. How then should dialogue be pursued in the light of this diversity?

Lois Lee (Chapter 14) questions the assumption of a simple divide between 'the religious' and 'the non-religious', and draws attention to the variety of positions and attitudes within those two categories and to the bearing which this has on the prospects for dialogue.

Dilwar Hussain (Chapter 15) reflects on the complex history of relations between Islam and the secular world, and suggests that it offers resources for dealing with potential areas of tension.

Ankur Barua (Chapter 16) looks at the ways in which the classical Hindu and Buddhist traditions complicate the picture of the divide between 'religion' and 'atheism' as it is understood in Western culture.

Simon Glendinning (Chapter 17) points to important continuities between Christianity and secular forms of a 'pilgrim's progress' in search of meaning, and to the way in which the inheritance of Marxism further complicates the picture.

Andrew Copson (Chapter 18) draws on his experience of opposition and cooperation between humanist and religious people and organisations to formulate some conclusions about how such encounters can succeed, what barriers stand in the way, and what principles could make dialogue more productive.

Ruth Abbey (Chapter 19) sets out the conceptual resources to be found in the work of the philosopher Charles Taylor for advancing engagement between religious and non-religious people, including in particular the ideas of 'transcendence' and 'fulfilment'.

Angie Hobbs (Chapter 20) suggests that Plato's approach to philosophy and his use of the dialogue form can provide a rich resource to promote dialogue between believers and atheists, and that encounters between religious ideas and secular thought can sometimes have surprising results.

14 Polar opposites?

Diversity and dialogue among the religious and non-religious

Lois Lee

Over the course of his premiership, David Cameron several times described Britain as a Christian country.[1] His claims were widely discussed – supported in some quarters, dismissed in others, and sometimes condemned amid concerns about exclusion and discrimination experienced by vulnerable non-Christian groups. Statements like these lend themselves to debate because they are often equivocal, phrased defensively (Britain is '*still* a Christian country') or in an attempt to mobilise Christians in some way ('As a Christian country, we must remember what [Jesus Christ's] birth represents') – and therefore suggesting not so much that Christianity is a robust and powerful force in the UK today as that it is on a low ebb. Thus, these comments and the discussions they provoke leave the somewhat confused sense that British culture is perhaps not as Christian as it might, or, in Cameron's view perhaps, ought to be.

Whatever political agendas are at work in statements such as Cameron's (and presumably this is a factor), in fact these kinds of confused messages about the nature of the 'religious landscape' in Britain today are echoed in wider debates. On the one hand, Cameron is far from alone in his sense that Britain is a broadly Christian country, and this view is supported by census data from the 2001 and 2011 surveys that asked about religion, in which majorities identified Christianity as their religion (Office for National Statistics (ONS) survey data). On the other hand, Britain is as often and as equivocally described as a 'secular country' (see Kettell 2015), and other major surveys show that those who describe themselves as 'not religious' are in the majority.[2] For yet other observers the real story about religion in Britain is neither the dominance of Christian nor of non-religious groups and cultures, but of religious diversity and pluralism. In this view, the growth of some Christian and non-Christian denominations and the increasing prominence of these groups within public life are highly significant. Whether perceived as a cause for celebration or a harbinger of doom, they suggest that what defines the UK's contemporary religious landscape is not its Christianity, atheism or secularity but rather its plurality and its multiculturalist and multi-faithist forms of pluralism.[3]

So what is *really* going on? Is Britain today fundamentally Christian, robustly non-religious, quietly secular or dynamically diverse? This book is about dialogue, but who *are* the believers and non-believers that might actually be participating in this dialogue? How do they think about themselves in relation to religion, and what do they actually believe and practice? When it comes to religion and its alternatives, what kinds of cultural resources do they benefit from, what kinds of vulnerability do they experience, and how do both of these things affect opportunities for dialogue and exchange?

This chapter provides a broad survey of the UK's 'religious landscape', broadly conceived. It charts the variety of religious traditions and groups now represented in the UK, and it highlights two particular features of this landscape that may have a bearing on prospects for dialogue. These are, firstly, the relatively even balance of Christian and non-religious constituencies in the UK today; and, secondly, the plurality of beliefs, attitudes and practices not only associated with religious people but with *non*-religious people, too. And, while the former might give us some clues as to why relations between the religious and the non-religious are so often strained in the UK, the latter is encouraging for dialogue, because it helps us to rethink the common notion that being religious and non-religious are fundamentally different states – that they are polar opposites. Instead, new social scientific research is laying increasing emphasis on what so-called believers and non-believers have in common – beliefs about the nature and meaning of life, social connections and ritual practices around these beliefs, and so on – and though we can still point to important differences between these 'worldviews' or 'existential cultures' (to use my preferred term),[4] understanding that both theists and non-theists are all believers in a wider sense is a great leveller – and, I would argue, a solid basis for dialogue.

The big picture: religious *and* non-religious?

Britain has been described as a country that is *neither* religious *nor* non-religious (Woodhead 2013).[5] The logic to this is that a relatively small number of Britons are clearly and actively religious according to a number of measures (religious identity, belief, participation in religious institutional and ritual life) while similarly few are clearly and affirmatively *non*-religious – that is, describing themselves as 'atheist', stating that they believe that Gods or higher powers definitely do not exist, and not participating in any religious culture. On the other hand, according to conventional measures, such roundly religious and roundly non-religious groups account for roughly a quarter share apiece of the British population, and 50 per cent in total.[6] Whether it is best to describe the UK as 'neither religious nor non-religious' or '*both* religious *and* non-religious' can therefore be seen as something of a glass-half-empty/glass-half-full proposition, and a matter of personal preference.

There are, though, a number of factors on the side of the 'both/and' view. For one, religious and non-religious *identities* are prevalent. In the 2001 and 2011 census, 92 and 93 per cent respectively responded to a voluntary question about religious affiliation, the vast majority describing themselves as part of a religion (ONS survey data). If the impression from the census data is that religious identities are by far the more commonplace, this needs to be weighed up against other large-scale survey data which have 'no religion' identities in the majority: the non-religious have counted as the largest single 'religious' group in the UK since 1993 and were an outright majority in 2009, 2010 and 2013.[7] Whatever the balance, the majority of Britons are willing to identify themselves in relation to religion, if only to affirm their distance from it.

These kinds of identifications might be seen as merely 'nominal' ones – the kind of identities we call on to describe ourselves only when prompted to do so, and which don't tell us very much about that person's lived life. And maybe it makes little sense to think about the apparently negative 'no religion' category as a form of identification. Yet, detailed qualitative research has shown that religious and non-religious nominal identities matter – that they are bound up with other social identities that mark out our relationships with our family, our friends, our cultural and national heritage (Day 2011). This work suggests that this is as true of non-religious identifications as of religious ones (ibid.), while other research points to a wide array of ways in which British non-religious people are actually quite committed to their identities as 'non-religious' (Lee 2015, 2016), and are not so indifferent to the issue that they would appreciate being identified in other terms.

Further evidence that Britain might be best considered *both* religious *and* non-religious concerns the particular influence that actively religious and actively non-religious portions of society have over British life. Perhaps this stands to figure: those who are actively religious or non-religious are presumably more likely to have articulated their thoughts in this area, and are often associated with organisations and institutions that can be readily identified and called upon to contribute to media, civic and other public discussions and debate. Those with explicit and coherent religious and non-religious identities have other advantages in the public sphere over others, too. For example, both groups are more likely to be highly educated (Voas and McAndrew 2014) as compared to those with 'fuzzier' positions. This means that several powerful institutions – including national and local government, education, the media and the arts – will be disproportionately shaped by the actively, that is, clearly, religious or non-religious.

Indeed, it is perhaps for some of these reasons that media and other public representations of religion tend to hone in on those involved with traditional and recognised religious groups and with organisations such as the British Humanist Association and the National Secular Society, as well as on individuals who have a powerful voice in cultural life as a result of other kinds of power and privilege; the new atheists, for example, largely occupy elite positions in society (Bullivant 2010), as do many prominent religious leaders. For reasons both practical and elitist, then, the 50 per cent who are perhaps not actively religious nor clearly non-religious are much less visible within the public sphere – at least when it comes to their perspectives on the role that religion should play in Britain today.

Another reason why the UK can be considered importantly 'both/and' when it comes to 'religion' and 'non-religion' is that the even balance between the two arguably plays a significant role in British society in its own right. Working with data from the turn of the millennium and also differentiating the explicitly religious and non-religious from 'fuzzy' groups, an analysis of eleven European countries shows that the UK was one of two to display this even balance of theistic and non-theistic populations – 23 and 27 per cent respectively (Siegers 2011).[8] When it comes to the two most prominent religious and non-religious cultures in the UK – the Church of England and the affirmed non-theists (or 'atheists') – these are likewise evenly balanced, at around the 20 per cent mark: 22.3 and 18.2 percent respectively (British Social Attitudes survey data for 2008).

It is possible that this balance can help us to understand a distinctive feature of the British religious landscape, namely its own particular brand of religion/non-religion conflict. Numerous places in the West are experiencing high-profile tensions between, on the one hand, religious and non-religious outlooks and, on the other hand, inclusivist and exclusivist forms of secularism (in which religious and sometimes non-religious beliefs are allowed to play a greater or much lesser role in public life and government, respectively); and these tensions have their distinctive contours – around sexual and reproductive politics in the US, for example, around laicity and Islam in France, around the Catholic Church in Ireland, and so on. In the UK, we have 'the God wars' – prominent, influential, often repetitive debates between new atheists and what might be called 'old (or at least traditional) theists'. These engagements undoubtedly facilitate dialogues of a sort, but have also had a profound impact on the contours of those dialogues and drawn attention to certain perspectives over others.

It seems likely that these God wars feed off the equal footing of religious and non-religious actors – both quite numerous, and both quite powerful in public life. The ability for *both* groups to have a sense of their own power as well as of their own weakness – exacerbated by the equivocal media assessments that I opened this chapter with – means that both are vulnerable in a way that might help us to understand why the power of these groups is the subject of so much dogged and bitter contestation. In reality, it is probably the case that, in particular ways and at particular moments, the religious and the non-religious are *both* marginalised – that is to say, treated as smaller or less significant than they really are. Certainly, each group is subject to the other's claims to dominance – that Britain is non-religious at heart or has Christianity in its veins. In a sense, both claims are right: non-religion is the growing force but its power must still be balanced against the role that religion, and Christianity especially, has played in British history, as well as the longer-term influence that that history must necessarily exert. Recognising that *both* are powerful and relatively secure in parts of contemporary society, and that *both* are ambivalent – capable of enriching life and of causing harm, too – is at once the more accurate way of describing the situation in Britain today and the approach most likely to move us away from the defensiveness and identity politics that have played such a prominent role in public life in recent years and which have sometimes undercut attempts at richer dialogue.

Britain in close-up: plurality and pluralism

To describe the UK as a 'both/and' nation when it comes to religion and non-religion is to paint that landscape with a very broad brush. As I have argued, there are important reasons to pay attention to what is going on in the UK at this level of generality, not least because this notion of the UK as a nation of two broad 'religious' groups has a powerful hold over the way we have thought about religious diversity, division and dialogue. But a more fine-grained brush is needed to describe the British landscape in more detail and the particular ways dialogue might – or might not – play out.

Religious plurality

The part of the population that may, for whatever reason, be described as religious is diverse. This is quite well known, albeit somewhat papered over in ideas about 'Christian Britain' or 'secular Britain'. Indeed, much of the plurality can be found from *within* the Christian category – now evenly split between Anglican and Catholic, and with non-Anglican Christians outnumbering those identifying with the UK's established church since 2005 (British Social Attitudes survey data).

While three Christian groups (C of E, Roman Catholic and those who give no denomination) outnumber them by some margin, other major religious identifications are also noteworthy, especially the Muslim, which now makes up 5 per cent of the UK population, and the Hindu, which accounts for another 1.5 per cent (British Social Attitudes survey data for 2014). Other major confessions are small – the number of Jews, Sikhs and Buddhists were all under 1 per cent in both the 2011 census and recent British Social Attitudes surveys (ibid.). But size is not everything, and there are various reasons why smaller religious groups exert a stronger influence than the number of their affiliates may imply. Religious groups are often regionally clustered, for example, meaning that even small populations can have a powerful presence in some areas of the country and in public life (ONS 2012; see also Modood 2015). Smaller religious groups are politically significant, too, through their collaboration in interfaith forums for dialogue and cultural exchange, their association with racialised discourses about Britishness and immigration, and their role in historic and contemporary geopolitical battles for power.

Thus, it is not as contradictory as it is sounds to say that the UK is at once dominated by two religious groups – the Christian and the non-religious – and at the same time profoundly shaped by its religious plurality and pluralism. And this is only to speak of plurality related to religious affiliation. Underlying and cutting across these identifications are variations of belief, practice and experience – referred to in other chapters in this volume, too.

Non-religious plurality

Though it is not always alluded to in public life, still the plurality of religion is widely recognised. Much less well known, however, is the diversity of non-religion. This is because we have historically thought about non-religion as merely the absence of religion – whether that is viewed as a sad and deprived condition to be in or a natural and beneficial one, in which the individual has been unleashed from the yoke of religion. This way of thinking is summed up in the overwhelming focus on 'atheism' in discussions of non-religion – on the state of simply being without (*a-*) belief in God (*theism*). As interest in the non-religious grows, however, this negative conception of non-religion is giving way to new, much more detailed accounts of non-religious attitudes, beliefs and cultures, and these are also highlighting the diversity of those who tick the 'no religion' box on whatever survey it might be. What is more, this diversity crosses all of the dimensions that we see with religious diversity: diversity of belief, practice, ritual, identity and so on.

Firstly, in terms of diversity of beliefs, the strong agnostic view – that there is no way for humans to know whether gods or higher powers exist – is consistently shown to be as commonplace as the non-theistic or 'positive atheist' (see Bullivant 2013) view that gods or higher powers certainly do not exist – both around 18 per cent of the population overall (British Social Attitudes survey data for 2008), and around 40 per cent apiece when it comes to those who identify themselves as not religious (Woodhead 2014). There is also a sizeable percentage of people who identify as non-religious and say that they believe in God, too. The almost total absence of research working with agnostics is surprising, though it perhaps has to do with the predominance of and fixation with non-theistic beliefs and atheist identities in public life, and with the common but probably false view that agnosticism implies indecision.[9] Even if we have more to learn about agnosticism, these very general measures point to at least three broad, but significant differences within the non-religious populations that we tend to treat as homogeneous.

Other research points to more diversity of belief, still. Non-religious affiliates can also fall into the increasingly significant 'spiritual but not religious' category. These people explore their spirituality outside of institutional religious settings (Heelas and Woodhead 2005), and probably account for around 10 per cent of the British population overall (e.g. Siegers 2011). Moreover, non-theistic and agnostic outlooks only scratch at the surface of the existential and philosophical cultures that people might draw on outside of religious and spiritual frameworks – romantic naturalism, nihilistic materialism, hedonism, existential or exclusive humanism, scepticism and agnosticism, and on and on. These are existential philosophies, worldviews and cultures (Lee 2015) that are developed outside of religious traditions but which still give people meaning as well as symbolic resources with which to negotiate life. To say that someone does not believe that God created the cosmos or humanity tells us something about them; but there are more possibilities here than some general form of materialism and therefore much more to be said.

There is also diversity of practice – of ritual, for example. As with the religious, the non-religious vary in their preference for different ways of marking the life course. Many prefer civil ceremonies (e.g. civil weddings, which became more common in the UK than religious ones in 1977 (ONS survey data)); an increasing number of people are exploring other non-religious alternatives such as Humanist ceremonies; while some people reject life cycle ceremonies in general or mark the life course in more intimate or informal ways. Yet others prefer to use religious ceremonies, pointing us towards an important implication of understanding non-religious positions in concrete and cultural terms – namely, the possibility of hybrid beliefs and identities that cut across religious/non-religious divides. Someone might, for example, combine their humanist materialist beliefs with a preference for Anglican rituals and Buddhist ethics and practices – and why not? On reflection, it seems likely that most individuals in the UK are influenced by not one but several religious cultures, not one but several non-religious cultures, and by secular concerns that direct attention away from existential matters and cultures altogether.

There is also sociocultural diversity along other dimensions. For example, demographers have begun to provide more detailed accounts of non-religious populations and, in the UK case, this is pointing to plurality along several lines. There is regional diversity, for example: like religious affiliations, non-religious affiliates tend to be clustered in certain places (Voas and McAndrew 2014), pointing to the ways in which we might start to think about an Islington humanist as possibly different in outlook and practice from a Brightonian humanist, say; or an English southerner's non-religious orientation as different from a Welsh one.

Finally, as with religious people, we should bear in mind that there is diversity in terms of the extent to which such beliefs, practices and cultures *matter*. For some, these kinds of beliefs and their cultural frameworks are of paramount significance; for others, they are significant in certain moments; and for yet others, they are hardly significant at all. Sometimes thought of as a type of non-religion, indifference is maybe best thought of as an independent attitude that can be combined with underlying religious or non-religious cultures, equally (or indeed with some combination of the two). Whether religious or non-religious, we are, most of us, more or less indifferent to such matters for at least some of the time; in this sense, indifference is a great leveller. If it does not feed into perceived religious/non-religious divides though, indifference may be significant to those interested in the prospects for dialogue as it marks out an important dimension to both.

Conclusion: equal but different

The surprising diversity of non-religious orientations points us towards what might be a forceful impediment to dialogue, namely, a fundamental asymmetry in the way that religious and non-religious actors are conceived of. On the one hand, we view religion as a rich cultural form, even something that is special – that should be set apart for special protections and special restrictions (Lee 2015, 197–200). By contrast, for most of our history, we have tended to view non-religion as a purely negative phenomenon – merely concerning the absence of religion and theistic experience and belief. Our tendency to pair 'religion and atheism' together in our thinking around these issues – a pairing taken up in the title of this volume – illustrates the point: whereas we think that there is more to religion than simply theism and theology, non-religious positions are thought about in terms of the mere absence of theistic belief (*theism*) (Lee 2015). We have tended to think that the non-religious do not believe or do anything in particular at all. These are naturalised accounts, which say that being non-religious is less a condition than it is a natural state, un-enriched and/or unfettered by religion. In this way of thinking, the idea of non-religious diversity makes little sense. 'Religion and atheism' is a phrase that tells us something important about the assumptions we tend to make, both about religion and about non-religion, too.

But these assumptions are unsettled by new cultural approaches to the non-religious, and by the new detailed studies of non-religious actors that have become possible as these populations have grown in size. (Long spoken of, it is easy to forget that widespread non-religiosity is a relatively recent phenomenon, dating only from quite well into the second half of the twentieth century.) Taking a cultural approach to the non-religious – paying attention to what it means to be alternatively spiritual, existentially humanist, romantically materialist, or hedonistically or nihilistically agnostic, and to what it means to be these things in different regional, demographic and other contexts – means that the idea of the religious and non-religious as polar opposites is harder and harder to maintain. If there is so much diversity, the idea of placing the religious and non-religious on a spectrum becomes as unpromising as trying to map religious confessions, movie tastes, food preferences or any other cultural formation onto a single spectrum.

Rather, binary approaches are likely to fail to do justice to the diverse and complicated ways in which humans understand the nature of life and the business of living. If we truly want to achieve understanding and dialogue, surely we need to understand existential experiences in their detail and diversity, the many and both theistic and atheistic cultural formations they manifest in, and the diverse ways in which these formations are both similar and different from one another. We need to recognise also the similarities that mean that religious and non-religious actors ought to be treated equally, and to recognise the significant variations that can make them different from another. And we need to recognise that, as sociocultural formations, they are both as likely to be ambivalent in their effects – neither wholly good nor wholly bad, neither all-powerful nor entirely put upon.

Given the prevalence of polarised accounts – most obviously but not only seen in God-wars-type debates – recognising the complexity of the British religious landscape is possibly a powerful resource for those interested in dialogue, because doing so undercuts simple oppositions and divisive asymmetries. Certainly dialogue requires two parties; but it does not – and perhaps should not – require two poles.[10]

Notes

1 E.g. 'David Cameron Declares: "Britain Is Still a Christian Country"', *Telegraph*, 5 April 2015, <http://www.telegraph.co.uk/news/general-election-2015/11516804/ David-Cameron-declares-Britain-is-still-a-Christian-country.html>; 'David Cameron AGAIN Calls Britain a Christian Country in His Annual Christmas Message', *Mirror*, 24 December 2015, <available at http://www.mirror.co.uk/news/uk- news/david-cameron-again-calls-britain-7064888>.

2 The non-religious has been the largest group in the Social Attitudes survey (see the British Social Attitudes Information System website, <http://www. britsocat.com/>) since 1993, and an outright majority in several years since 2010. Discussed in Lee 2016.

3 The distinction between diversity and methods of negotiating that diversity are often conflated in the concept of 'pluralism'. On the distinction between 'plurality' as a descriptive term and 'pluralism' as a normative one, see Bardon *et al.* 2015.

4 See Lee 2015, esp. ch. 7.

5 Woodhead actually says that the UK is 'neither religious nor secular'; the concept of 'secularity' is problematic, and I put this to one side for now, and return to this issue in more detail below.

6 Siegers (2011) suggests that 27 per cent of Britain are 'atheists' and 23 per cent are theists (if his 'church religion' and 'moderate religion' groups are combined), while Voas and Day (2007) suggest that a perfect 25 per cent are religious (15 per cent actively, 10 per cent privately) and 25 per cent unreligious.

7 For an explanation of the discrepancy between census and and British Social Attitudes data, see Voas and Day 2007. For a discussion of the majority status of the non-religious, see Lee 2016.

8 The other was Hungary.

9 Survey questions asking about belief in God tend to offer a 'don't know' or 'not sure' option alongside the strong agnostic view; the numbers mentioned here refer to the latter.

10 This chapter is made possible by the UCL (University College London) Scientific Study of Nonreligious Belief project, funded by the John Templeton Foundation.

Bibliography

Bardon, Aurélia, Maria Birnbaum, Lois Lee and Kristina Stoekl (2015) 'Introduction: Pluralism and Plurality', in Aurélia Bardon, Maria Birnbaum, Lois Lee and Kristina Stoeckl (eds), *Religious Pluralism: A Resource Book*. Florence: European University Institute.

Bullivant, Stephen (2010) 'The New Atheism and Sociology: Why Here? Why Now? What Next?', in A. Amarasingam (ed.), *Religion and the New Atheism: A Critical Appraisal*. Leiden: Brill, 109–24.

Bullivant, Stephen (2013) 'Defining Atheism', in S. Bullivant and M. Ruse (eds), *The Oxford Handbook of Atheism*. Oxford: Oxford University Press, 11–21.

Day, Abby (2011) *Believing in Belonging: Belief and Social Identity in the Modern World*. Oxford: Oxford University Press.

Heelas, Paul and Linda Woodhead (2005) *The Spiritual Revolution: Why Religion Is Giving Way to Spirituality*. London: Wiley-Blackwell.

Kettell, Steven (2015) 'Illiberal Secularism? Pro-faith Discourse in the United Kingdom', in Titus Hjelm (ed.), *Is God Back? Reconsidering the New Visibility of Religion*. London: Bloomsbury, 65–76.

Lee, Lois (2015) *Recognizing the Non-religious: Reimagining the Secular*. Oxford: Oxford University Press.

Lee, Lois (2016) 'The Nonreligious are Britain's Hidden Majority', *British Politics and Policy* [blog], London School of Economics and Political Science, <http://blogs.lse.ac.uk/politicsandpolicy/the-nonreligious-are-britains-hidden-majority/>.

Modood, Tariq (2015) 'Religion in Britain Today and Tomorrow', Theos website, <http://www.theosthinktank.co.uk/comment/2015/01/29/religion-in-britain-today-and-tomorrow>.

ONS (Office for National Statistics) (2012) 'Religion in England and Wales', ONS, 11 December, <http://www.ons.gov.uk/ons/dcp171776_290510.pdf>.

Siegers, Pascal (2011) 'A Multiple Group Latent Class Analysis of Religious Orientations in Europe', in Eldad Davidov, Peter Schmidt and Jaak Billiet (eds), *Cross-cultural Analysis: Methods and Applications*. New York: Routledge, 387–413.

Voas, David (2009) 'The Rise and Fall of Fuzzy Fidelity in Europe', *European Sociological Review* 25, no. 2: 155–68.

Voas, David and Abby Day (2007) 'Secularity in Great Britain', in Barry A. Kosmin and Ariela Keysar (eds), *Secularism and Secularity: Contemporary International Perspectives*. Hartford, CT: Trinity College Institute for the Study of Secularism in Society and Culture, 95–112.

Voas, David and Siobhan McAndrew (2014) 'Three Puzzles of Non-religion in Britain', E. Arweck, S. Bullivant and L. Lee (eds), *Secularity and Non-religion*. London: Routledge.

Woodhead, Linda (2013) 'Neither Religious or Secular: The British Situation and Its Implications for Religious–State Relations', in A. Berg-Sørenson (ed.), *Contesting Secularism: Comparative Perspectives*. Farnham, UK: Ashgate.

Woodhead, Linda (2014) 'The Fuzzy Nones', *Nonreligion and Secularity* [blog], Nonreligion and Secularity Research Network, 7 March, <http://blog.nsrn.net/2014/03/07/launch-series-the-fuzzy-nones/>.

15 Belonging without believing
Religion, atheism and Islam today

Dilwar Hussain

This chapter takes as its starting point the growing phenomenon of people choosing no longer to believe in the religion of their heritage, in this case Islam. The data on religious identification shows how this is a significant issue in many European countries, some of which have now gone beyond the 50 per cent threshold of people who do not express belief in a religion. In looking at some of the tensions this experience may create within debates on Islam, I was reflecting on Grace Davie's notion of 'believing without belonging', in her exploration of the transformation of Christianity and how people engage with it. I spoke at a conference a few years ago, when I deliberately changed that wording to talk about the need to find ways of 'belonging without believing'.

In contemporary debates around Islam in Western societies, often marred by politics of identity, one of the highly contentious issues that has emerged is the stigmatisation of people who leave their religion to convert to another, or move to a position of agnosticism or atheism. This can become a serious concern, with death threats, social isolation and a sense of being 'cut off' from one's community and even from one's family not unheard of. And yet the Qur'an asserts that 'there should be no compulsion in religion'. At the end of the chapter, I propose a framework for thinking about this tension further, but it raises the question of the relationship between Islam and terms such as 'freedom' (of religion), 'humanism', 'secularism' and 'the secular'.

The secular

The Qur'an is a scripture held as a divine source of light by Muslims, yet it should not follow from this, in automatic fashion, that it is at odds with the secular. In fact the earthly life is strongly affirmed and one could actually say that in some ways Islam is a 'secular religion' in the sense that secular means temporal and earthly. One often finds references to focus the mind on both this life and the next:

> And ordain for us good in the world and in the hereafter ...
>
> (Qur'an 7.156)

The metaphor of human creation, where Adam and Eve are sent to the earth, shows the 'divine plan' that they have been created for a temporal, earthly, secular existence. This was not a 'fall', but the purpose all along (as discussed below).

The promise that ensues is that light, or inspiration, will be 'sent' from the numinous to the earthly. Accordingly, the stated purpose or use of this light is to work within a secular setting. The European memory of its history of religion is not often narrated as one of a complementing dimension, but more as a 'run in' with the secular, and that constraining the force of religion was necessary for the expansion of secular, rational and scientific progress. To some secular reformers today, the Muslim world may often feel like that; the Qur'an can be read as an inoculation against the 'trappings of materialism'. But it can also be read as seeking a settlement on earth, fertilising the expansion of worldly progress, being a part of, and not apart from, the life of this world. In fact, the Qur'an appears to challenge other religious communities that it considers to be too 'other-worldly', saying: 'O People of the Book, do not go to excesses in your religion' (Qur'an 4.171).

Are these contrasting readings about the temporal existence – to ward off or to embrace – equally weighted in their claims? Both readings do at least exist and, across the passage of time, different Islamic subcultures have stressed one vision over the other.

Freedom

Free will is the very essence of the human spirit. According to the narrative of the Qur'an, and its story of creation, it is free will that differentiated humanity at the point of creation. The story begins with an announcement of intention by God to the assembly of angels:

> I wish to place a vicegerent upon the earth ...
>
> (Qur'an 2.30)

The angels suggested that (as a result of free will) man would 'cause mischief (on the earth) and shed blood'; God replied, 'I know that which you do not' – thus giving divine licence to this unique aspect of humanity and acknowledging that while freedom may lead to corruption, it is only through the exercise of free choice that the human spirit can reach the heights for which it was intended. This free choice, therefore, must include within it the ability to say 'no', even to God. A forced faith, or even a forced (or 'enforced') practice of religion can only be an inferior version of that practice, and temporal coercion can never truly convince the heart of a truth.

This is why the Qur'an asserts that there should be 'no compulsion' in faith. The opportunity to believe can only be truly realised and valued when there is also an opportunity to disbelieve. Of course, no freedom is absolute and all those involved in the debates acknowledge the need for some laws and rules to regulate behaviour – otherwise there would be chaos. But such laws should be about preventing harm, rather than enforcing religious practice.

While Eastern traditions have tended to focus more on responsibility and duty than on freedom, the European experience has been the struggle to win precious freedoms from monarchs, aristocrats, the church and others who wielded power – leaving Europeans with a particular penchant for the notions of individual freedoms and rights. It may be argued that Muslim notions of authority, hierarchy and respect tend to be romanticised, while Western conceptions of these values have come to be read with more sceptical undertones.

The notions of respect, for example, seem quite different. Muslims have learned to respect religious symbols and icons more than the people that follow those symbols – even though the Prophet Muhammad taught that the life of a single person is more precious than the most sacred site in Islam: 'the Kaba, and all its surroundings'. Yet today, an attack on the reputation of the Prophet or his family, or on a holy site, would cause outrage, but an attack on an ordinary Muslim may go unnoticed.

However, in the British climate of free speech, institutions and representatives of religion are often seen to be fair targets for ridicule, possibly because of the cynicism towards authority and power (especially of a religious nature), but laypeople are rarely subject to the same treatment. Our notions of freedom, and conversely of offence, are culturally contingent. They are not absolutes. The environment in Britain is one in which humour is often self-deprecating. Being able to laugh at oneself is a very British way of expressing self-confidence, and those unable to do so are seen as nervous and possibly having something to hide.

With the exception of anti-democracy activists who decry the Western political slogans of freedom as an anti-Islam plot, even orthodox Muslims speak a language of freedoms – at the very least an appeal to a freedom to practise their religion. Traditionally, a language of 'rights' or of passive tolerance or 'live and let live', inspired by verses such as 'to you your religion, to me mine' (Qur'an 109.6), and of freedom to choose one's religion as part of God's design, has emerged as the discourse. The tie-in of human 'freedom' with a central Qur'anic verse yields a discourse around 'freedom of religion' and, by extension, around a pseudo–human rights discourse. Atheism, for example, is thus framed as a choice. This does not alter the theological teachings around such a choice (that it falls short of recognising the gifts of God), but it does begin to reposition the social relationships that such an outlook can create. Furthermore, faith is seen as something that cannot be forced, it has to be a choice. Piety has to emerge from within and an attempt to feign it takes one into the territory of hypocrisy, which is seen to be worse than open disbelief because it involves deception.

Humans before believers

The voice of the Qur'an speaks to all human beings and one of the often-repeated configurations of its discourse is addressed to 'humanity/mankind'.

> O mankind! We created you from a single (pair) of a male and a female, and made you into nations and tribes, that you may know each other (not that you may despise each other).
>
> (Qur'an 49.13)

Such a verse seems to indicate an inclusive vision of humanity, in which ethnic and religious differences are to be celebrated and seen as a form of enrichment. A yet more explicit verse says:

> To every one of you We have appointed a way and an open road. If God had willed, He would have made you one nation; but that He may try you in what has come to you. So be forward in good works; unto God shall you return, all together; and He will inform you about that in which you used to differ.
>
> (Qur'an 5.48)

One is thus acutely aware that this life is one in which differences may be manifest, but such differences should not become the source of contention and division, let alone hatred or violence. We are to live in humility to carry out good works, and then when we return to God the truth claims of our positions will be finally resolved. Our focus in this life should therefore not be on judging others, but on our own performance. Another verse talks of the important identity of being human and how that in itself carries a tremendous dignity: 'We have conferred honour upon the Children of Adam ...'(Qur'an 17.70).

Belief in God was most often presumed in historical societies across the world, let alone the East. Early Islam encountered Christians, Jews, Zoroastrians (all three of whom were accepted as 'people of the book') and pagans but there is very little mention of encounter with atheism. Islamic history, therefore, provides little or no precedent for theological or social responses to atheism. The Madinan charter shows that Muhammad's instinct was to create a society where all the residents of the time were regarded as a single community (*ummah*), regardless of faith or belief.

Epistemological opening (and closing)

In his work on humanism and Islam, Ebrahim Moosa (2011) discusses the role of critical Muslim thinkers and scholars in learning from a wide range of sources. It was because they were open to learning from the Graeco-Roman, Persian, Indian, Chinese and other sources of knowledge that the translation movement at the time of the Abbasid 'House of Wisdom' (*Bayt al-Hikma*) was able to be so creative. This era led to a vast step-up in Islamic thought which had an impact on a wide range of scholarly disciplines including philosophy, science, mathematics, art and literature. Above all, one sees the tremendous role that reason played in Muslim thought at that time (and paved the way for influencing European thought).

To thinkers such as Miskawayh (d. 1030), the idea of *al-Insaniyya* (humanity/humanism) was the goal of an ethical outlook of Islam (Goodman 2003). Miskawayh charted out a premodern notion of 'evolution' in which he advocated that energy was infused into matter, which developed into mineral form, then into vegetable matter, which progressed to lower life forms and eventually became higher life forms. Similar ideas were also shared by the earlier Ikhwan al-Safa, a secretive intellectual and spiritual order around the tenth century.

Some Muslim thinkers advanced the idea that there are two forms of revelation – the type that one can read as the 'word of God' (scripture), and the type that one can 'read' from the natural world all around us. The epistemological work of Ibn Sina (d. 1037) on the latter influenced the Andalusian Ibn Tufayl (d. 1185), who borrowed from Ibn Sina and wrote his own version of a fictional work, *Hayy ibn Yaqdhan*, which tells the story of a boy who grew up on a remote island without human contact and how he came to develop knowledge of the truth (of God) through reason. This work was translated into Latin by Edward Pococke in 1671 (under the title, *Philosophus autodidactus*) and then into English by Simon Ockley in 1708 (entitled *The Improvement of Human Reason*). The text had a profound impact on, for example, Locke (d. 1704) (who was a student of Pococke) and his idea of the *tabula rasa* as well as on the theories of empiricism that developed in Western thought.

The point here is to illustrate that at a time of an open embrace and engagement with humanity and diverse sources of knowledge, a creative and vibrant interchange and evolution of learning can take place. Yet, when defensiveness, suspicion of others, fear and mistrust set in – as one may argue is currently a challenge for Muslim thought – that vibrancy dissipates, leading to a downward spiral of fear, mistrust and the closing of doors. How then does one prepare to engage with the challenges that the modern world presents, including the challenge of modernity and secularisation and what these mean to a religion that feels (correctly, or incorrectly) under threat? There are some Muslim thinkers in the last century, such as Iqbal (d. 1938), who have taken on the mantle of open intellectual engagement with the philosophical world around them, but many more of such figures are needed. From the late nineteenth century one could hear calls for renewed thinking (*ijtihad*) and reform (*islah*) in the Muslim world. Iqbal played a significant role in helping Muslims to think about the nature of the world after the demise of the Ottoman Empire and create a reasoned vision for a post-colonial society that could be based on a modern constitutional system.

Secularism

We often hear that Islam has no sense of separation of 'church and state', that there is an absence of the teaching of 'render unto Caesar what is Caesar's'. But a close scrutiny of Islam, and the life of Muhammad, shows that even in the teachings of someone who personified the 'religious' for Muslims, a compartmentalisation between 'worldly matters' and 'religious matters' was actually quite clear.

Muhammad once came across some people who were artificially pollinating palm trees. He disliked the idea and commented that it would be better not to do this. However, as a result of following his advice, the harvest in the following year was poor. When the farmers complained to him, he openly admitted the limitation of his knowledge regarding secular affairs and said: 'If a question relates to your worldly matters you would know better about it, but if it relates to your religion then it belongs to me' (Hadith collection *Sahih Muslim*).

In the early twentieth century a preoccupation with the caliphate, the 'Islamic state', was seen as a symbol of Muslim unity and its restoration as vital in defending Muslim interests and procuring justice in a post-colonial context. However, in reality, there has been a well-established normative distinction (albeit in premodern settings) between the temporal, sovereign authority and the institutions of religion in the Muslim world, with the latter mainly advocating autonomy and resenting their co-option by the state whenever that did happen. In *The Failure of Political Islam*, Olivier Roy (1994) argues that 'a de facto separation between political power' of sultans and emirs and the religious power of the caliph was 'created and institutionalized ... as early as the end of the first century of the hegira'. Roy points to an early separation of powers in which the state's religious functions and worldly administrative arms, including systems of legal arbitration, were organised as distinct organs. Muhammad Abduh (d. 1905) asserted more than a century ago that Islam is not a theocracy and that there is a distinction between the 'religious' and the 'worldly'.

With the immense disappointment of Muslims with the various national projects often couched (even if at times with little more than lip service) in the terms of Islam – Saudi Arabia, Pakistan, Iran, Sudan, Afghanistan, etc. – there is a growing recognition that a liberal, secular democracy is a good model for ensuring accountable, open societies that can protect the rights of all citizens of the state.

This may go some way in explaining why Islamic parties contesting modern political debate through a democratic national election have historically fared very poorly, even in a country like Pakistan, which is arguably the only modern nation state to emerge as an independent Islamic country (though this is a contested description), and where the emotion of a Muslim identity runs deep, the most established and organised religious parties make little impact in their chief aim of forming a majority government. Cries of corruption and foul play, among other factors, are commonly cited as a reason, but any objective assessment of political (as opposed to moral) offerings points to stark and obvious limitations in the quest for government. In setting out their democratic case for government, religious parties have very little to offer by way of a secure economic policy, national aspiration or welfare reform.

The instinct of the demos, the national vote bank, is not to trust religious parties with the national purse any more than they would with a surgical operation. Religion after all has always had a medicinal as well as a moral offering, yet it would be considered absurd to leave an advanced physical ailment in the hands of religious teachers. The application of scientific disciplines to human affairs within the economically and socially advanced nations of the world is thus an emergent challenge to an Islamic thought that makes an inconsistent qualification of human progress, by embracing material scientific enquiry but resisting world advancement in the human sciences. This dichotomy, already sensed by the Muslim populace, will inevitably have to give way to a more coherent approach.

Within the nation state, there is a growing, if unappreciated, list of Muslim majority countries that wear a secular political system on their sleeve. Turkey is routinely cited as the example, and it is significant in key ways, not least because it is within Europe and had a central role in the latter part of Islamic political history. But Turkey upholds a strident narrative of its own enlightenment struggle and therefore presents a contentious and questionable model of harmonising faith and secularism. In addition to Turkey, states which do not claim a religious name for their system, and can be considered as variants of a secular model for a Muslim majority population, include Albania, Azerbaijan, Burkina Faso, Chad, Gambia, Guinea, Kazakhstan, Kosovo, Kyrgyzstan, Mali, Senegal, Tajikistan, Turkmenistan and Uzbekistan.

Even within the largest Muslim populations, there are strong undertones of a secular approach to national governance. Indonesia's five founding principles, the Pancasila, which forms the philosophical foundation of the nation state, is a confident attempt to 'square' secularism with a majority Islamic faith. Indonesia has the largest Muslim population in the world, and consists in fact of a multiplicity of distinct island cultures. The Pancasila is a concept that has invited differing opinions regarding its religiosity, but successive Indonesian leaders have shown it to be flexible enough to assert a strong secular dimension despite its first principle proclaiming belief in God (not 'Allah' or 'Islam') as the national faith. The Pancasila has allowed the largest Muslim population to assert itself as a country for Muslims but not an Islamic nation state, in a way that the second largest nation, Pakistan, has not been able to.

It is precisely around this question of the whole Pakistan 'project' that the philosophical basis of Pakistan politics and the politics of its national identity revolve. The founder Muhammad Ali Jinnah insisted on a white column on Pakistan's national flag, to symbolise its minority population of other faith communities as a clear indicator of purpose – indeed, within his immediate family there were cross-religious marriages that were free of family taboo. Twenty years after Pakistan was founded (Jinnah died a year after independence), the Pakistan People's Party emerged as a progressive socialist party. It began as a communist-leaning political force in opposition to the then government's support for America, with strong socialist messages and goals. By the 1970s, its rallying cry of 'Roti, Kapra aur Makan' (food, clothing and housing) saw it form a government on a secular basis.

Pakistan and Indonesia then, represent large-scale, complex examples of a popular will and a political determination to find a civil space for religious neutrality where the national framework is dominated by a single religion. Through their challenges and policy aims, and while they remain far from having a religiously neutral basis by Western standards, they do point to a quest for a modern existence where Islam can thrive as a religion and the state can thrive as a plural society.

However, the story is more complex than that; an absence of religious rule (and an 'on-paper' separation of religion and state) does not automatically imply genuine freedom and liberty, given the role of the military and authoritarian tendencies in many Muslim countries. Furthermore, 'secularism' in the Muslim world has, in the past, been associated with forced 'westernisation' (Turkey for example) and/or double standards (e.g. support for dictatorships). This means that Muslim publics are often very sceptical of the term 'secularism' (though, as mentioned previously, not necessarily the notion of separation).

While advocating secularism, I am not for the disappearance of religion, nor for an anticlerical and closed-minded laicity (see Birt *et al.* 2011). Rather, I see secularism as a good way of managing the public debate and structuring society, especially where multiple religious, ideological and belief positions may collide. So there is a conversation to be had about the extent, nature and mode of religious presence in the public sphere. The differentiation made by Rowan Williams between procedural secularism and programmatic (anticlerical) secularism is a helpful one here. Given the plural nature of that presence, perhaps the Rawlsian notion of 'public reason' can help – especially in a culture with very low religious literacy. But it seems that we also need to reach a point where religious voices can be given adequate consideration and not automatically disregarded as 'superstitious'.

Conclusion

We have looked at some of the ideas that could be important building blocks within Muslim thought for a more nuanced and compassionate interaction between people who find themselves on different sides of the religion and atheism divide. Based on this, we can see that some of the potential areas of tension could be negotiated by using resources that are deeply embedded in the Muslim heritage and tradition. The idea of whether a person is free to believe or not believe; the choice of how much they should observe if they believe; the notion of fundamental human rights and equality of human beings; non-discrimination between people on the basis of their religious identity; how a secular society can both protect religions and the rights of individuals; the use of reason in the interpretation of sacred texts to allow for more contextually rooted religious discourses – all these are based on traditional views, but can also lay the ground for a set of open and inclusive interpretations of Islam that can help to look ahead to meet the challenges we face in society.

The Western world is home not just to significant numbers of Muslims, but also to significant subgroups of Muslims. There is no such thing as a singular 'Muslim community'. Within that diversity, a wide spectrum of religious practice can be found in a very dynamic landscape that has come to represent 'Muslim identity'. The idea that belonging, being part of something, is based on a common and shared belief may be a useful one, but in my view it is not enough in the very complex hyper-diversity that we live in today.

The greatest challenge of the future is about how we live with difference, not how we promote similarity. Such a future has an amazingly bright and exciting prospect, but it needs to be based on a sense of openness, compassion and respect that allows people to be themselves, without judgment, without prejudice, without pigeonholes. I am passionate about my beliefs. But equally passionately, I feel that we need spaces where I, and others who may not believe in the way that I do, or choose not to believe in anything 'religious', can share a sense of belonging, commonality and mutuality. Before we are believers, we are human. There is a distinction between 'being' and 'believing'. And we need to find ways in which we can *be* human together, even if we don't *believe* together.

> 'Shall I tell you what is better than much prayer and charity?' They said, 'Yes.' He said, 'mending discord between people. And beware of hatred – it strips away your religion.'
>
> (Hadith collection *Muwatta Imam Malik*)

Bibliography

Birt, Yahya, Dilwar Hussain and Ataullah Siddiqui (eds) (2011) *British Secularism and Religion: Islam, Society and the State*. Markfield, UK: Kube Publishing.

Goodman, Len (2003) *Islamic Humanism*. Oxford: Oxford University Press.

Moosa, Ebrahim (2011) 'The Spirit of Islamic Humanism', in John Gruchy (ed.), *The Humanist Imperative in South Africa*. Stellenbosch: African Sun MeDIA.

Roy, Olivier (1994) *The Failure of Political Islam*. Cambridge, MA: Harvard University Press.

16 The Ocean of Being and the Web of Becomings

The pilgrim's progress on Indic horizons

Ankur Barua

The classical Indic intellectual traditions can be a source of both promise and dismay for interpreters who approach them with the categories of 'religion' and 'atheism'. On the one hand, we have the fairly widespread image of India as a land steeped in perennial wisdom, one that has been appropriated in complex ways by the conceptual structures of Theosophy, deep ecology, vegetarianism, new religious movements, transnational yoga, and so on. For more than a century now, certain Indian forms of spirituality have been hailed for their promissory note of a *via media* for Westerners seeking to dismantle the Abrahamic binary of institutionalised religion versus militant atheism. On the other hand, several lines of post-colonial critiques have pointed out that the association of India with 'spirituality' is a complex product partly of the British colonial exoticisation of the Orient as sunk into an ahistorical passivity and partly of some Indian intellectuals' projection of the Orient as the saviour of the fallen soul of a materialistically depraved West. Consequently, if according to the first representation of India, its atmosphere has forever been saturated with spirituality, according to the second deflationary account, its aura of spirituality is a social construct that emerged under the conditions of colonial modernity. Clearly, then, before we begin to explore whether classical Indian thought can illuminate contemporary Western debates relating to 'religion' and 'atheism', we have to address the methodological issue of whether its diverse universes possess any equivalents or correlates for these terms.

a

Skirting the conceptual minefield of attempts at defining 'religion', we will venture into the relatively more tractable field of definitions of 'atheism'. We take 'negative atheism' to be the view that no good reasons or valid arguments are available to demonstrate the reality of trans-spatio-temporal entities or states or processes, and its metaphysically more robust cousin 'positive atheism' the view that the non-reality of such entities or states or processes can be rationally demonstrated. If we examine the metaphysical horizons of three classical Indic systems – Advaita Vedanta associated with Shankara (*c*.800 CE), the theistic Vedanta of Ramanuja (*c*.1100 CE), and Buddhism – in the light of these distinctions, we can notice certain overlaps as well as disjunctions across them.[1]

None of them are forms of either 'positive atheism' or 'negative atheism': each affirms a distinctive trans-spatio-temporal X as the highest good of human endeavour, points to a certain scriptural text or foundational experience as the source of our human knowledge of X, and develops patterns of rational argumentation to undercut defeaters of belief in X. However, since the ineffable X does not easily lend itself to rational discourse, unpacking the nature or structure of X leads us to the conceptual dilemma, familiar to students of Christian mysticism, of trying to speak about X which, by definition, transcends human speech. For Advaita Vedanta, X is the eternal, indivisible and immutable self-luminous Consciousness which is the foundational ground of all empirical reality, such that the constituents of our everyday world structured by difference – chairs, tables, horses, aeroplanes, and laptops – are essentially this X. To elaborate the metaphor indicated in the title of the essay, just as a drop in a wavelet in a wave in the ocean is essentially water, so too all finite spatio-temporal entities, in their truest essence, are non-dual (*advaita*) with X. Crucially, X is transpersonal, that is, personal qualities such as omniscience, omnipotence, and others do not characterise its ultimate essence (Rambachan 2006). Therefore, while human beings may approach X through personalised images possessing such qualities, these attributes have to be gradually discarded on the way towards the interiorised realisation of oneself as essentially X. As one progresses up the rungs of a ladder towards the summit – an ascent structured by the development of virtues such as self-control, the contemplative interiorisation of the content of the Upanishads, and so on – the realisation dawns on the aspirant that she and the ladder itself are essentially X, so that at the apex she and ladder, which are metaphysically unreal, fall away. For Ramanuja's theistic Vedanta, in contrast, X is the fully personal Lord Vishnu-Narayana who is free from all worldly defects but possesses empirical qualities such as knowledge, joy, sovereignty, and others in their supereminent form. The Lord indwells the world which is the divine body in the 'pan-en-theistic' sense that the Lord, who is ontologically distinct from the world, abides as its transcendental ruler as well as its immanent presence (Lipner 1986). While the multiple strands of Vedantic thought are at times sharply divergent from one another (and we have noted one such instance in the disagreement between Shankara and Ramanuja regarding their views of X), they converge in their affirmation that X is that which *subsists* while everything that is empirical is subject to change, mutation, and suffering. The multiple doctrinal forms of Buddhism – originating in India and moving outwards to Southeast Asia, China, and Japan – share in common the assertion that the world is not composed of any permanent entities, and that X is to be understood not through the Vedantic vocabulary of *endurance* but (merely) as the cessation of the world of impermanence.

More concisely, while for Vedantic thought, Brahman (the scriptural name for X) is that which abides in the midst of empirical change and decay, a Buddhist thinker such as Nagarjuna (*c.*200 CE) would speak of *nirvana*, the highest good, simply as the passing away of this world riddled with transience, decay, and suffering. To develop the other metaphor in the title, all empirical reality is a gigantic and enormously intricate web of mutually criss-crossing interrelations, and the entities of everyday life are but shifting nodes in this dynamic matrix of fleeting becomings (Harvey 2012). While *nirvana* is, in some sense that words struggle to convey, 'outside' this matrix, Buddhist thinkers emphasise that *nirvana* is not quite the still point of the Vedantic Brahman but the utter dissolution of the very language of permanence.

Crucial to these Vedantic–Buddhist dialectics is the role of the Vedic horizon in their argumentative structures: the Vedantic argument for the existence of Brahman, in the Vedic schools (*astika*) of Advaita Vedanta and theistic Vedanta, is that the Vedic revelation indicates to us that the world is encompassed by and grounded in Brahman, a scriptural datum that the anti-Vedic (*nastika*) Buddhist traditions did not accept. Thus, Ramanuja rejects a certain argument based on a general relation between 'products' and an 'intelligent maker' – the inference, for instance, from perceived pots to the unseen potter – and argues that scripture alone is the epistemic means to the divine. Ramanuja argues that such an inference will not lead us to the Lord Vishnu-Narayana, because the two cases – one potter from many pots, and the Lord from the world – are not analogous. Ramanuja points out in an intriguingly Humean fashion that while we can infer a producer from the artefacts, we cannot infer a single omnipotent and omniscient maker from the natural features of the universe, nor can we treat the universe itself as a unitary entity (Bartley 2011, 172–3).

With this somewhat fine-grained analysis of the conceptual bases of Vedantic thought and Buddhism, we can return to the definitional enterprise. First, it is crucial to note that since our definitions do not refer specifically to 'God', as the term is understood in Abrahamic theisms, Buddhism does not fall into the category of 'atheism'. While from the perspective of metaphysical naturalism, atheism would involve the rejection of anything that is trans-empirical, Buddhism affirms the reality of trans-empirical processes such as the moral order of *karma* that governs rebirths across several lifetimes. Further, certain configurations of Mahayana Buddhism speak of the Bodhisattvas who are supramundane beings assisting worldly humans in their pathways through the cycles of rebirth (*samsara*). While the Bodhisattvas are not the Buddhist equivalent of the sempiternal angels of Christian imagination and a fortiori the eternal God of Catholic doctrine, they possess certain forms of superhuman mental stabilisation, omniscience, and so on. Second, theistic Vedanta (of which there are many forms in classical and contemporary India) offers more ready parallels with Abrahamic theisms: they speak, from within their distinctive universes, of a unitary and supremely personal Deity as the source of being, goodness, and value, and of single-minded devotion to the Deity as an integral aspect of one's return to the Deity. Third, however, Advaita Vedanta presents an intriguing challenge to our definitional mapping: on the one hand, it is not 'atheistic', since Brahman is the supra-empirical reality that is non-dual with all empirical beings, and, on the other hand, it is not 'religious' either in the Abrahamic sense, since the transcategorial Brahman, the ultimate end that human devotional worship points towards, is devoid of all personal attributes.

b

Against this conceptual backdrop, we can begin to explore the theme of the 'pilgrim's progress' that is central to the multiple forms of Buddhism and Vedantic Hinduism, even though they often diverge in their responses to the basic questions of 'who is the pilgrim?' and 'what is the goal of this progress?' Notwithstanding the vital divergences that we have outlined in the preceding section, their practices of the 'care of the self' are structured by certain axiomatic equivalences. If we were to engage in conversations with classical Indian figures such as Shankara, Ramanuja, and Nagarjuna about the ingredients of a meaningful life we would discover that the following presupposition structures their responses.

First axiom of impermanence (FAOI): If P is impermanent, then P cannot be the source of true satisfaction.

All our conversation partners agree that the empirical world structured by suffering (*samsara*) is indeed such a P, and hence cannot provide true happiness to someone who is involved in a quest for a meaningful life. To add another classical Indian partner to this dialogue, the set of beliefs and practices clubbed together as Samkhya-Yoga puts forward the thesis that there is a preponderance of suffering over happiness in this world, and that even moments of happiness are, in fact, mixed with pain or tend to change into pain. According to its metaphysical picture, outlined in the *Samkhya-Karika* of Isvarakrishna (*c.*300 CE) and the *Yoga Sutra* of Patanjali, the world has evolved from the conjunction of two independent principles: pure, inactive, and contentless consciousness (*purusha*) and the primordial source of physicality (*prakriti*). The essential self (*purusha*), which is non-agential witness, forgets that it is metaphysically distinct from the mind–body complex which is a product of dynamic *prakriti*, and this misidentification leads to a succession of lives which are mired in suffering. The remedy lies in learning to distinguish (*viveka*) between oneself as translucent witness of the ever-changing states of the psychophysiological complex, so as to reach the final destination of disassociation (*kaivalya*) from all insentient *prakritic* entities. This therapeutic structure is announced at the very beginning of the *Samkhya-Karika* which states that because of the torment of the three types of suffering (psychophysical, natural, and cosmic) there arises in human beings the desire to know the means to terminate them. As one gains a deeper insight into the way that things really are, one sees all phenomenal-*prakritic* existence as suffused with suffering. As Patanjali's *Yoga Sutra* (2.15) notes: to the one who discerns correctly, all indeed is suffering (Feuerstein 1979).

The first noble truth of Buddhism too declares that 'all is suffering' (*sarvam duhkham*), and hammers home the point in the following clear terms: 'Birth is painful, old age is painful, sickness is painful, death is painful, sorrow, lamentation, dejection, and despair are painful. Contact with unpleasant things is painful, not getting what one wishes is painful' (Radhakrishnan and Moore 1957, 274). However, while at first glance Samkhya-Yoga and Buddhism seem to overwhelm us with detailed descriptions of our lives as mired in pain, suffering, and misery, this exhortation to view the world *as* permeated with dissatisfaction is propaedeutic to the resolution of the ills that beset us. These traditions, structured by FAOI, offer highly specific diagnostic approaches to the human condition: only *after* we have realised the true depths of our misery shall we also wish to put an end to it, and reach out for the remedy that has been offered to us. That is, this sort of an *experience-as*, in which one learns to *experience* suffering *as* omnipresent, plays a therapeutic role, for a physician may not be able to heal a patient who does not grasp the true extent of her *disease*.

To facilitate the attainment and deepening of this 'healing' insight, the *Yoga Sutra* lays down an eightfold path through which the diseased individual is led back to full health. Some scholars have highlighted the parallels between this Samkhya-Yoga 'technology of the self' and the structure of classical Indian medicine: corresponding to the four sections of the latter, Samkhya-Yoga too speaks of suffering, its cause, liberation from it, and the means to its cessation (Warrier 1981, 56–7). A similar diagnostic structure, founded again on the thesis of the ubiquity of suffering, is present in classical Buddhism, which holds that all conditioned phenomena can only lead to a deep dissatisfaction (*duhkha*). Once again, when Buddhism's FAOI is placed within the overall structure of the three other noble truths, its therapeutic thrust becomes clear. Having urged us to see suffering as permeating the very fabric of phenomenal existence, the Buddha goes on to identify the *cause* of suffering as craving (the second noble truth), specify that a *remedy* is available through the cessation of this craving in *nirvana* (the third noble truth), and lay down a *path* towards the restoration of health comprising the eightfold path (the fourth noble truth). In fact, the depiction of the Buddha as a physician is a vital aspect of both Theravada and Mahayana Buddhist self-understandings: while the Pali Canon speaks of the Buddha as the Great Physician and his *Dhamma* as the therapeutic training for his disciples, the Mahayana text *Saddharmapundarika Sutra* speaks of the Buddha as a benevolent doctor who seeks to dispense the proper medicine to his sons (Burton 2010, 187). More specifically, the Mahayana thinker Shantideva (*c*.800 CE) argues that the Buddha's teaching is 'the sole medicine for the ailments of the world, the mine of all success and happiness'; and points out that just as medicine tastes unpleasant to the ill, likewise Buddhist practice, which is in fact directed to the health of enlightenment, often turns out initially to be unpleasant or difficult (Crosby and Skilton 1995, 143, 69, 101).

The analytic equivalence indicated in FAOI between 'impermanence' and 'lack of true happiness', however, did not go unchallenged in classical India. The metaphysically naturalist tradition of the Charvaka which denied the existence of all trans-empirical entities and events – such as the spiritual self, the process of rebirth, and Brahman – also rejected FAOI. While Buddhism claims that absolutely every form of phenomenal existence is suffused by suffering, it is possible for a critic to retort that 'happiness' and 'sadness' both constitute the fabric of our fragile existence, and by being prudent we can learn to increase the former and decrease the latter. Such indeed would have been the response of the Charvakas who endorsed a hedonistic ethic of attaining the greatest amount of pleasure in this life. They held that it was

> wisdom to enjoy the pure pleasures as far as we can, and to avoid the pain which invariably accompanies it; ... just as the man who desires rice, takes the rice, straw and all, and having taken as much as he wants, desists.
>
> (Radhakrishnan and Moore 1957, 229)

The hard-nosed Charvaka therefore mocks the individual aspiring for liberation as a fool who would refuse to eat rice because it comes encased in husks or consume fish because they contain bones or grow crops because animals might destroy them. The Charvaka is claiming, in other words, that what FAOI refers to as 'true satisfaction' is an unreal fiction, and that human beings can, if they are careful enough, attain limited but genuine satisfactions. The Charvaka claim is based on the following presupposition:

> Second axiom of impermanence (SAOI): If *P* is impermanent, *P* can be the source of limited – and yet genuine – satisfaction.

Now we may be urged, in response to SAOI, to perceive the pervasiveness of suffering by counting the number of our happy hours free from anguish, and consider how they constitute a minuscule fraction of our misery-laden lives. Such a hedonistic calculus would not unambiguously yield the conclusion required by Buddhism, for different individuals would add up the pluses and the minuses in their own ways and place different weights on the entries in the two columns, depending on the specific circumstances of their lives. Therefore, the first noble truth of Buddhism, which asserts, via FAOI, the ubiquity of suffering, needs to be disentangled from its hedonist associations, so that 'pleasure' and 'pain' are regarded primarily not as hedonic terms but as objectively evaluative terms which are grounded in a metaphysics of impermanence. That is, one should read the therapeutic structure of Buddhism as based not on quasi-utilitarian considerations of the predominance of pains over pleasures (or vice versa), but in a metaphysical claim about the very nature of *all* phenomenal existence – namely, that it is characterised by impermanence (*anitya*), suffering (*duhkha*), and not-self (*anatman*). According to Buddhism, people who claim to have found some limited amount of happiness (though not entirely unmixed with pain) and, via SAOI, view the whole as positively good are in a state of spiritual ignorance. The metaphysical assumption that lies at the basis of this evaluative thesis is, of course, FAOI: that which is impermanent or subject to transmutation is (ultimately) utterly deficient in worth.

While Advaita Vedanta, Mahayana Buddhism, theistic Vedanta, and Samkhya-Yoga all accept FAOI, only the first two on this list accept the somewhat more philosophically provocative linkage of 'impermanence' and 'metaphysical unreality'.

Axiom of reality (AOR): If Q is impermanent, Q is metaphysically unreal.

Before we proceed, a few comments on this axiom. An entity is empirically or phenomenally real to the extent that it is accessible to one or more of the five sensory modes. Thus, the book that I am reading at the moment is (at least) empirically real in the sense that it is not the content of a hallucination. An entity is (also) metaphysically real if it turns up in the final inventory list of things that constitute the universe. Thus, unicorns, dragons, and phlogiston are – undisputedly – metaphysically unreal; the interesting philosophical question is whether the book too is metaphysically unreal. Advaita Vedanta employs AOR as part of its demonstration that the book, and indeed the whole empirical world, *because* they are subject to transformations, have only a dreamlike phenomenal reality (*maya*) which rests on the sole metaphysical reality of the immutable Brahman (Mahadevan 1985). That is, while the empirical world within which pilgrim selves seek to attain Brahman – the world structured by a *karmic* order that operates across lifetimes – is not a mere hallucination, it is not substantially real. As Keith Yandell (2001, 173) has pointed out: 'There is a tendency in Indian metaphysics (as well as elsewhere) to think in terms of what exists permanently or everlastingly as really existing and of what exists only for a time as existing defectively or not at all'. While this axiomatic presupposition also operates in Nagarjuna's understanding of the world structured by *karmic* processes, he would reject, as we have noted, Advaita's postulation of a timeless Ground underlying worldly appearances. Notwithstanding this foundational divergence, both Shankara and Nagarjuna agree that the psychophysical organism is metaphysically unreal, *because* it is subject to change.

We will illustrate the significance of AOR for the question of what makes life meaningful by discussing the Buddhist attempt to critique our everyday sense of an enduring self. The belief in some kind of a substantial self (the 'I') that glues together one's cognitions and volitions is a deep-seated error, and the Buddhist scholastic centuries were devoted partly to the task of dismantling the belief in all enduring entities. The 'I-conceit' that unifies the discrete impermanent aggregates into a self is the source of attachment to 'my-self' and also desires for impermanent physical objects which are regarded – and aggrandised – as 'mine'. However, these desires of the 'I' directed at the world are not brute forces but are responsive to our beliefs. The reason that desires produce suffering is because they are rooted in false views about the nature of reality, such as the belief in a permanent self. Therefore, Buddhist philosophical therapy has a strong cognitive dimension: we need to overcome our ignorant ways of viewing the world as a domain of substantial things. The world is correctly viewed not as composed of permanent substrata with their contingent qualities, but as a collection of interdependent processes, none of which bears the mark of substance, but which are related to one another through dependent origination (*pratitya-samutpada*). Just as the 'continuity' that we observe on the cinema screen is an emergent product, due to an optical illusion, of discrete slides rapidly succeeding one another, likewise the sense of a durable 'I' emerges from a rapid flux of cognitions, emotions, and volitions. Therefore, in place of a substantial self that is ontologically distinct from its properties such as thoughts and feelings, there are simply interrelated processes of cognitions and feelings, and no 'I' that possesses or comprehends these events as 'mine'. An individual who is trained to 'mindfully' see one-self as an aggregate of transient events is on the way to Buddhist enlightenment (Gowans 2014).

c

Let us summarise our argument in the preceding section. A predominant note that Samkhya-Yoga, Buddhism, and the multiple configurations of Vedanta strike is that human beings have to be trained to perceive everything around them as incapable of providing them with genuine contentment (FAOI), and this training involves careful reflection and discriminative understanding of the nature of reality, the structure of human personhood, and the shape of meditative praxis. These traditions agree on these points: the phenomenal world is not a locus of lasting value but neither is it a purely hallucinatory domain (even for systems which accept AOR), and through ethical-meditative praxis, underpinned by the *karmic* moral order, human beings can be gradually extricated from the mesh of rebirth and sorrow.

With this survey of some classical Indic systems, let us turn to one aspect of the religion-versus-atheism divide in the contemporary West: namely, the question of what constitutes the meaning of life (Eagleton 2008). The literature on this question, often highly polemical, presents a sharp contrast between two viewpoints which we will label 'strong objectivist' and 'strong subjectivist'. According to the former, there is the grand Meaning of Life out there, etched on to the fabric of reality, and human beings must bow servilely to this eternal template if their lives are to be meaningful. The latter states that there are as many meanings of life as there are humans who may care to raise this question, so that human beings generate meanings entirely from within the dense textures of their distinctive forms of life. If we express the difference with some metaphors, the strong subjectivists argue that meaning is not an ingredient that we extract from the world in the manner in which we excavate (pre-existing) gold from mines; rather it is an artefact with which we ornament our worlds in the way in which we insert chocolate into cakes, while keeping in mind that chocolate does not suit everyone's subjective tastes. However, as several writers have pointed out, this polarisation only caricatures both viewpoints. On the one hand, strong objectivists need not deny that individuals have to subjectively appropriate what is claimed to be the objective goal that suffuses human existence with being, goodness, and value. Thus, on most understandings of the Christian doctrine of grace, God's offer of salvation operates not on human automata but on active recipients who must appropriate this gift with inner commitment, and from within the distinctive contexts of their lives. On the other hand, strong subjectivists do not (usually) conclude that a life spent counting the number of blades of grass on Midsummer Common is as meaningful as one that involves caring for the sick and the dying in a hospice. Therefore, even they operate with some weakly objective – in the sense of trans-subjective – standards as to which lifeworlds are relatively more meaningful than the others.

Consequently, the central debate between the two groups is not primarily an epistemological one about how we acquire, order, and regulate our beliefs, but a metaphysical one about what constitutes the fabric of reality. The debate between the two groups over 'what there is' can therefore be phrased in the following manner:

Metaphysical naturalism: if by utilising the five empirical senses you cannot perceive any meaning in the world (in the manner in which you can 'directly' perceive the cat on the mat and can 'indirectly' perceive subatomic phenomena through electron microscopes), then this absence of perception demonstrates that life is objectively meaningless.

Christian theism: if by utilising the five empirical senses you cannot perceive any meaning in the world, then this failure of perception demonstrates *not* that life is objectively meaningless but that you have not yet developed, under divine grace, the 'trans-empirical' senses.

We may emphasise this point about the primacy of metaphysics in these disputes in the following way: according to (most) Christian theologians, God's existence is not dependent on how many humans affirm the divine existence, just as according to atheists, metaphysical naturalism is not falsified merely by the fact that many humans believe in God.

d

Let us return to our classical Indic dialogical partners after this detour through contemporary debates over the meaning(s) of life. The Charvakas are the nearest equivalent to the tough-minded empiricist type of our times: they rejected all beliefs not only in the substantial self and the eternal Brahman (the Buddhists did too) but also in the *karmic* ordering of reality across lifetimes (the Buddhists did not). According to the metaphysical naturalism of the Charvakas, the explanation for the orderly patterns of cosmological phenomena is not that there is a transcendental governor who supervises them, but simply that physical entities are structured with intrinsic natures (*svabhava*). Thus, to explain why fire can burn wood we do not need to postulate any spiritual essences or divine governors: it is the very nature of fire to burn things, and that brute fact is the end of the matter. However, Advaita Vedanta, theistic Vedanta, Samkhya-Yoga, and Buddhism, in their somewhat divergent ways, argue that an inventory of the universe includes trans-empirical entities, states, or processes which remain inaccessible to worldly pilgrims until they undergo an education of the senses and develop a fine-tuned 'trans-empirical' insight into the essence – or non-essence – of reality.

The observer of the religion-versus-atheism debates in the West might be struck by the fact that the classical Indian dialectical debates were often not so much about the question whether 'God exists' but about what should be included in a list of the fundamental constituents of reality. Many of the foundational texts (*sutras* or *karikas*) of these systems begin with the statement that human beings seek to overcome the suffering they are currently subject to, and thereupon embark on their meticulous analysis or deconstruction, sometimes guided by scriptural horizons, of the structures of the universe. Thus, while the contemporary Western debates often portray religion and atheism as two hostile camps, with the forces of scientific reason liberating the bastions of recalcitrant unreason, the Indian systems help us to see how debates relating to FAOI, SAOI, and AOR can bring together disputants from a wide range of metaphysical perspectives. These systems agree that seeking to grasp Z generates suffering if Z is metaphysically unreal, though, as we have seen, they sharply disagree over precisely what this Z is: all trans-empirical entities (the Charvakas), the personal divine as an ultimate reality (all forms of Buddhism and Advaita Vedanta, but not theistic Vedanta), the substantial 'I' (all forms of Buddhism and Advaita Vedanta, but not theistic Vedanta), the eternal Brahman (all forms of Buddhism but not Advaita Vedanta or theistic Vedanta), and so on.

Therefore, the association in some Western circles of 'spirituality beyond religion' with 'Oriental mysticism' needs to be carefully examined. The nebulous phrase 'Oriental mysticism' is a portmanteau term for a hybrid product of numerous strands of Western esotericism, Indic yoga, naturopathy, critiques of the military–industrial complex, transpersonal psychology, vegetarianism, green movements, New Age spirituality, and so on (King 1999). However, as our discussion has indicated, Indic systems are, in fact, structured by a highly dense system of metaphysical doctrines such as FAOI and (sometimes) AOR, which do not always shape the ongoing appropriations of 'Oriental mysticism' in the West.[2] Further, Vedantic theisms (which accept FAOI but reject AOR) continue to flourish not only on the Indian subcontinent but also in the West through movements such as the Hare Krishna (ISKCON, International Society for Krishna Consciousness), so that the somewhat popular equivalence between 'anti-theism/anti-religion' and 'Indian spirituality' should not be accepted.

With these caveats in mind, however, we may note a historical point about why the label 'spirituality without religion' has become widely associated with the 'turn to the East'. The rise of secularism in the West has been shaped by the European enlightenment's rejection of religion as the source of superstition, dogma, and persecution of dissent. Many French, English, and Scottish freethinkers viewed religious belief as a relic from the superstitious and barbaric infancy of the human race. A survey of influential strands of philosophical thought from Descartes to Spinoza to Hegel to Russell (and beyond) demonstrates at first a gradual waning, and subsequently a vehement denunciation, of belief in a transcendent God as conceptualised in Christian theism. A defining moment in this narrative of unbelief was Nietzsche's apocalyptic claim that 'God is dead', and that with the demise of the divine, all the transcendental securities that had underpinned human existence have been washed away. Human beings have finally 'come of age', and having thrown away the yoke of divine providence they should be bold enough to forge their own destinies. Around this time, a particularly devastating critique was launched first by Marxists and then by feminists to the effect that Christian establishments are guilty of colluding with ideologies of domination, oppression, and subjugation, whether these are capitalist or patriarchal.

In the light of this historical background, we can see that the appeal of the Eastern turn lies in the promise of 'Oriental mysticism' to package 'religion' without the virulent appendices of dogmatism, irrationalism, persecution, intolerance, authoritarianism, and so on. Whether 'Oriental mysticism' indeed delivers on this promise is, of course, a topic for future historians. On this occasion, however, we will conclude with three remarks. First, we should avoid romanticising classical and contemporary India as a domain of idyllic harmony, for 'religious' structures in India, as elsewhere, have alternately legitimised, supported, interrogated, opposed, and (partially) subverted deeply entrenched structures of caste, gender, class, ethnicity, and so on. Second, we should resist the 'imagination' of India as permeated by an essentially mystical ethos that appears in many introductory texts to Indian civilisations, for they ignore or marginalise the presence of a multiplicity of not specifically spiritual strands in the Indian traditions. Not only the vigorous arguments between Hindu and Buddhist philosophers over the issues of scepticism, idealism, and realism, but also the contributions of the classical Indians to mathematics, grammar, medicine, and political analysis, the presence of practical concerns in various streams of epic poetry such as the Mahabharata, the Buddha's agnostic stance towards metaphysical speculation, and so on should be highlighted to counter the popular perception of India as a land of undiluted spirituality. As Amartya Sen (1999, 24; emphasis added) notes:

> Indian traditions are often taken to be intimately associated with religion, and indeed *in many ways* they are, and yet Sanskrit and Pali have larger literatures on systematic atheism and agnosticism than perhaps in any other classical language – Greek, Roman, Hebrew, or Arabic.[3]

Third, however, Indic 'religious' spaces are indeed relatively free from the organised, institutionalised, and systematic persecution of dissent of the kind associated, for instance, with the Albigensian crusade or the Spanish Inquisition. To explain this absence with the motto 'Indic spirituality is intrinsically peaceful' would be another version of the romanticisation of an 'essential India' indicated in the previous comments. A specifically philosophical/theological reason why the (medieval Catholic) 'crusading mentality' does not have any direct Indic analogues is, in fact, another metaphysical presupposition.

> Axiom of liberation (AOL): Not all who wander in this lifetime are lost. Some of these wayward individuals may, over a number of successive lifetimes, ultimately arrive at the true Goal of all humanity.

Thus, while Abrahamic theisms, which reject AOL – though the medieval Catholic doctrine of purgatory could be seen as a specifically Christian version of AOL – have sometimes been characterised by an apocalyptic fervour directed at the unbelievers, the multiple configurations of Indic spirituality, all of which accept AOL, display a more relaxed attitude to the 'salvation of the neighbour'. Consequently, the binary 'in Christianity you are compelled to believe certain dogmas, while in Indic spirituality you are free to believe whatever you wish' turns out to be a caricature of both sides. Since Indic spirituality is structured by FAOI, (sometimes) AOR, and AOL, the real debate between religion and atheism – in India as in other locations – is one over what are the ultimate threads that constitute the fabric of the universe.

Notes

1 The term 'Vedanta' refers to various scholastic attempts to systematise the diverse body of scriptures such as the Vedas (*c.*1200 BCE), the Upanishads (*c.*800 BCE), and the Bhagavad Gita (*c.*400 CE). Vedantic thought in classical India often developed through dense dialectical debates with Buddhist opponents who rejected some of its foundational presuppositions.
2 This is a sociological comment about the transnational circuits of Indian spirituality. Whether these appropriations are 'authentic' to the classical Indian materials is a topic for another day. We must, however, keep in mind in discussions of 'authenticity' that many Indians themselves are now active members of these circuits.
3 Sen is using the term 'atheism' in the sense of the rejection of a personal God.

Bibliography

Bartley, C. (2011) *An Introduction to Indian Philosophy*. London: Continuum.
Burton, D. (2010) 'Curing Diseases of Belief and Desire: Buddhist Philosophical Therapy', in C. Carlisle and J. Ganeri (eds), *Philosophy as Therapeia*. Cambridge: Cambridge University Press, 187–217.
Crosby, K. and A. Skilton (trans.) (1995) *The Bodhicāryāvatara*. Oxford: Oxford University Press.
Eagleton, T. (2008) *The Meaning of Life: A Very Short Introduction*. Oxford: Oxford University Press.
Feuerstein, G. (1979) *The Yoga-sūtra of Patañjali: A New Translation and Commentary*. Folkestone, UK: Dawson.
Gowans, C. (2014) *Buddhist Moral Philosophy*. London: Routledge.
Harvey, P. (2012) *An Introduction to Buddhism*. Cambridge: Cambridge University Press.
King, R. (1999) *Orientalism and Religion*. London: Routledge.
Lipner, J. (1986) *The Face of Truth: A Study of Meaning and Metaphysics in the Vedāntic Theology of Rāmānuja*. Basingtoke: Macmillan.
Mahadevan, T. M. P. (1985) *Superimposition in Advaita Vedānta*. New Delhi: Sterling Publishers.
Radhakrishnan, S. and C. A. Moore (eds) (1957) *A Sourcebook in Indian Philosophy*. Princeton, NJ: Princeton University Press.
Rambachan, A. (2006) *The Advaita Worldview: God, World, and Humanity*. Abany, NY: SUNY Press.
Sen, A. (1999) *Reason before Identity: The Romanes Lecture for 1998*. Oxford: Oxford University Press.
Warrier, A. G. K. (1981) *The Concept of Mukti in Advaita Vedānta*. Madras: University of Madras.
Yandell, K. (2001) 'Some Reflections on Indian Metaphysics', *International Journal for Philosophy of Religion* 50: 171–90.

17 Religiosity and secularity in Europe

Simon Glendinning

The secularisation thesis

In post-war Britain, academic philosophers did not talk about the meaning of life. Analytic philosophy dominated British philosophy, and this kind of philosophy was, at the time, dominated by investigations of logic, language, mind and knowledge. Moral philosophy, along with aesthetics, mostly hid in a corner. But creeping out of that corner, discussion of meaning in a richer sense than occupied most philosophy of language began to make its way. In 1976 a distinguished analytic philosopher, David Wiggins, delivered a paper called 'Truth, Invention and the Meaning of Life'. He began in these words:

> Even now, in an age not given much to mysticism, there are people who ask 'What is the meaning of life?' Not a few of them make the simple 'un-philosophical' assumption that there is something to be known here. (One might say they are 'cognitivists' with regard to this sort of question.) And most of these same people make the equally unguarded assumption that the whole issue of life's meaning presupposes some positive answer to the question whether it can be plainly and straightforwardly *true* that this or that thing or activity or pursuit is good, or has value, or is worth something. Finally, something even harder, they suppose that questions like that of life's meaning must be among the central questions of moral philosophy.
>
> The question of life's having a meaning and the question of truth are not at the centre of moral philosophy as we now have it.[1]

Not at the centre of moral philosophy – and nowhere near the centre of philosophy in general. Not in 1976. Not in Britain. And while it is true that in Continental Europe philosophy was being done in ways that were at least more congenial to raising the question, still, there too, generally speaking, such ambitious efforts were rare.

They are still rare but not so rare today, neither in Continental Europe nor in Britain. And I know of a number of professional philosophers who are grateful that they can now write about the deepest questions of human life without embarrassment. It is an interesting question why this has happened at this time, why it has become possible to discuss this kind of theme again.

If we set this situation in moral philosophy in the context of wider questions of the culture of Europe's modernity we might become aware of a new shift in recent years, a shift that is really quite profound, and which sheds light on the question of what is or has been 'at the centre of moral philosophy as we now have it'.

Why might it be that discussion about the meaning of life went off the radar in philosophy during the twentieth century – and also off the radar beyond academia too, off the radar in Europe during the last hundred years or so?

At the risk of both gross simplification and a certain academic dullness, I want to suggest that the background to that state of affairs can be framed in terms of the acceptance by European intellectuals of what has been called 'the secularisation thesis'. This thesis was developed by different thinkers in different ways, but social theorists like Weber, Durkheim and, in his own fashion, Marx, led the way in thinking we could describe the historical movement of modernity in Europe in terms of a transition from a society dominated by magic, myth, superstition and religion, into one with a cognitively superior outlook in which these things are disclosed as illusions and delusions which we shed in the name of reason, criticism and science.

This story belonged within an even more long-run historical narrative: one which conceived the movement of the whole history of the world in terms of a transition from an origin that was primitive, barbarian, savage – and basically animal – moving slowly and in stages through developments in human society towards a modern, rational and scientific end. There is here the idea of History as Progress towards an ideal End of Man and towards an ideally civilised form of social and individual life. The secularisation thesis dovetails with that wider discourse of world history: it is the idea that the movement into a rational and scientific age is one which is likely to see primitive and traditional conceptions not only of the world but also of the significance of our lives increasingly give way to rational and scientific ones. The old illusions will in all likelihood wither away, and in the future, soon, we will have *finally* emancipated ourselves from myth, superstition and religion. We will have finally learned how to live.

The secularisation thesis became increasingly matter of course for European intellectuals in the late nineteenth and twentieth centuries. So when people were writing at that time – in philosophy, in history, in politics and in sociology – there was this unquestioned background that, while there were still some foolish believers around, the proper methods were finally making their way; and the methods with a future were rational and scientific. In principle, they would leave nothing unexplained, and such explanations would have nothing to do with religion (or 'God and Fate') *at all*.

Before I explore this thesis – a thesis which concerns nothing less than the becoming-secular of the world – we should pause to acknowledge that for many people the claimed changeover in our thinking and believing that the secularisation thesis presents was a cause for considerable anxiety. For many, though they may have kept quiet about it, the sense of loss of a religiously articulated understanding of the significance of our lives was not the loss of an illusion or delusion at all, but rather the loss of a way, perhaps finally the only intelligible way, through which we could make sense of the idea that, with respect to the question of the meaning of life, there really is *something to be known*. What seemed to be disappearing was the most profound, rich and satisfying discourse through which we might hope to come to know what is to be known about the meaning of life. And when religion falls away or is eclipsed then all you are left with is an utterly mundane life in which it is totally unclear why, ultimately, we should think that there is anything more to life than shopping. And this really is the bottom line. As some people might want to put it: today we worship only the Molten Calf of the Standard of Living. In a world that is becoming-secular we are all becoming-shoppers.

Of course, many of the proponents of the secularisation thesis thought there was a promised land ahead too: an end of history to come which would be some kind of ultimate realisation of human flourishing without illusion. So they wouldn't have thought at all that the disappearance of religion was leading towards a life without the means to grasp the meaning of life. But for many people the apparent eclipse of religion was a profoundly worrying event for European humanity. They felt that secularisation would leave us with a life deprived and devoid of meaning: a nihilistic postmodern condition, where anything goes.

Today, however, something else is swimming into view. Today, the question is not whether there is anything left to value in an increasingly secular world, but whether we should regard the secularisation thesis, independently of an optimistic conception of an end to come it may harbour for some, as in any sense worth giving credence to any more.

I mean: religion, religiosity, a sense of spirituality, has simply *not* gone away.

Nietzsche, looking at his fellow Europeans in the late nineteenth century, found in the self-professed atheism he increasingly saw around him nothing but a retreat from the authoritarian idea of God as the 'father' or the 'judge'.[2] That apart, the religious instinct seemed to him still 'in vigorous growth'. And this was in Europe, not in parts of the world where religion in various forms was more obviously still thriving and not withering.

I do not think that there have been any fundamental changes since Nietzsche was observing Europeans. It is becoming evident that in reality there has been little or no weakening in religiosity, even if there is a weakening of a certain difficult idea of God. The weakening of that difficult idea is leading, no doubt, to some weakening of ties to those ecclesiastical authorities which carry it. And as a result we see a decline in religious practices of certain kinds (regular churchgoing, for example). But this is a decline in certain forms of religious authority, without a parallel decline in religiosity.

Europe, the supposed vanguard of world secularisation, is, we should now accept, simply not the exception in the world, not the vanguard of secular reason surrounded by great swathes of humanity still going on in its infantile ways as if nothing has happened. No, Europe, like everywhere else, has remained solidly religiously committed. Indeed, even in traditional terms the picture is not the one we might have been led to believe: self-identifying as a believer of some kind is still incredibly high among Europeans. In Britain in 2002, for example, over 70 per cent of those responding to the census declared they were Christians – with about 45 per cent or so still saying they believe in God too. (That's a great comparative statistic.)

Instead of increasing atheism, we should perhaps talk more neutrally of a decline in traditional religious theism. Rather than being part of a congregation or seeing oneself as being bound to a given ecclesiastical authority, we have new forms of *the pilgrim*, the one who is on a personal spiritual path. What one 'finds' along the way may or may not be construed as a matter of finding God. Nevertheless, for most Europeans or those whose life is saturated with the European heritage, it is most likely that one finds that one is a Christian of sorts.

For me, then, the secularisation thesis has simply been blown away – and blown away both by the facts about continuing religiosity and by its own utterly dismal understanding of what religiosity actually amounts to (namely, as akin to a belief in the existence of fairies). People today have turned around to see that this religion thing which was meant to be going away has not gone away at all, and it is not in any case what we thought it was.

The end of the end of man

On the other hand, there has been a change. It is a change that the secularisation thesis was an attempt to come to terms with and to which it itself belonged: a movement or mutation within the default construal of the world and the significance of our lives.

What we need now is a new way of thinking about the change that has taken place in Europe during the last two or three hundred years. Three hundred years ago God and God's plan for Man was at the centre of the self-understanding usual among Europeans. We now live in a time when that is no longer true. The secularisation thesis was one way of trying to grasp that change. But it was inadequate. I think David Wiggins began a helpful kind of rewriting of that inadequate idea in his essay on the meaning of life when in the heat of the Cold War, and writing now of our time as a time after Darwin, he said this:

> Unless we are Marxists, we are more resistant [today] than the eighteenth- or nineteenth-centuries knew how to be [to] attempts to locate the meaning of human life or human history in mystical or metaphysical

conceptions – in the emancipation of mankind, or progress, or the onward advance of Absolute Spirit. It is not that we have lost interest in emancipation or progress themselves. But whether temporarily or permanently, we have more or less abandoned the idea that the importance of emancipation or progress (or a correct conception of spiritual advance) is that these are marks by which our minute speck in the universe can distinguish itself as the spiritual focus of the cosmos.[3]

That's a big 'shift' as he says: a seismic decentring of our self-understanding.[4] But the crucial point, it seems to me, is Wiggins' insistence that we should not interpret this shift as a loss of interest in emancipation or progress – or indeed of spiritual advance. In short, whatever changes we are looking at in Europe in the last 300 years, the mistake is to interpret these changes either along the lines of postmodern nihilism or along the lines of the classic secularisation thesis. For my own part, what I would propose is that we conceive the becoming-secular of Europe not as a movement of the becoming-atheist of humanity (a movement towards our becoming, one and all, rational humanists) but as a moment *within* the long-run event of the becoming-Christian of the world: it is a mutation within that movement, an alteration within an event that we can call the Christianisation of the world.

Reflecting on the fact that Gustave Flaubert was writing in the second half of the nineteenth century, Jean-Paul Sartre, who was writing in the second half of the twentieth century, sketches the outline of this kind of conception:

> Flaubert writes for a Western world which is Christian. And we are all Christians, even today; the most radical disbelief is still Christian atheism. In other words it retains, in spite of its destructive power, schemata which are controlling—very slightly for our thinking, more for our imagination, above all for our sensibility. And the origins of these schemata are to be sought in the centuries of Christianity of which we are the heirs, whether we like it or not.[5]

And, indeed, one might add to this: not only whether we like it or not but also whether we know it or not. So this movement of becoming-secular of the world has to be seen as unfolding within the fabric of a world forged from the centuries of Christianity. It did not fall from the sky as some kind of ready-made alternative to a Christian worldview – nor did it arrive from outside Europe, as an import of sorts. It grew from a European cultural tree, 'which is Christian' – or, since Sartre leaves a place open for other controlling schemata, especially 'for our thinking', we might better say which is Graeco-Christian or Pagano-Christian.

The missionary culture and messianic vision of an 'end of History' held within the outlook of the secularisation thesis inherits the Christian eschatological heritage. The picture of the long run of history that I introduced at the beginning – the discourse of Europe's modernity that tells of a transition from a primitive distant past, through ages which were given to magic, myths, superstition and religion, breaking finally, and first in Europe, into an age which is not – that story runs profoundly parallel to the idea of providential history that belongs squarely within the Christian tradition. All the terrible things that we see going on in the world today and everyday – for the Christian we are to understand that there is compensation for all this, compensation for past and present suffering, in the idea that there is a redemptive end to come, that this is all part of God's plan for Man, and that there will be some final end of things in which believers find their just reward. If we can only spread this good news we can *all* learn, finally, how to live. That Christian religious idea of providence can be translated very rapidly into the sort of conception of history implied by the secularisation thesis: a history in which 'modern' Europeans belong to an advance guard in the emancipation of the rational subject or the emancipation of the working (universal) subject, a revolutionary movement that will lead towards some triumphantly final end of history where all the terrible things that have happened will have worked themselves out. These are secularisations of distinctively Christian conceptions of providence. It is not that secular concepts have come to *replace* theological ones. On the contrary: they *are* secularised theological concepts.

So I think one of the most important points we need to learn today is quite how fundamentally Christian is this secular world in general, and its secularisation thesis in particular.

Indeed, Christianity carries within itself the decisive conceptual resources for advancing the idea of a distribution between the secular and the sacred that we find everywhere in Europe today. In the Bible we read, for example, Jesus saying 'Render to Caesar the things that are Caesar's, and to God the things that are God's' (Mark 12:17). That idea of the possibility of some form of 'separation of church and state' – what one might also call the death of God *in the world* – is already inside the Christian understanding of the world.

Developing this thought even more strongly, Jacques Derrida argues for seeing how the modern preference for political secularity is connected to a thesis in Kant on the essential connection between *morality* – what it means to make decisions and conduct oneself morally as a rational human being – and *religion*, a link that will make this European political space *both* secular *and* Christian. The Kantian thesis could not be more simple, but Derrida asks us to 'measure without flinching' the implications of it.[6] If we follow Kant we will have to accept that Christian revelation teaches us something essential about the very idea of morality: 'in order to conduct oneself in a moral manner, one must act as though God did not exist or no longer concerned himself with our salvation'.[7] The crucial point here is that decisions on right conduct should not be made on the basis of any assumption that, by acting in a certain way, we know we are doing God's will. The Christian is thus the one who 'no longer turns towards God at the moment of acting in good faith'.[8] In short, the good Christian, the Christian acting in good faith, is precisely the one who must decide in a fundamentally secular way. And so Derrida asks, regarding Kant's thesis, 'is it not also, at the core of its content, Nietzsche's thesis':[9] that, in the world, God is dead?

Derrida does not flinch: this thesis – the thesis that Christians are those who are called to endure the death of God in the world – tells us 'something about the history of the world – nothing less':

> Is this not another way of saying that Christianity can only answer to its moral calling and morality, to its Christian calling, if it endures in this world, in phenomenal history, the death of God, well beyond the figure of the Passion? ... Judaism and Islam would thus be perhaps the last two monotheisms to revolt against everything that, in the Christianising of our world, signifies the death of God, two non-pagan monotheisms that do not accept death any more than multiplicity in God (the Passion, the Trinity etc.), two monotheisms still alien enough at the heart of Greco-Christian, Pagano-Christian Europe that signifies the death of God, by recalling at all costs that 'monotheism' signifies no less faith in the One, and in the living One, than belief in a single God.[10]

We should not understand the secularity of European societies that we see today as a kind of external imposition onto a Christian conception which is basically alien to it. Again, the deep flaw in the secularisation thesis is to conceive the movement of recent history as a break from a religious and especially Christian epoch. On the contrary, it belongs to the movement of the Christian world in mutation ... in deconstruction.

How, then, might we begin to think about the question of the meaning of life if we forgo the traditional picture embodied in the secularisation thesis? First, we no longer need to regard the becoming-secular of the world as a radical loss of religious meaning, or as a movement into nihilism and shopping. On the other hand, in an age not given to mysticism or metaphysics, and in the light, I would add, of the horrors of Nazism and Stalinism, it is clearly no longer so credible to conceive our lives in terms of some other grand historical narrative either. The old ('cognitivist') idea that the World or History or Man has 'an intrinsic meaning' that is on the way to realisation is not, in my view, the lens through which the meaning of life should be assessed.

How might we think about this issue otherwise? I want to recommend that we make a change in the vocabulary of this debate, and propose rethinking questions concerning 'the meaning of life' in terms of the idea of *a life worth living* or *living a worthwhile life*. This, I want to say, is not something that can be assessed except from the inside, and from the inside not just anything will count as living such a life, though nor will only one kind of life be regarded as such either. It is not, I want to suggest, a matter of finally *knowing* how to live but of *creating* a life ('experiments in living') that can be experienced as worthwhile.

This may be regarded as yet another secularisation of a religiously significant construal. However, we do not have to think in terms of that (anyway problematic) contrast at all. One of the things I want to affirm is that a *non-believer* can accept that a *believer's* attempt to understand the significance of our lives does not need to be regarded as something that prevents us making a step forward in the ambition to create a worthwhile life. Someone who has no or little instinct for religiosity need no longer think, as the modern secularisation theorist still must, that he or she is, at bottom, an enemy of a life that cleaves faithfully to God.

On the other hand, I am suggesting that someone today who is still interested in forming, say, a correct conception of spiritual advance, is going to have to do so without the old idea that what makes a life worth living is its alignment with a Truth about the Good Life for Man to which our thinking about the worth of our lives is finally answerable. We have to accept that the kinds of things that people say give their life meaning are not 'discoveries about the moral universe' but belong to an effort to create a life worth living. I am, I hope, aware of the extent to which we have – as becoming-shoppers – *failed*, individually and collectively, to achieve that.

Unless we are Marxists

There is a serious objection to the position I am defending here. Given that we are no longer to be 'cognitivists' about the meaning of life, can we, today, give an account that would really allow us to make sense of the contemporary failure I have just asserted *as a failure*? To do so would seem to presuppose a standard against which to compare our life, a standard which could be regarded as capturing what is genuinely proper for human existence: an idea of the good life. Earlier in this discussion we saw that David Wiggins identifies as no longer available to us two conspicuously objective conceptions of what is proper to the good life: metaphysical and mystical conceptions of Man and History. We are more resistant today than people in the eighteenth or nineteenth centuries knew how to be to such conceptions, 'unless we are Marxists'. He means, of course, unless we think of ourselves as Marxists. But one might worry that unless we *are* Marxists – or, at the very least, unless we can frame an objective and not exclusively religious conception of what is proper to the good life for Man – we have no basis on which to assess whether we are moving towards or away from the attainment of any kind of life worth living whatsoever. Any continued interest in 'emancipation and progress' (which Wiggins affirms that we *are* still interested in) would be strictly nonsensical.

Wiggins claims that our increased resistance to teleo-messianic narratives does *not* imply that we have lost interest in 'emancipation or progress themselves'. But can we retain that interest – and not be Marxist in the sense I am giving that here? Perhaps *we*, in our time, are Marxist just to the extent to which we can retain that classic interest.

This is not to invite yet another Marxist revival. Rather it is to acknowledge that we belong to societies with a history whose self-understanding *today* cannot be radically dissociated from a Marxist heritage. As Derrida notes, echoing Sartre on our being Christians, 'whether they wish it or know it or not, all men and women, all over the earth, are today to a certain extent the heirs of Marx and Marxism'.[11] There is a complication to every discourse that would say that our continued interest in emancipation or progress could be radically non-Marxist or can simply do without Marx. Especially if we think we are not Marxist. Here is Derrida again:

> A messianic promise, even if it was not fulfilled, at least in the form in which it was uttered, even if it rushed headlong toward an ontological content, will have imprinted an inaugural and unique mark in history. And whether we like it or not, whatever consciousness we have of it, we cannot not be its heirs.[12]

Unless we are going to be naively unwitting Marxists we had better attend to this inheritance. We need to attend to the spectres of Marx and Marxism in our time. Especially today, when it is so often announced that Marxism is dead.

I will come back to this, but first we need to acknowledge that Wiggins' political naivety is coupled with a deep historical insight. It is, I think, plainly true that

> we are more resistant [today] than the eighteenth- or nineteenth-centuries knew how to be [to] attempts to locate the meaning of human life or human history in mystical or metaphysical conceptions – in the emancipation of mankind, or progress, or the onward advance of Absolute Spirit.

And it is as one of the last great attempts to elaborate a grand teleo-messianic narrative of emancipation and progress of this kind that Marxism has its place in Wiggin's account. If I was a Marxist, or a Marxist through and through, I would have an understanding of world history which showed our present condition as alienated, and which pointed towards the promise of a historical movement of de-alienation – a historical movement in which it would all come right in the end, if we can only get our collective act together and build that revolution.

Would I be taking unjustified advantage of the 'we' if I were to say ('unless we are Marxists') *we don't believe that*, we can't fall back on a philosophy of the teleo-messianic history of the alienation and de-alienation of Man like that? I don't think so. However, and with the greatest trepidation, I am inclined to think that what *we would* still really like to see, beyond minimal expectations for a life free of want, is effective in-the-world engagement in the creation of conditions for living a life worth living. I want this to be understood as an 'end' that is not conceived as a matter of achieving finality with regard to the question 'How to live?', but a way of living its inheritance that gives it a future *as always remaining to be thought*. ('The unexamined life is not worth living.')

If this ambition retains the classic interest in emancipation and progress in a non-theological, non-mystical form, then it seems to me undeniable that it belongs 'to a certain extent' to the inheritance of the first *great* discourse of this type: the interest in emancipation and progress elaborated in Marx. Here, for the first time in history, what has made its way is an undeniably world-affecting engagement (headlong to disaster, let's not forget) in the creation of conditions for living a life worth living *in a form that was in principle philosophical and scientific, not theological and mystical*.

But, and this is to restate the problem that I began this section with, can we, the inheritors 'to a certain extent' of this inaugural contribution, can we retain its 'messianic *promise*' without inheriting its disastrous teleo-messianic *programme* of an end? Let me put this another way: can there be a discourse of emancipation and progress that is, precisely, emancipated not only from the old providential conception but also from the whole modern conception of the *telos* of Man? The objection to that (let's say still-Marxist) ambition is that without *some* conception of the Truth of Man and History, and hence of the proper heading of Man, we cannot make *any* sense of the idea that not every way of living a life will *be* a life worth living. Have we resources for that kind of discrimination? We have (inherited) *plenty*.

To illustrate this, I want to return once more to Wiggins' discussion of the meaning of life, and to an example he gives of a contrast between two lives – a discussion in which he invites his reader to accept that, yes, only one of these people is actually living a worthwhile life, and of *you* dear reader (that is to say, you as someone who belongs to and is a participant in a particular society with a continuing history) judging this *without more ado*. His example is this:

> There is a difference, which we as participants insist upon, between the life of a man who contributes something to society with a continuing history and a life lived on a plan of a southern pig-breeder who (in the economics textbooks, if not in real life) buys more land to grow more corn to feed more hogs, to buy more land to grow more corn to feed more hogs ... The practical concerns of this man are regressive and circular. And we are keenly interested, on the inner view, in the *difference* between these concerns and non-circular practical reasoning or life plans.[13]

The latter (a life lived on the basis of non-circular life plans), Wiggins suggests, 'fans out into a whole arborescence of concerns'.[14] This kind of image is important to us in considering our own lives and the lives of those with whom we live. If we live in a society in which, by our lights, such a life is increasingly unavailable to most of us, then we will have failed to create conditions in which we can *think* we are living a life that *keenly sustains* the question of the worthwhile life – *and hence singularly failed to create the conditions of actually living such a life*. Equally, however, to suppose we know what the proper (ideal) form of that arborescence must take for a life to be 'genuinely worthwhile' is to reduce the 'messianic promise' internal to the experience of present inadequacy and failure to the heading of a 'teleo-messianic programme', reducing the always non-ideal ideal of the worthwhile life (construed, remember, as something *always* remaining to be thought) to the dogmatic faith in the 'purity of a path' towards a definite end.

Within the limits in which any such judgement is possible, the lives that are most worth living today will belong to those who are *keenest* to 'insist upon [the difference]' that Wiggins sees as available without more ado to 'we as participants' in a community with a history, *those who keep it alive*. That is to say, the lives that are most worth living today will belong to those participants for whom *the idea of finally having done with the question* is experienced most intensely or most keenly as something *to resist*.

Notes

1 David Wiggins, 'Truth, Invention and the Meaning of Life', in *Needs, Values, Truth: Essays in the Philosophy of Value* (Oxford: Oxford University Press, 1987), 87.
2 Friedrich Nietzsche, *Beyond Good and Evil* (Harmondsworth: Penguin, 1973), 62.
3 Wiggins, 'Truth, Invention and the Meaning of Life', 91.
4 Ibid., 88.
5 Jean-Paul Sartre, *L'Idiot de la famille*, vol. 2 (Paris: Gallimard, 1972), 2124, cited and translated in Robert Cumming, *Starting Point* (Chicago: Chicago University Press, 1979), 225.
6 Jacques Derrida, 'Faith and Knowledge', in J. Derrida and G. Vattimo (eds), *Religion* (Stanford, CA: Stanford University Press, 1998), 10.
7 Derrida, 'Faith and Knowledge', 11.
8 Ibid.
9 Ibid.
10 Ibid., 12.
11 Jacques Derrida, *Specters of Marx* (London: Routledge, 1994), 113.
12 Ibid., 114.
13 Wiggins, 'Truth, Invention and the Meaning of Life', 100.
14 Ibid., 101.

18 Engagement between religious and non-religious in a plural society

Andrew Copson

After ten years of debating, opposing, and criticising, but also of discussing, agreeing, and cooperating with religious people and religious organisations in a professional capacity, it's interesting to take time to reflect on these experiences in the round and be asked to contribute to this volume. The recent history of structured and institutionalised engagement and dialogue between those with different worldviews has largely focused on the religious. Why is it important that the non-religious should be involved? Universal answers could be given, but there is one answer that is very specific to Britain. Unusually in a global context, the non-religious in Britain are on course to being a majority, if they are not already.

One of the most robust and long-standing trends in recent decades in the religious demography of Britain is the growth in the number of those who self-identify as having no religion. Between 1983 and today, in response to the question, 'Do you regard yourself as belonging to any particular religion?' this proportion has increased from being 30 per cent of the population to being 50 per cent. With the exception of the equally striking decline in Anglican self-identification (down from 40 per cent to 16 per cent), no trends are as significant: the rise in non-denominational Christianity from 5 per cent to 11 per cent and of non-Christian religions from 3 per cent to 8 per cent pale in comparison. These figures are from the British Social Attitudes survey and refer to religious identity, but other measures – of belief and of practice, for example – indicate the same social reality. As just one example of each: the increase of firm non-belief in any gods is a clear generational trend, growing from 27 per cent amongst over-60s to 47 per cent in18–24-year-olds, according to YouGov in 2015; weekly attendance at a place of worship is at all-time low levels, with just over 90 per cent of the population not attending in 2015. Nor is it the case that those abandoning religious beliefs, identities, and practices are mostly adopting 'spiritual' ones. YouGov in 2013 found that most people (51 per cent) said 'I would not describe myself, or my values and beliefs, as spiritual or religious', with 'spiritual' at 11 per cent and 'religious' at 10 per cent. No one has the gift of truthful prophecy, but all these trends seem set to characterise the social landscape of Britain for at least the near future.

Any social movement that genuinely has mutual understanding between people of different worldviews as its aim cannot afford to ignore the non-religious in light of this demographic reality. Thankfully, the foundational principles of the 'interfaith' movement within the UK prima facie do so in only one respect – the specific use of the word 'faith'. There is nothing elsewhere in its principles that could not in theory be extended to include the non-religious. The stated 'vision' of the Inter Faith Network for the UK, for example, is to achieve a society 'where we live and work together with mutual respect and shared commitment to the common good' and it sees its 'mission' as being to 'increase understanding and cooperation between people of different faiths' and 'helping create opportunities for mutual learning and tackling prejudice'. Although its own work is purely with those who regard themselves as religious, plainly this vision and these aims can apply equally to encounters and cooperation between non-religious and religious people as well. In light of the large and growing presence of the non-religious in the UK, and the impact that has and will have on the types of 'prejudice' and barriers to 'mutual respect and shared commitment' that might exist, we might say not only that these aims can apply, but that they urgently ought to.

Nonetheless, there are of course challenges facing the involvement of the non-religious in work of this sort, and some re-examination of principles to accommodate this within existing modes of engagement is certainly essential. To try and get a sense of the non-religious experience on the ground, I questioned thirty humanist participants in local dialogue and engagement on their experiences of this. I asked them about their motivations for becoming involved, what they thought had been successful about their work, and what barriers they had experienced to that success. I asked them my questions in 2015 on experiences that they had in recent years and uncovered a wide range of activity. Many had participated in interfaith groups and committees convened explicitly for the purpose of dialogue, either by local public authorities in the interest of cohesion or by local media for broadcast, or in structured social activities within the private sphere, such as in a 'multi-faith' book club. Others had experience of dialogue and encounter as part of a team of individuals of different religions and worldviews assembled to deliver a particular project or programme. Again, this could be either public (the provision of pastoral support to patients in hospitals or hospices, in prisons, or in the police force; the organising of educational days for school pupils; the provision of an inclusive civic event in a time of crisis) or private (a fund-raising committee for a local church hall that functioned as a general community asset; the setting up of a 'peace camp'). A few were pioneering 'bilateral' forms of engagement in privately organised events open to the public which paired humanists with Muslims, Buddhists, or Catholics for discussions and debates.

Motivations

There were clear similarities between the motivations reported by the humanists involved and those that are often reported by religious people who get involved in dialogue and engagement.

Participants wanted:

- To dispel what they felt were unfair prejudices and misconceptions about their own beliefs and values. 'I hoped to show that non-religious people were not all "evil"', reported one participant. 'I had attended a public event at which terrible things were said about the morality of non-religious people', reported another, adding that it prompted her to get involved and that she has now been so for many years. 'I hoped to show that not all non-religious people are "militant atheists"', which was certainly the prejudice', said another.
- To advance social cohesion and mutual understanding. 'I live in a diverse community where there is much lack of understanding between the various groups', said one, typical of many responses. This concern for mutual understanding was both a concern for non-religious people to be understood ('well over 50 per cent of young people in my area are from a deeply religious ethnic background and have had little if any exposure to non-religious belief systems') and a concern to understand others ('I wanted to learn more about my neighbours'). In almost every case it was expressed as reciprocal: 'I wanted to learn about religious attitudes and to present humanist views to them.'
- To ensure equal treatment for those who shared their beliefs. Participants spoke of a 'desire to be more visible' and especially to make the point, particularly in public-authority circles, that 'not everyone who is white is a Christian'. 'I wanted to increase understanding of all faiths and beliefs, and to ensure fair treatment across the board', said one participant, reflecting a common coupling of this motivation with the aim of advancing mutual understanding. There was a common assumption that the advancement of understanding would lead to fairer treatment of all.
- To gain personal fulfilment and enjoyment out of their work. One reported attending the first meeting out of 'curiosity', another reflected on how much she 'enjoy[s] learning about faiths and feeling able to express views about a range of beliefs' and another on how the encounters he had were all 'stimulating'.

Successes

Most respondents felt they had been at least partially successful in their aims. Common successes reported were:

- Changes in perception of non-religious people from negative to positive. This was the most commonly reported success. 'I have had several young people say things along lines of "you've changed what I think about atheists for the better"', said one participant. Also typical was, 'I think I was able to show that not all non-religious people are militant atheists or aggressive secularists.'

- An increase in mutual understanding and inclusion. Much of this manifested itself on a personal level, with one participant reporting, 'I am now greeted with enthusiasm by the Ahmadi Muslims.' 'I am now greeted with open arms', reported one participant. However, there were more general successes reported: 'I think other participants are more informed about and more respectful of humanists'; 'broader understanding of and tolerance for alternative views [has emerged]'. There were also more measurable policy changes reported: 'I was able to organise a public talk by staff at the local hospice about end-of-life issues'; '[there was a] change of language in official documents and initiatives'; and one participant was asked to chair the committee producing the religious education syllabus for local schools on the strength of his contributions.
- Personal enrichment and development. Dialogue changes people, even if they do not think it will or don't expect it to. 'I have become more enthusiastic and less dogmatic – I hope', said one participant who did not go into the work for this reason. Others had 'learned a better debating style and approach' and 'found quite a few friends'.

About a third of the participants, however, believed they had not been successful in their aims. 'What success? Not much!', 'Negligible', 'Very few successes sadly'. 'My presence is tolerated but I am not allowed to speak in the main discussions', said one, and another at this extreme end of the spectrum, 'I experienced constant insults and hostility'. Even where some successes had been achieved there were bad experiences, and significant barriers to success had required overcoming.

Barriers

The barriers reported were different depending on what type of group, programme, or project the respondent was involved in but all respondents said they had faced barriers. For some those barriers had proved insuperable, but even those reporting successes had faced significant barriers. They included:

- Needing to overcome the perception that they're looking to persuade. 'It was very clear at the start that the majority view was that I was only there to try to convince them all they were wrong. I did nothing of the sort and was soon accepted, but new members from religions still bring this assumption with them', said one participant whose involvement had spanned many years.

- Simple hostility. Sometimes this was expressed very mildly by respondents, as in one respondent's experience that 'representatives of particular faiths are uncomfortable with atheists and agnostics'; sometimes it was more outright: 'he told me that if I didn't believe in the Ten Commandments then I couldn't have any morality'.
- Claims that their inclusion is inappropriate. Many participants in 'interfaith' dialogue simply don't accept that such dialogue should include those with non-religious worldviews and identities. 'One participant said I shouldn't be involved because "who do humanists pray to?"'; '[my humanism was seen] as absence of belief more than an alternative worldview'; 'at the beginning there was suspicion and resentment at my being included' – these were all typical experiences. Sometimes this lack of a welcome generated resentment in the humanist participants to an extent that they no longer wished to be involved.
- Superficial engagement. Much frustration was reported with the atmosphere of 'smiling faces, no real thoughts of changing' and one participant's view that 'there is a lot of talk but not much action and each representative is mainly concerned with putting their own point of view', was typical. 'It is nice people talking to nice people', complained one respondent.

Principles for the future

The experience of these humanists surveyed certainly chimes with my own these last ten years and helps to shape some principles that should make engagements between religious and non-religious people more productive. In general, many of the principles that apply are those that apply to dialogue and cooperation between religious people. Many non-religious participants in these activities are starting with the assumption that they will be judged and stereotyped. Religious people often feel the same and any measures that reduce this likelihood are useful. In 1993 the Inter Faith Network for the UK produced principles for building good relations. The current version of this document, *Building Good Relations with People of Different Faiths and Beliefs*, read inclusively, will serve as a good basis for any such work between the religious and non-religious:

> As members of the human family, we should show each other respect and courtesy. In our dealings with people of other faiths and beliefs, this means exercising good will and:
>
> - Respecting other people's freedom within the law to express their beliefs and convictions
> - Learning to understand what others actually believe and value, and letting them express this in their own terms
> - Respecting the convictions of others about food, dress and social etiquette and not behaving in ways which cause needless offence

- Recognising that all of us at times fall short of the ideals of our own traditions and never comparing our own ideals with other people's practices
- Working to prevent disagreement from leading to conflict
- Always seeking to avoid violence in our relationships

When we talk about matters of faith with one another, we need to do so with sensitivity, honesty and straightforwardness. This means:

- Recognising that listening as well as speaking is necessary for a genuine conversation
- Being honest about our beliefs and religious allegiances
- Not misrepresenting or disparaging other people's beliefs and practices
- Correcting misunderstanding or misrepresentations not only of our own but also of other faiths whenever we come across them
- Being straightforward about our intentions
- Accepting that in formal inter faith meetings there is a particular responsibility to ensure that the religious commitment of all those who are present will be respected

All of us want others to understand and respect our views. Some people will also want to persuade others to join their faith. In a multi faith society where this is permitted, the attempt should always be characterised by self-restraint and a concern for the other's freedom and dignity. This means:

- Respecting another person's expressed wish to be left alone
- Avoiding imposing ourselves and our views on individuals or communities who are in vulnerable situations in ways which exploit these
- Being sensitive and courteous
- Avoiding violent action or language, threats, manipulation, improper inducements, or the misuse of any kind of power
- Respecting the right of others to disagree with us.[1]

However useful these general principles are, there are undoubtedly areas that need more attention once the non-religious are introduced into the equation.

Dialogue should not be allergic to disagreement

In theory, there is no reason why this should be of greater importance in relation to the religious and non-religious in dialogue than in relation to interfaith dialogue. Disagreements between people of different religions can be as intense if not more so than those between the religious and humanists. In practice, however, there is much polite papering over of the cracks of the, 'Oh well, we all believe in the same god really' sort in 'interfaith' groups that the presence of a non-believer disrupts. In addition, many non-religious people do not see anything special about religious practices and customs as against any other cultural practices, and so are more likely than religious people to be actively critical of those they see as morally and socially harmful. It is no doubt because of this that one of the principles espoused by the British Humanist Association in its dialogue work is that it

> [does] not mean failing to challenge ideas and activities we believe to be harmful, or failing to recognise areas of disagreement. Mutual understanding means understanding differences as well as common ground. If dialogue achieves no more than box-ticking, photo-opportunities, or mutual admiration, it is of little value.[2]

This is a vital principle, not least because apparent consensus is often false and correspondingly fragile in times of crisis. Respectful but clear disagreement can be the only truthful way to build successful relationships with integrity and wider community resilience and I have certainly found it to be so in practice. I have often built more productive and lasting working relationships with religious believers with whom I disagree than with those with whom I have more views in common. Where this has happened it has invariably been when the former have not been reluctant to identify where we disagree, but been upfront about it in away that has allowed us both to know where we stood.

At the same time, there is no need to jump straight into the most controversial topics

This is a principle for both religious and non-religious participants. If the first conversational gambit by a religious participant is a demand of their humanist interlocutor that she denounce Richard Dawkins, in response to which the humanist insists that the religious participant apologise for the Catholic anti-Semitism that led to the Holocaust, then what follows is unlikely to be enjoyable, productive, or socially useful. One local humanist participant in response to the survey went further and said that 'for dialogue to be meaningful it needs to be on a subject on which both parties' views are not already highly polarised'. That may or may not be true (my own experience is that radical disagreement is not necessarily a barrier to fruitful engagement), but it is certainly the case that some self-restraint is called for in light of the polarised 'religious vs non-religious' narrative fuelled by almost all of our media and many of our politicians and religious leaders. That context is what needs to be overcome and it will not be overcome by jumping in at the deep end, even if the deep end is where we arrive eventually.

Everybody has beliefs; everybody has a worldview

Again, this is a principle for both religious and non-religious participants. It is not the case that the non-religious are a homogeneous army of calculators, whose mental toolbox contains only logic and reason. This assumption is held by religious people who see the non-religious as deficient and desiccated as a result, characterising them primarily by what they do not believe in. It is also held by non-religious people who see themselves as superior, untainted by assumptions, beliefs, and unfounded values which are the baggage of the religious alone. This is probably the area in which the phrase 'interfaith' is at its most unhelpful, with its implication that people engage with each other from within their own impermeable silos. The reality is that every person is a unique entity in terms of their values and beliefs and the experiences that have led to their possession of those values and beliefs – and we have to engage with people on that basis. One of the projects which recognises this very clearly is the Encountering Faiths and Beliefs programme of the London-based NGO 3FF (Three Faiths Forum), an organisation which 'works to build good relations between people of different faiths, beliefs and cultures'. It trains speakers from different beliefs to go into schools together on panels, talk about their own beliefs, and then reply to questions. So far, so typical, but the difference comes in that the programme, although it aims for a diversity of confessions (providing a Muslim, a Christian, a humanist, and a Hindu, for example) specifically denies that its speakers should be seen as 'representatives' of their worldview and trains its speakers instead to tell their own personal story and in response to questions about 'what Muslims believe', for example, to reply in terms of 'what *I* believe'.

Don't make a fetish of the religious/non-religious distinction

I have been at meetings on education policy where representatives of different worldviews have been brought together as part of the policy-making process and found that I agree most with the Hindu or Sikh representatives and that they and I all disagree with the Christian representatives. The specific question, in the first instance of that, was on the notion of pluralism within the religious education curriculum, but the general point is that the religious/non-religious distinction is less hard and fast than many claim. Points of comparison and reference and commonality cut across such a putative divide. In fact there is no simple religious/non-religious divide when it comes to the building of mutual understanding through common reference points. On a panel speaking in front of one audience of school pupils, the Buddhist representative and I had a long and fruitful discussion of our respective approaches to morality without a divinity, and found we had much in common which she did not share with her fellow 'religious' panellists. If we map the frontiers of encounter as being between people and ideas rather than between monolithic worldviews, we will end up with more constructive and deeper encounters as well as those that are more capable of including the non-religious.

Have a clear purpose and a concrete end

I used to think that to engage in mere talking-shops was unproductive and that bringing people together for face-to-face encounter just to discuss beliefs was fruitless compared with bringing them together for 'side-by-side' working jointly in a common cause. There were many reasons for this: a fear that face-to-face encounters overemphasised what divides us; an assumption that cooperative working where the fact that participants are of different convictions was incidental, and the common aim the thing, was more likely to produce unforced recognition of commonalities and hence break down prejudices. I no longer think that, but what the experience of others and my own makes evident is that every activity should have a clear purpose. If the purpose is greater understanding of specific similarities and differences between respective worldviews on particular philosophical, ethical, or political questions, and the medium for achieving this is intellectual discussion face to face, that's fine – but the purpose should be clear. Many of the frustrations reported by non-religious people reflect this fact that interfaith institutions have no clear purpose and much of the disruption experienced as a result of the presence of an incoming non-religious person is because their presence exposes this. I have a clear preference still for endeavours that are to produce a particular output ('we are here to write a syllabus about worldviews for local schools that will be educationally rigorous and personally fulfilling') over those that are to achieve a particular outcome ('we will all leave this room understanding each other's perspective on mortality'), but I accept that is because of my own personality, and that it is simply clarity as to either outcome or output that is the necessity.

Christian senses of entitlement are a significant barrier to engagement

I have been invited to so many self-described 'inclusive' memorials and ceremonies in which the only formal act of worship is a Christian prayer that I have lost count. It is a point of pride for the Church of England in particular that it seeks to make itself the spokesman not just of its own denomination but of 'faith' per se. I have seen this reflected in many structures of interfaith engagement in England, where the Church is so often seen as host and it is one of the features of the 'interfaith' landscape which has led to so many engagements between humanists and religious people being bilateral ones with non-Christians (there have been no structured dialogue programmes between Anglicans and humanists in recent decades at all). Rather as with the question of disagreement above, there is no theoretical reason why this should be more of a problem for the non-religious than it is for the non-Christian religious. The reality, however, is that many non-Christian religious participants do feel themselves to be recent incomers to a Christian country, and they see the pre-eminence of the Church of England as natural and acceptable. The majority of non-religious people, who have a white British ethnic background and who either turned away from Christianity themselves or whose parents or grandparents (or, as in my case, great-grandparents) did, inevitably feel differently. Many feel that the attention paid to Christianity in the interfaith world is excessive and find the Anglican claim to hold the ring implausible and overweening. In my own experience, younger participants from non-Christian religions also feel this. In Scotland, this is less of an issue. Perhaps it is the fact that Scotland is unencumbered by an established church that enables its government to be so genuinely inclusive, saying in its national guidance on dialogue that Scotland in the past was a Christian country but is now 'a small and diverse country with many nationalities, cultures and beliefs'. That guidance also says that people should not be expected to pray at gatherings designed to bring people together and is generally more inclusive of the non-religious. The aspiration of the Church of England to be a powerful political, cultural, and social body rather than just a religious one will probably hold back the same sort of inclusive progress in England, but it can still be worked for.

Recognise actively religious people have a lot of misconceptions about the non-religious

Although there is still much work to be done to increase understanding and overturn prejudices about religious people, the fact is that there has been considerable progress in this work, not least as a result of the statutory school curriculum. There has been almost no serious work at the same level to address the religious prejudices about and lack of understanding of the non-religious and attempts to involve the non-religious in dialogue and engagement face the barrier of this ignorance. One of the tactics sometimes used to advance the inclusion of non-religious people in dialogue is to reconfigure their worldview as a 'faith' just like other 'faiths'. Sometimes this is done from the best of intentions, but under normal definitions of the words 'religion' and 'faith', the common-sense humanism of most non-religious people is not included. Aside from this, there are many specific ways in which the non-religious and humanists in particular are misunderstood. I have often encountered the view that humanism is a very recent or just a 'Western' belief. Although western Europe certainly has a tradition of humanist thought and action that can be traced back more than 2,500 years, especially to the people of Greece and the west coast of Asia at that time, this way of understanding the world, of finding meaning in life, and of grounding moral thinking can also be found in China at the same time (for example, amongst followers of Confucius) and just as long ago in India (for example, in writings of the Lokayata or Charvaka) and many other cultures for just as long. (This is one area in which well-versed Hindu participants are often extremely useful to non-religious participants!) Non-Christian participants in particular sometimes see white people's humanism as just Christianity without god, or as somehow dependent on the religious moralities of previous centuries; in fact, many people have thought and expressed humanist ideas over many centuries all over the world, contributing to a humanist tradition. Today, the largest humanist organisations are in Norway and India and the fastest growing in Uganda and Nigeria. Most typical is the idea that non-religious people have no morality or that they think that science answers ethical questions or is the only discipline needed to understand everything. Of course, most non-religious people do believe that the provisional answers arising out of the application of the scientific method are the only way to understand the material reality of the universe. However, they typically also give a special emphasis to the importance of human beings and those things that make us special, such as the 'inner' human life of emotion, imagination, and creativity. And, as is well known, the evidence shows that they are as moral or more so than self-identifying religious people.

It's not just the non-religious who are not religious

Reconfiguring dialogue and engagement in a way that reflects the principles suggested here would be a benefit not only in terms of involving the non-religious in the essential work of mutual understanding between citizens with different worldviews. The fact that programmes and projects of dialogue and engagement currently touch the lives of only a minority is not just because they are only inclusive of religious people. The reality is that they don't include most religious people either. British society is plural not in the sense that it is divided into denominations and congregations of many diverse types, but in an individual sense. Even one self-described Sunni Muslim's or Roman Catholic Christian's or Theravada Buddhist's or Orthodox Jew's beliefs and values and practices may be strikingly, even diametrically, different from their theoretical co-religionists. This is the sort of plural society we live in, and in adjusting itself towards the principles that will best ensure non-religious involvement, the project of interfaith dialogue will find itself better suited to involving more religious people too.

Notes

1 'Building Good Relations – Principles', Inter Faith Network for the UK, <http://www.interfaith.org.uk/about-ifn/values-of-ifn> (accessed 6 January 2016).
2 'Dialogue with Others', British Humanist Association, <https://humanism.org.uk/community/dialogue-with-others/> (accessed 6 January 2016).

19 Siblings under the skin

Charles Taylor on religious believers and non-believers in *A Secular Age*

Ruth Abbey

Charles Taylor is a major figure in the English-language tradition of philosophy and many of his works have been translated into other languages. His recent large work, *A Secular Age* (2007; henceforth *ASA*), extended and intensified the religious turn in his writing which began towards the end of his 1989 book, *Sources of the Self*.[1] *ASA* has received a great deal of attention, commentary and criticism and has introduced Taylor's thought to some new audiences.[2] This chapter explores whether a discussion of Taylor's work on religion and secularity belongs in a volume designed to advance and enhance the exchange between religious believers and atheists in a productive manner. It proposes several ways in which Taylor's thought does provide valuable resources for this project. These include his capacious conception of religion, the weight he gives to exclusive humanism in affecting all forms of religious belief, his eschewal of what he calls subtraction stories, his insistence that the immanent frame (this term is explained below) permits both openness and closure to transcendence, and his notion of fullness. At the end, this chapter touches on some countervailing considerations which raise complications for and qualifications of this mostly positive assessment.

It is well known that Taylor's central ambition in *ASA* is to shed light on what he calls Secularity 3, or the current conditions of religious belief and experience in Western societies. This is what, in Taylor's eyes, sets his approach apart from other analyses which see secularity as referring either to the evacuation of religion from the public and other social spheres, which he calls Secularity 1, or to the decline in the number of people expressing allegiance to traditional religious views and engaging in traditional religious practices and institutions, which he dubs Secularity 2. While Taylor cannot ignore either of these developments entirely, his approach is preoccupied with what it is like to be a religious believer or non-believer in contemporary Western societies. At the work's outset he declares his intention to 'focus attention on the different kinds of lived experience involved in understanding your life in one way or the other, on what it's like to live as a believer or an unbeliever' (Taylor 2007, 5; see also 2–4, 8, 13–14, 423). Immediately we see that his ambition is to speak of, and to, both groups – those who harbour religious commitments and those who do not. These opening remarks suggest that Taylor's work could be a very valuable resource for the purposes of this volume which is to promote dialogue between religious believers and atheists.

Defining religion

There are myriad ways of defining religion and the choice of definition is crucial to how the debate is conducted. A foundational point in this discussion must therefore be what Taylor means when he refers to religion. Taylor operates with an original and strikingly capacious conception, counting any perspective or worldview that remains open to transcendence of the human, all too human, as religious. As he says early in *ASA*, 'a reading of "religion" in terms of the distinction transcendent/immanent is going to serve our purposes here' (15; see also 16, 20, 544). What matters for him is whether an outlook has a transcendent or vertical axis and whether its sense of the transcendent comes back to inform its conception of human flourishing. As Taylor later says, he defines religious faith 'by a double criterion: the belief in transcendent reality, on one hand, and the connected aspiration to a transformation which goes beyond ordinary human flourishing on the other' (510). He defines religious longing as 'the longing for and response to a more-than-immanent transformation perspective' (530).

By this logic, the category of religion embraces much more than theism – theism is but one form of religion. And religion is much more than institutions, doctrines or rituals: for Taylor it can include those things but need not. And even if it does include these more traditional aspects, his working conception of religion goes well beyond them. This broad and inclusive – perhaps even permissive – approach to what counts as religion is helpful in hosting a fruitful conversation between those who are religious and those who are not because of its relaxed attitude to who qualifies as a religious person. Following Taylor's approach, many and varied perspectives can be brought to the table on the side of religion and such hospitality obviates any rigid, restrictive or essentialist idea of what or who is religious.

Exclusive humanism

Another feature of Taylor's definition of religion that is both interesting in itself and relevant for the present discussion is that he effectively defines religion in contrast to what he calls exclusive humanism. (He sometimes calls this self-sufficient or self-sufficing or atheistic or reductive humanism but the term exclusive humanism will be used here to stand for all of these.) As Taylor says in the introduction to *ASA*,

> the coming of modern secularity in my sense has been coterminous with the rise of a society in which for the first time in history a purely

self-sufficient humanism came to be a widely available option ... a humanism accepting no final goals beyond human flourishing; nor any allegiance to anything else beyond this flourishing. Of no previous society was this true.

(18; see also 245)

Although Taylor repeatedly refers to exclusive humanism in the singular, this term is best understood as embracing a family of doctrines and approaches which, whatever their differences, share the common feature of positing a purely horizontal picture of human life, meaning and fulfilment.[3]

The advent of exclusive humanism means that religious non-belief or indifference has become a live option, permitting people to now live without any personal connection or aspiration to religion or any form of transcendence (19–21, 322, 423). And this in turn has strong knock-on effects for those who are religious, for being religious cannot be taken for granted in the Western world in the twenty-first century in the way it could in the sixteenth. Exclusive humanism constantly reminds religious believers of a viable alternative to their orientation toward transcendence. Exclusive humanism is thus a massively powerful force in Taylor's analysis, for it changes the sociocultural experience and meaning of being religious. In his hands, moreover, exclusive humanism serves not only a crucial role in signalling the arrival of a secular age but provides religion's constitutive other. All religion becomes what exclusive humanism is not: a worldview with an orientation toward transcendence. So in this sense, even though exclusive humanists comprise a minority in all Western societies, this category wields huge influence in Taylor's analysis.[4] Investing the category with such weight can be productive for the dialogue between religious believers and non-believers because although a believer himself, Taylor is imbuing non-religious positions with a fundamental gravity and (Western) world historical significance.

Subtraction stories

A related feature of Taylor's analysis of exclusive humanism that is promising for the debate between religious believers and non-believers lies in his rejection of subtraction stories as a way to explain the absence of religious belief in a person's life and in the culture more generally.[5] Subtraction stories see modernity in general and religious non-belief in particular as simply sloughing off old ideas and understandings to make space for options and possibilities that were always there waiting in the wings. For the subtraction thesis, '[w]hat emerges from this process – modernity or secularity – is to be understood in terms of underlying features of human nature which were there all along, but had been impeded by what is now set aside' (22; see also 157, 571–2). Subtraction stories, whatever form they take, fail to appreciate just how much creative and innovative intellectual, normative and imaginative effort has been required to render human life meaningful, devoid of any vertical axis. In contrast to such stories, Taylor insists that 'Western modernity, including its secularity, is the fruit of new inventions, newly constructed self-understandings and related practices' (22; see also 157, 294, 572–3). This also strikes me as a helpful move for fostering productive debate between religious believers and non-believers because it creates a sort of level hermeneutical playing field, casting both sides as constructed interpretations of meaning that change over time. There is no room for either believers or non-believers to claim that their positions are natural, necessary, self-evident or indubitable.

The immanent frame

This brings us to a larger point Taylor makes which is also potentially beneficial for furthering and deepening the debate between believers and non-believers. What Taylor dubs 'the immanent frame' offers modern Westerners a way of making sense of their lives without reference to God, the divine or the transcendent (594). The major institutions of modern life – the market economy, the public sphere, popular sovereignty, the family – can be understood as self-constituting and self-regulating, as not necessarily relying on any conception of God, religion or transcendence for their legitimacy or smooth functioning. The immanent frame is not, however, synonymous with exclusive humanism. Modern Westerners might have little or no choice but to live within the immanent frame, but this does not necessitate excluding religion. Exclusive humanism is but one option within the immanent frame. It is possible to live within the immanent frame while remaining open to religion and the transcendent: this frame 'permits closure, without demanding it' (544; see also 545, 556). For those who are religious, the immanent frame need not be an iron cage. Taylor's target throughout much of *ASA* is those who portray the closing of the transcendent window as necessary and inevitable in modernity (and often, according to him, as desirable) (548, 555–6, 579, 595). He tries to combat this not by producing a counter-spin toward openness, but by showing that neither openness nor closure is compelled by the immanent frame which all modern Westerners inhabit.

But continuing his theme of what the immanent frame permits rather than compels, Taylor argues that those who assert that God (or any equivalent deity) exists and should be acknowledged by all are spinning the immanent frame in an open way, just as those who assert that God (or any deity) does not exist and that exclusive humanism should be acknowledged by all are spinning the immanent frame in a closed way. While he understands the temptation to both types of spinning, he sees neither as legitimate. In reality, apodictic certainty is unavailable to either side: all that each can have is faith that their view is correct. When it comes to questions of religious belief and non-belief, 'we never move to a point beyond all anticipation, beyond all hunches, to the kind of certainty that we can enjoy in certain narrower questions, say, in natural science or ordinary life' (551). Whatever their self-understandings, believers and non-believers alike actually share the epistemological condition of anticipatory confidence (548–9, 550–1, 555–6, 579, 593, 674, 703, 833 n. 17). Such faith can grow stronger or weaker over time but it can never harden into absolute confidence in the rightness of one's position. This insistence that certainty is available to neither side once again levels the epistemic playing field between those who are and those who are not religious and seems to hold promise for advancing the debate between them, for neither side is a priori disadvantaged or on the defensive.

Fullness

Complementing Taylor's critique of subtraction stories as a way of explaining secularity is his discussion of the concept of fullness. Taylor maintains that 'there is no escaping some version of ... "fullness"; for any liveable understanding of human life, there must be some way in which this life looks good, whole, proper, really being lived as it should' (600). He insists that all humans harbour some conception of fullness somewhere in their lives:

> We all see our lives, and/or the space wherein we live our lives, as having a certain moral/spiritual shape. Somewhere, in some activity, or condition, lies a fullness, a richness; that is, in that place (activity or condition), life is fuller, richer, deeper, more worth while, more admirable, more what it should be ... Perhaps this sense of fullness is something we just catch glimpses of from afar off; we have the powerful intuition of what fullness would be, were we to be in that condition, e.g.; of peace or wholeness, or able to act on that level, of integrity or generosity or abandonment or self-forgetfulness.
>
> (5; see also 16, 677)

The 'utter absence of some such [ideal of fullness] would', conversely, 'leave us in abject, unbearable despair' (600; see also 597). Individuals do not need to have articulated, nor even be fully conscious of, the conception (or conceptions) of fullness that guide their actions and choices, but Taylor would argue that some idea of fullness could be reconstructed from their life (16).

The ideals of fullness harboured by those who are religious will differ one from another but will all be informed in some way by their religious beliefs (11). Yet even those whose life includes no transcendent dimension have ideas about what makes their lives more fulfilling according to Taylor. The dignity conferred by a life lived in accordance with reason is one such non-transcendent ideal of fullness; working for the betterment of one's fellow human beings is another (8–9, 694); working to protect and preserve the well-being of animals and the environment would be another. Indeed, one of the things that marks the secular age is that exclusive humanism has advanced a number of ideals of fullness that make no reference to the divine or transcendent (15, 19). Insisting that exclusive humanist positions must include, even if tacitly, some conception of fullness helps Taylor to explain the tremendous attraction that they have exercised over the last two hundred or so years. Rather than locating their drawing power in their repudiation of religion alone, he identifies elements of their positive appeal. In doing so, Taylor also pays tribute to the intellectual and imaginative effort expended in developing exclusive humanist doctrines (244–5), which harks back to his critique of subtraction stories.

Along with demonstrating the creative and affirmative dimensions of exclusive humanist positions, the invocation of an ideal or intimation of fullness also has the effect of levelling the playing field in the debate between those who are religious believers and those who are not, although this time it is the normative, rather than the hermeneutical or epistemic, playing field that is so levelled, at least in the first instance. Taylor is showing both sides that they share a very important normative structure with one another. Indeed, Taylor himself offers his idea of fullness as a heuristic device in the current debate about and between religious and non-religious positions, proposing that '[t]he swirling debate [can] ... be seen as a debate about what real fullness consists in' (600). He reiterates this when responding to some of the reactions to *ASA*, urging that 'what we badly need is a conversation between a host of different positions, religious, nonreligious, anti-religious, humanistic, antihumanistic, and so on, in which we eschew mutual caricature and try to understand what "fullness" means for the other' (Taylor 2013, 318).

Taylorean tools

My suggestion that a number of elements of Taylor's thought are salutary for developing the debate between religious believers and non-believers finds some support in recent work by George Levine. Levine does not, to be sure, deploy Taylor's ideas in quite this way: rather, he utilises them for the articulation of what Taylor would call a form of exclusive humanism. In his editor's introduction to *The Joy of Secularism*, Levine echoes a number of Taylor's themes by trying to bring to light what is positive and affirmative about non-belief and by demonstrating that what he calls secularism can nourish forms of fullness. Levine declares his desire to adduce a form of secularism that represents

> a positive, not a negative, condition, not a denial of the world of spirit and religion, but an affirmation of the world we're living in now ... such a world is capable of bringing us to the condition of 'fullness' that religion has always promised.
>
> (Levine 2012, 1; see also 6, 7, 8, 9)

Levine also follows Taylor in emphasising the existential, rather than the purely cognitive, dimensions of living as a non-religious, or secular, person (2). Levine's work illustrates that Taylorean tools can profitably be taken up by both sides of the debate.

As a secular illustration of Taylor's conception of fullness, Levine alludes to Amy Clampitt's poem 'The Sun Underfoot among the Sundews' (13). Turning to poetry as a source of ideals of fullness is very concordant with Taylor's approach, because he is the first to admit that the arts can be crucial vehicles for these ideals. In this vein, I find that Marie Howe's 1994 poem 'What the Living Do' captures a secular, or exclusive humanist, moment of fullness. Dedicated to her brother Johnny who died of Aids-related complications five years earlier, the poem begins by relaying all the mundane minutiae that so easily oppress the spirit: a clogged kitchen sink, a plumber not called, accumulating dirty dishes, a malfunctioning heater, the shopping bag that breaks mid-load, the coffee spilt down one's arm. And then there is the insatiable yearning. 'We want the spring to come and the winter to pass. We want whoever to call or not call, a letter, a kiss – we want more and more and then more of it.' None of the poem's initial litany of complaints about daily life seems propitious for illustrating the lofty condition of fullness. Then comes the 'but'.

> But there are moments, walking, when I catch a glimpse of myself in the window glass,
>   say, the window of the corner video store, and I'm gripped by a cherishing so deep
>   for my own blowing hair, chapped face, and unbuttoned coat that I'm speechless:
>   I am living. I remember you.

The speaker's being 'gripped by a cherishing so deep' resonates with Taylor's description of fullness as 'that ... condition [where] life is fuller, richer, deeper, more worth while, more admirable, more what it should be ...' (Taylor 2007, 5). In Howe's case, however, this sense of fullness is not 'something we just catch glimpses of from afar off' as per Taylor, but, as befitting an exclusive humanist conception, it is something seen close up, in the window of the local video store. The speaker's powerful affirmation of the mere fact of being alive conveyed in the poem's turn from complaint to celebration is, as I read it, the affirmation of a life untouched by transcendence. What renders the speaker speechless is just the reflection of herself alive and its vivid contrast with her absent dead brother. In addition to revelling in simply being alive, the poem suggests that this fact of existence affords her the power and privilege to remember her deceased brother. Johnny does not speak to her from beyond; there is no epiphany of posthumous reunion. Instead what the poem asserts is 'I am living. I remember you.'

Dilemmas and cross pressures

Not only are there a number of ways in which elements of Taylor's analysis of secularity can enhance the debate between those who are and those who are not religious, but Taylor himself sees his work as having this function. His remarks, quoted above, about his conception of fullness facilitating a much needed conversation between a host of religious and non-religious positions testifies to his ambition on this score. More generally, part of his purpose in *ASA* is to reduce the perceived distance between those who are and those who are not religious. In part 5 of the book in particular, whose subheadings include 'Cross Pressures', 'Dilemmas 1' and 'Dilemmas 2', he strives to reveal that the supposed antagonists in the debate have more in common than either side realises, and to expose a more fertile, complex, uncertain middle ground (674–5).

As part of this agenda Taylor identifies a number of dilemmas each side in the debate shares (673). These include whether all forms of transcendence can really be eschewed (630); whether Christianity or exclusive humanism stifle human flourishing in some way (675); how to make sense of violence (639, 668, 688–9); how to understand death (720–7); and how to strive for high ethical standards without mutilating the ordinary goods of human life (623–4, 627, 640–1, 656). Identifying these dilemmas is designed not only to deconstruct the supposed binary oppositions of belief and non-belief but also to create a space for beginning to articulate the experience of many people who recognise themselves in neither of these opposing positions. Taylor is attempting to shift the parameters of debate, for at the moment partisans of polarised standpoints define themselves against one another, largely ignoring this middle, cross-pressured ground occupied by many (431, 627). It is in the context of one such discussion of the shared terrain between believers and exclusive humanists that Taylor declares '[w]e are brothers under the skin' (675). That sentence not only provides the title for the present chapter but also alludes to the shared history between contemporary Christian and exclusive humanist positions. He traces both to reform movements within Christianity (636), which he spends a large portion of the book tracking.

Conclusion

This chapter has pointed to some of the ways in which Taylor's thought contains the potential to host a fruitful dialogue between those who are and those who are not religious. These include his capacious conception of religion, the weight accorded to exclusive humanism as a social and cultural force, the critique of subtraction stories, the emphasis on the insuperable ambiguity of the immanent frame, Taylor's conception of fullness, and his identification of a number of dilemmas that must be grappled with by those who are and those who are not religious. However, before closing, it must be acknowledged that other features of Taylor's work make it less suited for this purpose.

Taylor's broad and inclusive approach to what counts as religion was numbered as one of his work's helpful features in hosting a fruitful conversation between those who are religious and those who are not. Yet conversely, his very gesture of defining religion in such a broad and sweeping way has the effect of minoritising (to coin an ugly but useful term) those who are not religious. Perhaps this minoritising doesn't matter when one is mounting a philosophical debate where all that counts is the strength of the arguments. But it does matter when one is taking a more sociological or phenomenological approach in the way Taylor is, because those who show up as not religious according to the way he draws religion's boundaries are consigned to a numerical minority whose experiences and orientations are very different from the vast, if internally heterogeneous, majority who are religious. Those who are not religious by Taylor's reckoning because they live their lives without pointing their compass toward the transcendent are rendered rare and exotic by his capacious conception of what counts as religion.

Taylor has long been a practising Catholic and his personal religious orientation has assumed greater visibility in his writings over the last two decades. There are a number of moments when he appears as less of an even-handed arbiter in the debate between those who are and those who are not religious and becomes instead the active proponent of an open, and thus pro-religious, reading of the immanent frame (436–7). One of his major aspirations in *ASA* is to demonstrate that religion is neither dead nor dying in the modern West and to make room for the recognition of faith and orientations toward transcendence in all their variety and motility. As he says, 'the developments of Western modernity have destabilized and rendered virtually unsustainable earlier forms of religious life, but … new forms have sprung up. Moreover this process of destabilization and recomposition is not a once-for-all change, but is continuing' (594; see also 437, 461). At times this sounds like a celebration and vindication of religion's persistence rather than simply a correct sociological observation.

Another way in which Taylor's tilt toward religion manifests itself is in the criteria he lays out to decide whether living the immanent frame in an open or closed way is better. Although he insists, as indicated above, that there is no definitive way of deciding whether the immanent frame is best occupied in an open or a closed way, his criteria suggest a preferential option for religion. One such criterion is to see which alternative – exclusive humanism or religion – provides the best account of the full gamut of human experience. Because it refuses to speak of interpellation by outside forces, Taylor deems exclusive humanism to be poorly equipped to make sense of 'the specific force of creative agency; or ethical demands, or … the power of artistic experience' (597; see also 589). A view of human existence that is open to transcendence is, in his estimation, better placed to describe and give some account of such aesthetic and ethical experiences. Taylor also claims that theism provides a more robust moral source for the very demanding modern ethic of universal solidarity and assistance (677–8, 695). He concludes that 'this kind of response to the image of God in others ... can be real for us, but only to the extent that we open ourselves to God ...'. This sort of opening provides 'a path towards a much more powerful and effective healing action in history' (703). Here Taylor is overtly arguing in favour of the attractions and advantages of inhabiting the immanent frame in an open, and indeed specifically Christian, way. Moments like these make his work less appealing as a venue for conducting a conversation between those who are and those who are not religious.

Elsewhere (Abbey 2014) I have suggested that Taylor accords ontological status to the human orientation toward transcendence, and insofar as my interpretation is correct, it also tips his scales in favour of religion. I close with a remark from *ASA* which similarly reduces Taylor's ability to host a free and fair conversation between those who are and those who are not religious. At the close of chapter 10 he says, 'A race of humans has arisen which has managed to experience its world entirely as immanent. In some respects, we may judge this achievement as a victory for darkness, but it is a remarkable achievement nonetheless' (376; see also 255, 257). In the context of the current project, this remark is disturbing for three reasons. First, it casts exclusive humanists as 'a race of humans', which both exaggerates their number and separates them – from other races of humans? – in a way that compounds the depiction of them as a rare and exotic group indicated above. Second, it invokes a 'we' who are not exclusive humanists, which flies in the face of Taylor's ambition elsewhere to underscore what exclusive humanists and those who are religious have in common. Third, and most disturbing, it associates exclusive humanism with forces of darkness. This demonising of exclusive humanists, even if a throw away remark, collides directly with many of Taylor's other gestures toward respectful and equal exchange between those who are and are not religious.

Notes

1 Since then Taylor has written about religion in his short work from 1999, *A Catholic Modernity?*, in *Varieties of Religion Today* (2002), and in *Modern Social Imaginaries* (2004). However, for the purposes of this discussion, I draw primarily from *ASA*.
2 Smith (2014) provides a reliable synopsis of *ASA*.
3 As the adjective 'exclusive' suggests, not all humanism is of this sort. Taylor makes room, briefly, for a non-exclusive form of humanism, taking as his example the idea of deep ecology and its belief that humans can experience a form of transcendence in communing with the natural world (19). According to this perspective, nature's value is intrinsic rather than instrumental and it provides an eminently valuable good above and beyond human life.
4 For data supporting the claim that very few people in even Western societies adhere to any form of exclusive humanism, see Abbey 2010.

5 References to this appear throughout the book – there is an index entry for 'subtraction stories', which lists the page numbers.

Bibliography

Abbey, Ruth (2010) 'A Secular Age: The Missing Question Mark', in Ian Leask, with Eoin Cassidy, Alan Kearns, Fainche Ryan and Mary Shanahan (ed.), *The Taylor Effect: Responding to a Secular Age*. Newcastle upon Tyne: Cambridge Scholars, 8–25.

Abbey, Ruth (2014) 'Theorizing Secularity 3: Authenticity, Ontology, Fragilization', in Carlos D. Colorado and Justin D. Klassen (eds), *Aspiring to Fullness in a Secular Age: Essays on Religion and Theology in the Work of Charles Taylor*. Notre Dame, IN: University of Notre Dame Press, 98–124.

Howe, Marie (1994) 'What the Living Do', *Atlantic Monthly*, April, <http://www.theatlantic.com/past/docs/unbound/poetry/atlpoets/howe9404.htm>.

Levine, George (ed.) (2012) *The Joy of Secularism: 11 Essays for How We Live Now*. Princeton, NJ: Princeton University Press.

Smith, James K. A. (2014) *How (Not) to Be Secular: Reading Charles Taylor*. Grand Rapids, MI: William B. Eerdmans Publishing Co.

Taylor, Charles (1989) *Sources of the Self: The Making of the Modern Identity*. Cambridge, MA: Harvard University Press.

Taylor, Charles (1999) *A Catholic Modernity?*, ed. James L. Heft. New York: Oxford University Press.

Taylor, Charles (2002) *Varieties of Religion Today*. Cambridge, MA: Harvard University Press.

Taylor, Charles (2004) *Modern Social Imaginaries*. Durham, NC: Duke University Press.

Taylor, Charles (2007) *A Secular Age*. Cambridge, MA: Belknap Press of Harvard University Press.

Taylor, Charles (2013) 'Afterword: *Apologia pro Libro suo*', in Michael Warner, Jonathan VanAntwerpen and Craig Calhoun (eds), *Varieties of Secularism in a Secular Age*. Cambridge, MA: Harvard University Press, 300–24.

20 Filling the space between

What we can learn from Plato

Angie Hobbs

It might initially seem surprising to claim that Plato is a rich resource for people concerned to promote dialogue between believers and atheists. Does not the imaginary state depicted in his final work, the *Laws*, say that certain kinds of deceitful and unrepentant atheists are to be put to death (907d–909d)? Nor does the imaginary state of the *Laws* appear to permit any genuine dialogue between believers and atheists.[1] Yet I want to propose that if we take Plato's works as a whole (including the *Laws*) we will find that they provide an excellent resource for those who are interested in such a dialogue. And this is for three reasons: firstly, he provides a model of how such a dialogue might be conducted (even though he does not give us an example of precisely such a dialogue himself); secondly, he provides us with the materials to construct a case for the potential benefits of dialogue to both parties (not simply the atheists who might be converted); and, thirdly, he writes about religious beliefs in such a way that those beliefs can be (and, I shall suggest, have been) fruitfully reworked within a secular framework.

To understand how this might be so, we need some context. The first point to emphasise is obvious yet still frequently overlooked. Although the precise nature of Plato's own religious beliefs are much debated (a point we shall be returning to below),[2] he wrote in the fourth century BCE and did not adhere to any of the current dominant world religions; he is thus not directly implicated in any of the current conflicts in which the participants claim allegiance to one of those religions. His dialogues can therefore function to some extent as a shared cultural resource and offer an inclusive space in which religious and ethical issues can be robustly debated without the participants in the debate feeling so keenly that their specific beliefs and identities are being immediately threatened.

The term 'dialogues' is key here. Although Plato at no point gives us a true dialogue between believers and atheists,[3] it is nevertheless of fundamental importance that he chooses the dialogue form as his literary vehicle, and populates these dialogues with such a varied cast of characters. One of the reasons for this choice is almost certainly to emulate as far as possible his mentor and friend Socrates' adherence to the spoken word: Socrates always steadfastly refused to write down any of his teachings, believing that oral debate – ideally one-to-one – was far more effective at producing real change in the interlocutor. Such concerns about the limitations of the written word are vividly articulated by Plato in the *Phaedrus* 274b–275e in the myth of Theuth: one cannot converse properly with a book, as the book will keep saying the same thing (and the fact that the shortcomings of writing are here written down is yet another means by which Plato aims through irony to stimulate active thought and response in his readers).

And the debates can be genuinely robust: Plato does not simply think that dialogue in general is good; in the early and middle stages of his career at least, he positively searches out the toughest opponents for Socrates that he can find. In the *Gorgias*, for example, Callicles argues eloquently that the naturally strong and resourceful few both can and should take more power, wealth and sensual pleasure than those weaker than themselves, simply because they can: might is, literally, right.[4] In the *Republic*, Thrasymachus maintains with equal force that what we term 'justice' is simply the interest of the stronger: rulers make the laws in their own interest and then say that it is 'just' to obey those laws; so if the ruled do obey them and act 'justly', they are simply serving the interests of the stronger party and more fool them.[5] The character of Socrates is given real opposition, voiced by tough, clever and charismatic opponents.

It is also important to note that the 'character of Socrates' is precisely that: a character in a dramatic dialogue. Plato may have chosen the dialogue form partly as a tribute to the oral style of his mentor, but the 'Socrates' of the dialogues is not to be confused with the historical Socrates, and nor should we assume that he is simply Plato's mouthpiece. The same is true of the Eleatic Stranger in the *Sophist*. The *Laws* is admittedly rather different, in that the views of its central character, the Athenian Stranger, are not scrutinised and questioned by the other characters in the way that the views of Socrates are in the earlier dialogues; it seems reasonable to infer that the Athenian Stranger is at least closer to being a mouthpiece for Plato. But even here it would be wise to allow for a little distance. For the fact remains that Plato never appears as a speaking character in any of his works (and there are only two brief references to 'Plato' in the entire corpus: he is mentioned as present at Socrates' trial at *Apology* 38b (and offering money for Socrates' penalty), and, significantly, as absent and 'sick' on the day that Socrates is put to death in prison in the *Phaedo* 59b). We can thus never know for sure whether Plato the author unequivocally agrees with any of the views he puts into the mouths of his characters, even though it is very likely that he finds the views of the principal characters most sympathetic to his own: hoping that a view is true, and thinking that it is likely to be closest to the truth, is not the same as unequivocal agreement. So we cannot be absolutely certain what Plato thinks of the Athenian Stranger recommending the death penalty for some atheists in the *Laws*, although it is likely that he is sympathetic to the Stranger's position. The critical point remains, even in the *Laws*:

namely that the distance between Plato the author and his characters invites discussion and debate; the distance opens a space for the reader.

To sum up so far: Plato writes in a way which does not simply show dialogues and debate taking place between various characters, but which is also designed to promote dialogue with his present and future readers. It follows that although we do not witness a dialogue in *Laws* 10 between believers and atheists, the topics discussed are, I would contend, still intended to be debated by us, even though the *Laws* is far less aporetic in tone than earlier works. Furthermore, despite its more proclamatory style, the *Laws* still provides us, in both theory and practice, with perhaps the clearest examples in the entire Platonic corpus of a central feature of all good dialogue, namely the attempt to *persuade* one's interlocutor rather than simply bludgeon them into submission. In 719e–723d the Athenian Stranger says that it is vital that a persuasive prelude should introduce every law as it is only through such preludes that the lawgiver(s) can hope to elicit true consent from those they govern. And the Stranger remains true to his word: the space allocated to these persuasive preludes throughout the *Laws* far exceeds the space allocated to the laws themselves. *Laws* 10 is a case in point: by far the greater part of the book is taken up with the preamble to the laws on religion, in which the Stranger seeks to persuade atheists and doubters, through careful rational argument, that the gods exist, that they care about humans and that they cannot be bribed.

This is not the place to assess the quality of these arguments;[6] what matters for our purposes is that such arguments exist, and I wish to propose that they exist because Plato thinks their existence will benefit both parties. Certainly, the Athenian Stranger believes that such attempts to persuade the atheist will, if successful, be of benefit to the atheist – and not just because the former atheist would now no longer be at risk of the death penalty: their soul will be in a much better state for both this life and the afterlife. At 909a he says explicitly that atheists who are otherwise of good character are to be sent to a reform centre and visited by members of the Nocturnal Council who will try to effect their 'spiritual salvation'.[7] And there is every reason to think that on this issue Plato is fully in accord with the views of the Stranger: the atheist's soul will be in a vastly better state if they become a believer irrespective of whether they live in a theocracy which puts some atheists to death and imprisons others.[8] All this seems straightforward. What is perhaps more striking is that, as I argue below, Plato also thinks (i) that making such arguments will be of benefit to the *believer*, and that they will be of benefit whether or not the attempts at persuasion are successful. Indeed, we may even be able to extrapolate from his views – although this is a conclusion that Plato himself does not explicitly draw – and claim (ii) that engaging with the arguments and ideally engaging in dialogue may be of benefit even to the atheist who remains unpersuaded. In the imagined state depicted in the *Laws*, of course, such potential benefits from engaging with the arguments will not be enough to save the recalcitrant atheist from death; nor, as we have seen, does there seem to be the possibility of a genuine, open-minded dialogue between the atheist and the theist in the imaginary state itself (rather than the atheist just listening to the arguments). But that should not stop a modern reader from looking at the *foundations* of Plato's belief in the value of trying to persuade atheists and concluding that – the draconian *Laws* notwithstanding – there are good Platonic reasons why dialogue between believers and non-believers should take place for the benefit of both parties, whether or not the former convert (or even seek to convert) the latter to a religious viewpoint.

Why do I think that (i) and even (ii) are the case? The answer lies in two points that are absolutely fundamental to Plato's conception of the divine and our human relation to it, and which underlie any attempts to persuade the hearer or reader through rational argument of the existence and nature of the gods. It is true, as we have seen, that the precise nature of Plato's religious beliefs is much disputed – not simply because he never writes in his own voice, but also because the main characters, particularly Socrates and the Athenian Stranger, speak at times of 'the gods' and at others of 'God' with seeming indifference.[9] Nevertheless, the evidence in favour of these two fundamental points seems overwhelming. The first is that there is a rational controlling intelligence (*nous*) and that the universe is divinely and providentially ordered. There are so many passages which attest to this that it is hard to think that it is not Plato's own view: see, for example, *Phaedo* 97b–98b, *Cratylus* 400a, *Philebus* 28d–30e, *Laws* 967d–e. Socrates' censorship in *Republic* 2 and 3 of the portraits of the traditional Olympic gods in Homer and elsewhere is also highly relevant here: the portrayals are critiqued not simply because they depict the gods behaving immorally, but also because they show the gods to be irrational and capricious, whimsically dispensing good and bad fortunes on humans without any consideration of merit.[10]

The second fundamental belief is that human reason is akin to this divine controlling reason (e.g. *Republic* 611e, *Timaeus* 90a; this may also be what is meant at *Philebus* 29b–c where Socrates says that there is a small spark of cosmic fire within humans). It is the divine element within us, and it follows that humans both can and should try to hone their rational powers: this is the essence of the 'assimilation to God' as far as is humanly possible which we are told is our chief human task (*Theaetetus* 176a–c, *Republic* 613a–b, *Timaeus* 90a–d, *Laws* 716c). The lyric poet Pindar, writing in the fifth century BCE, may have claimed that 'mortals should think mortal thoughts' and that trying to exceed those boundaries is hubristic and dangerous, but for Plato our divinely appointed mission is to exercise our divinely sourced reason to scale the heights:

> We should think of the most authoritative part of our soul [i.e. reason] as a guardian spirit[11] given to each of us by god, living in the summit of the body, which can properly be said to lift us from the earth towards

our home in heaven, as if we were a heavenly and not an earthbound plant. For where the soul first grew into being, from there our divine part attaches us by the head to heaven, like a plant by its roots, and keeps our body upright.

(*Timaeus* 90a–b)[12]

However – and this is the crucial move for our present concerns – honing our rational powers and 'becoming like God' is not just a matter of contemplating the heavens, important though that is; it also involves questioning and reflecting on all matters of import, including matters of divinity and religion: *pace* Stephen Hawking,[13] in Plato there is no inevitable conflict, or even tension, between religious belief and philosophy, or religious belief and science. This is one of the reasons why Socrates in the *Apology* is able to portray his work of engaging Athenians in debate about key concepts as the fulfilment of a divine mission from Apollo (23b, 30a, 30e–31a). Furthermore, the concepts under scrutiny are not only ethical and aesthetic; they also include the nature of the divine itself, and the proper human attitude towards it. Witness the seminal discussion in the *Euthyphro* about whether things can be called holy because they are loved by God, or whether God loves things because they are holy (9e–10a). As the dialogue unfolds, it is strongly suggested that the latter is the case; and it is further implied that holiness is the assistance humans provide to the gods in producing the noble product of human virtue[14] – which would in turn suggest that Socrates' practice of questioning his fellow humans to help them understand the nature and importance of virtue is indeed a holy task. Witness, too, the attempts to prove through a series of careful arguments the immortality of the *psychê* in the *Phaedo* (a dialogue in which Socrates talks explicitly of his life's work as his attempt to fulfil the commands of certain dreams (60d–61a): it seems very probable that these dreams are to be thought of as divinely inspired). And, to return to our starting point, witness the need to try to persuade atheists through argument in the *Laws* that the gods exist, are incorruptible, and care for humankind. In all these cases the ultimate aim is the salvation of the soul of both the speaker and hearer,[15] but this can only be achieved through the development and proper use of the rational powers of both, because only reason can apprehend knowledge of the good[16] and put it into effect. In short, it is a key part of our divinely appointed task to ask questions about the divine.

It is true that Plato does not go on to say explicitly that engaging in genuine faith/secular debate (as opposed to the atheist simply stating his case and the theist responding) would be a good way of going about such questioning; he might even deny that it is the case. Yet it is, I think, a fair conclusion to draw, both from his beliefs in a rational cosmos of which each human's reason is a part, and also from the rational and exploratory methods of the dialogues.

Debates about the existence and nature of God/the gods, therefore, and our relation to the divine both play an intrinsic role in the flourishing life in their own right and in addition help us come to a clearer view of what that flourishing life could be like. Nevertheless, becoming as much like God as a human can is not the same as actually becoming God, and Plato is always keenly aware of the necessary limits of human knowledge and language, particularly in matters of the divine itself. At *Meno* 86b, for example, Socrates admits that he cannot confidently assert most of the claims he has just made about the immortality and reincarnation of the soul – points which have grounded the entire argument that what we call learning is in fact nothing other than recollection of what we have already learned in previous lives and discarnate states – while at *Apology* 40c–41c Socrates freely admits how little we know of what happens after death, and carefully delineates the various possibilities (his favoured scenario is one where he is able to interrogate the semi-divine heroes such as Agamemnon or Odysseus). Earlier in the *Apology* (21a–22a) he also tells of his long struggle to try to ascertain what the Delphic oracle meant when it said that there was no one wiser than Socrates, eventually concluding that it means that he is the only person who does not claim to know what he does not know. He may conceive of his work as a service to God, but he also says that he is wise with no more than 'human wisdom' (20d–e). In later dialogues, Plato's ambitions for human wisdom may grow and he may think that we can get ever closer to God, but it is not clear that Plato ever thinks that that boundary can be fully crossed, at least in our bodily lifetimes.[17]

Most significantly of all for our current concerns, at the beginning of the *Critias* (107b) Critias tellingly says that when we are reflecting on divine matters, we must of necessity employ representation (*mimêsis*) and comparison (*apeikasia*): our thinking about the divine must inevitably be metaphorical.[18] Plato follows this advice on many occasions: depictions of the afterlife are couched in mythical form at the end of the *Gorgias*, *Phaedo* and *Republic*[19] and the divine Form of the Good – and the other perfect, unchanging insensible Forms – is described through the similes of the Sun and the Divided Line and Cave in *Republic* 507a–517e. Again, the message is the same: although our rational powers can be ever more fully actualised, and although we can assimilate ourselves ever more closely to God, our embodied human thinking about divine matters must always be articulated through metaphor which requires interpretation. It therefore follows that the debate cannot ever be finally closed.

This leads us to the third way in which Plato's works provide fertile territory for interactions between believers and atheists, as it is the avowedly metaphorical nature of his religious language that allows Plato's writings on religious matters to be so richly reimagined, reinterpreted and reused by subsequent generations of believers and non-believers alike. Witness how the ascent up the ladder of love towards the divine Form of Beauty at *Symposium* 210–212 has captured the imaginations of subsequent philosophers, theologians, poets and psychologists;[20] and witness too the manifold uses made of the account of our guided ascent from the shadowy cave of this phenomenal world towards the sun's light of the divine Form of the Good in the *Republic* 514a–517c.[21] A particularly intriguing case is Plato's treatment of the daimonic realm in the *Symposium* and its subsequent history.[22] The setting of the dialogue is a drinking party where assorted guests – a comic and tragic poet, a philosopher, a doctor amongst others – give speeches in praise of *erôs*, erotic love. When it is his turn to speak, Socrates recounts how as a young man he was taught about *erôs* by an older woman named Diotima, whom he portrays as some kind of priestess and seer. According to Diotima, *erôs* is not a god (as the previous speakers had depicted him), but a *daimôn*, and

> everything daimonic lies between the divine and mortal realms ... its power being that of interpreting and conveying things from humans to gods and gods to humans: entreaties and sacrifices from the former, and commands and returns for sacrifices from the latter. Being in the middle, it fills in the space between them, so that the whole is bound together into one continuum.
>
> (202d–e)

Daimons cannot be seen by humans, but – as portrayed here by Plato – they interpenetrate and interconnect the entire cosmos. And Plato's portrayal of them in the *Symposium*[23] has had a rich history. The Neoplatonists Plotinus, Iamblichus and Proclus were all much preoccupied with what fills and connects the space between mortal and immortal realms and the key role played by daimons in this respect,[24] and Porphyry *On Abstinence* 2.38 explicitly references *Symposium* 202e:

> Among these good daimons are to be numbered 'the transmitters' as Plato calls them, who convey and announce the concerns of men to the gods and divine matters to men. They convey our prayers to the gods as if to judges; they also bring down to us their commands and guidance together with prophecy.[25]

The range of Platonic and Neoplatonic interpretations of daimons, including the one explored here in the *Symposium* and *On Abstinence*, was later taken up by the Renaissance philosopher Ficino in the latter years of the fifteenth century. With particular regard to the daimonic role in *Symposium* 202e, it is significant that Ficino not only translated the *Symposium* into Latin but wrote a commentary on it, the *De Amore*, which discusses Diotima's notion of daimons in book 6, chapters 2–5 and 8 (these daimons are sometimes referred to specifically by Ficino as 'good daemons' and distinguished by him from the bad daemons/demons of Christian thought). Although Ficino's account brings in many other Platonic and ancient texts in addition to the *Symposium*, it is still true that Diotima's portrayal of daimons as intermediary beings who complete the whole is the driving force of his discussion. Indeed, the *De Amore* as a whole is – to our eyes[26] – a synthesis of many different philosophical treatises on love, which Ficino brews up into his own idiosyncratic and rich concoction, but again all that need concern us here is that he pays especial attention to Diotima's account of the daimonic realm. The *De Amore* was first published in 1484 and for 200 years it was one of the most widely read and respected books in Europe, being studied not just by philosophers, but poets and scientists and almost everyone of learning.[27] Ficino also writes about the interconnective role of daimons (good daemons) in other works, particularly the *Three Books on Life* and the *Platonic Theology* – they are absolutely central to his view of the cosmos.[28]

Plato, the Neoplatonists and Ficino, of course, are all, in their different ways, profoundly religious thinkers. Yet my claim above was that the deliberately metaphorical nature of many of Plato's religious writings meant that such writings have a particular capacity to spark the imaginations of believers and non-believers alike, and I cited the images of the ladder of love and the cave as instances where this has happened. Can we also say the same of the picture of daimons flitting between the mortal and immortal realms and connecting the whole? I believe that we can, and, if I am right, the implications are profound. What follows involves some speculation, but it is speculation of such import that I think it is very much worth including as a coda and invitation to further research; and I shall indicate clearly what is known for sure and what is (I believe credible) guesswork.

For one particularly notable student of ancient philosophies and religions, including ancient daimonology, and magical and alchemical practices, was Newton: it was his extensive collections of papers in these subjects that prompted John Maynard Keynes to call him 'the last magician'.[29] Newton owned Ficino's translation of Plato,[30] and there is at least one place in his manuscripts where he incontrovertibly cites Ficino.[31] Ficino usually treats of daimons as guardian angels (e.g. *De Amore* 6.3), and Newton too developed a doctrine of angels as spiritual intermediaries throughout the cosmos.[32] All this is a matter of fact, but I think we can go further. Some historians of science have proposed that Newton's fascination with ancient notions of active spirits as mediators – and I would add very possibly this passage in the *Symposium* in particular, perhaps also with the support of Ficino's *De Amore* – profoundly influenced his vision in the *Principia* of a world interpenetrated and connected by unseen physical forces acting at a distance.[33] It is notable that Ficino himself explicitly discusses action at a distance in the form of magnetic attraction in *De Amore* 6.2, at the beginning of his discussion of Diotima's claim that eros is a daimon and her account of the connective daimonic realm. It certainly seems well within the bounds of possibility that Newton's fecund imagination has taken hold of an ancient religious worldview, which he understands to be couched in metaphorical language, and he wonders how such a worldview could be translated into modern scientific terms. Even if his direct sources are Neoplatonic rather than Platonic, Plato still lies at the heart of the Neoplatonic notion of daimons and Plato would still be a vital indirect source. This should not surprise us: as Plato's metaphorical language is always employed to express his vision of a divinely rational cosmos, his dialogues may be particularly fruitful territory for any scientist to explore.

Newton was not an atheist (even though his version of Christianity – which denied the Trinity – was regarded as heretical by some at the time). But his physical theories have clearly been adopted (and in some respects usefully contested) by non-believers as well as believers. The message is clear. If it is indeed the case that some of these scientific theories were either sparked or reinforced by his study of ancient religions, then there could not be more powerful testimony for why believers of different faiths, non-believers and agnostics need to keep channels of communication open, either through direct debate or simply through being aware of what others are saying, or have said. Seeking to extend the bounds of human knowledge and possibility through rational enquiry is a vital component of the human condition, and it is happily impossible to predict whose idea, or which anonymous collective vision, will set the imagination of future thinkers alight.

Notes

1 At *Laws* 885c–e a hypothetical atheist is permitted to make a brief statement of his case, but when the Athenian Stranger (the main interlocutor in the work) attempts to change his mind – on which more below – the atheist is not allowed any riposte: it is not a genuine exchange of views.

2 See, for example, Morgan 1992, 227–47; Dodds 1951, 207–35 and *passim*; Tarrant 2012, 251–3; Solmsen 1942.

3 Apart from the hypothetical atheist in *Laws* 10 cited in note 1, above, who is only allowed an opening statement, the closest is perhaps the examination by Socrates of Protagoras' man-measure doctrine in the *Theaetetus* (151d–172c, 177c–179d), in which words are sometimes put into the mouth of an imaginary Protagoras, including an explicit profession of his agnosticism (162d–e).

4 *Gorgias* 481b–492c.

5 *Republic* 338c–339a, 343a–344c.

6 See the very helpful bibliography provided by Saunders and Brisson 2000.

7 See also 903d and 904c–905c; at 905b it is made very clear that impiety is a vice that the gods will punish.

8 The point is made with vivid eloquence in the eschatological myths at the end of the *Gorgias*, *Phaedo* and *Republic*.

9 For example, *Laws* 902e refers to 'God' in the singular, while immediately following in 903a we have 'the gods'; again, at 903d the Stranger talks of the 'divine draughts-player', but at 903e reverts back to 'the gods'. See Tarrant 2012, 252. For the purposes of this chapter the distinction does not greatly matter, providing both 'God' and 'the gods' are viewed as rational (see below).

10 *Republic* 379c–380c, quoting from (amongst other passages) *Iliad* 24.525–33 and Aeschylus frag. 160.

11 *Daimôn*; see below for the account of the vital intermediary role played by *daimônes* in the *Symposium*.

12 Trans. Lee and Johansen 2008 (Penguin Classics).
13 E.g. in Hawking and Mlodinow, *The Grand Design* (2010).
14 See Roslyn Weiss 2012, 55–6.
15 See notes 7 and 8 above.
16 The form this knowledge takes is discussed below.
17 A possible exception is the lover who reaches the top of the ladder of love at *Symposium* 212a: 'it belongs to him to be loved by the gods and to him, if to any human being, to be immortal'. But the precise interpretation of this passage is highly complex.
18 And see also *Timaeus* 22c–d, where the Egyptian priest who allegedly tells Solon the tale of the island of Atlantis (founded by the union between the god Poseidon and a mortal woman) says explicitly that a myth may symbolize a cosmological or historical event.
19 *Gorgias* 523a–526d (though it is interesting that Socrates says to his interlocutor – Callicles – more than once that although he will probably dismiss the tale as a '*mythos*', he, Socrates, regards it as a true account (*logos*)), *Phaedo* 110b–115d, *Republic* 614b–621b.
20 To take just two examples from very many: Freud treats the ladder as providing the inspiration for his theories of libido and sublimation in *Three Essays* and *Group Psychology and the Analysis of the Ego* (for detailed references see Santas 1988, 153–88); and the Greek Orthodox theologian Kallistos Ware (1979) discusses the relation between the ladder of love in the *Symposium* and John Climacus' (seventh century CE) *Ladder of Divine Ascent* in *The Orthodox Way*.
21 Again, to take just a few examples from many: the imagery of the allegory of the cave infuses C. S. Lewis' work, Wallace Stevens, *The Man with the Blue Guitar*, and Iris Murdoch, *The Fire and the Sun*; see also Stephen Dunn's fine poem *The Allegory of the Cave*. The allegory has also inspired many paintings and cartoons: there is a striking example from the sixteenth-century Flemish School in the Musée de la Chartreuse at Douai in France. Cinema, too, has proved a fertile medium: both *The Matrix* and *The Truman Show* are indebted to it.
22 I am currently writing about this at much more length in 'Socrates, Eros and Magic'.
23 Plato in fact writes about daimons in a number of works, and his thoughts on them are not always easy to reconcile, but it is this passage from the *Symposium* that is our focus here. For other mentions and discussions, see *Phaedo* 107d–108b and 113d, *Cratylus* 397d–398c8 (quoting Hesiod, *Works and Days* 120ff.), *Timaeus* 40d and 90a (the latter quoted above), *Statesman* 271d.
24 There are many discussions, but see especially Plotinus, *Enneads* 3.4; Iamblichus, *On the Mysteries* 3.18; Proclus, *Elements of Theology*, propositions 7, 11, 14, 15, 32 and 33.
25 In the edition of Clark 2000 (translation modified by Rees 2013).
26 This was not Ficino's understanding of his enterprise; he saw his work as an uncovering of the one, true, ancient religio-philosophical worldview.
27 See Rees 2013, 30 and 225 n. 27.
28 *Three Books on Life* 3.23, trans. Kaske and Clark 1989, esp. 375; *Platonic Theology* 10.2, trans. Allen and Hankins 2001–6; see also *In Apologiam Socratis Epitome*, in *Opera Omnia* (Basel, 1576), 1387; *Letters*, trans. Members of the Language Department of the School of Economic Science 1975–, vol. 7, letter 5 (to the poet Callimachus). See Rees 2013, 183–5 and 246 n. 26.
29 For the references that follow I am indebted to Simon Shaffer, though Professor Shaffer cannot of course be held responsible for my interpretation.
30 The 1602 Frankfurt edition of Ficino's Plato is listed in Newton's library catalogue.

31 This is in a group of manuscripts, probably compiled in the mid-1680s, which are notes for a treatise on the *prisca* which Newton never completed, and which he provisionally called *Philosophiae gentilis origines philosophicae*. The manuscripts are in the American Philosophical Library, and in MSS Temp.3 Miss, folio 19. Newton refers to Ficino's 'De sole et lumina libri duo' for the view that 'The old physicists called the sun the heart of heaven and earth'.

32 See Shaffer 2011, 90–112.

33 See B. Dobbs in *Janus Faces of Genius* (1991), ch. 5: 'Modes of Divine Activity in the World: The *Principia* Period'; and J. E. McGuire, 'Neoplatonism and Active Principles', in McGuire and Westman, *Hermeticism and the Scientific Revolution* (1977).

Bibliography

Allen, M. J. B. (trans.) and J. Hankins (ed.) (2001–6) *Platonic Theology*. 6. vols. I Tatti Renaissance Library. Cambridge, MA: Harvard University Press.

Brisson, L. and T. Saunders (2000) *Bibliography on Plato's Laws*. Sankt Augustin: Academia.

Clark, G. (ed.) (2000) *On Abstinence from Killing Animals*. London: Duckworth.

Climacus, J. (seventh century CE) *The Ladder of Divine Ascent*, trans. C. Luibheid and N. Russell, with an introduction by K. Ware. Mahwah, NJ: Paulist Press, in association with the Missionary Society of St Paul the Apostle in the State of New York, 1982.

Dobbs, B. (1991) *The Janus Faces of Genius: The Role of Alchemy in Newton's Thought*. Cambridge: Cambridge University Press.

Dodds, E. R. (1951) *The Greeks and the Irrational*. Berkeley and Los Angeles: University of California Press.

Hawking, S. and L. Mlodinow (2010) *The Grand Design*. New York: Bantam.

Lee, H. D. P. and T. K. Johansen (trans.) (2008) *Timaeus and Critias*, new edn. London: Penguin.

McGuire, J. E. and R. S. Westman (1977) *Hermeticism and the Scientific Revolution*. Los Angeles: William Andrews Clark Memorial Library, University of California.

Members of the Language Department of the School of Economic Science (trans.) (1975–) *The Letters of Marsilio Ficino*. London: Shepheard-Walwyn.

Morgan, M. L. (1992) 'Plato and Greek Religion', in R. Kraut (ed.), *The Cambridge Companion to Plato*. Cambridge: Cambridge University Press, 227–47.

Rees, V. (2013) *From Gabriel to Lucifer*. London: I. B.Tauris.

Santas, G. (1988) *Plato and Freud: Two Theories of Love*. Oxford: Basil Blackwell.

Saunders, T. J. (trans. and ed.) (1970) *Plato: The Laws*. Harmondsworth: Penguin.

Shaffer, S. (2011) 'Newtonian Angels', in J. Raymond (ed.), *Conversations with Angels*. Basingstoke: Palgrave Macmillan, 90–122.

Solmsen, F. (1942) *Plato's Theology*. Ithaca, NY: Cornell University Press.

Tarrant, H. (2012) 'Theology', in G. A. Press (ed.), *The Continuum Companion to Plato*. London and New York: Continuum, 251–3.

Ware, K. (1979) *The Orthodox Way*. London: Mowbray.

Weiss, R. (2012) 'Euthyphro', in G. A. Press (ed.), *The Continuum Companion to Plato*. London and New York: Continuum, 55–6.

Part V

Conclusion

In this concluding section the editors attempt to draw out some lessons for how dialogue between religious and non-religious people can usefully proceed. They identify some questions about language and metaphysics on which believers and non-believers need to seek clarification if they are to understand one another's beliefs better. They examine the idea that the practical and existential dimensions of life may provide more scope for building bridges, while recognising that there is no simple separation between practices and beliefs. Finally, they attempt to clarify the value and purpose of continuing dialogue between religious believers and non-believers.

21 Continuing the dialogue

Anthony Carroll and Richard Norman

'Conclusion' is a misnomer. We are hugely grateful to all the contributors for the range and diversity of their ideas. Looking for conclusions would be premature, but we hope that they will open up a continuing dialogue. What we want to do in this final chapter is to suggest some fruitful directions which that dialogue might take.

Beliefs and 'epistemic status'

One important theme to emerge is that a religious commitment is not simply a matter of theoretical beliefs. Religion is not best seen as a set of explanatory hypotheses about the nature and origin of the universe. Its practical dimension is vital, and that in turn means more than just providing ethical guidance. Commitment to a religion, with its practices and rituals and symbolism, furnishes a way of 'being in the world', making sense of one's life and articulating one's deepest emotions and experiences. We'll refer to this as the 'existential' dimension. For this reason abandonment of a religious commitment would not simply be rejecting a set of beliefs but rather adopting a new way of life. This also poses a challenge to the non-religious, to explore alternatives to religion at the existential level. We'll come back to this later.

Beliefs are not the whole of religion, then. Nevertheless they are an irreducible component. Religion shorn of its distinctive beliefs ceases to be religion. There is a factual as well as an existential dimension. That is not necessarily to draw a sharp line between the two. Religious believers will often say that their beliefs emerge out of their practices – that it is through engaging in the rituals and the way of life that they come to see the world as imbued with religious meaning. However, while practices may *disclose*, for them, the presence of God in the world, most religious believers are committed to at least some of these factual claims. They are beliefs which (most) religious people accept and which (most) non-religious people reject. Any serious attempt at dialogue therefore has to address the question of how so many sensitive and intelligent human beings can disagree so radically over such fundamental beliefs.

Stephen Law says that '[a]theists should not suggest that religious folk are stupid' (Chapter 4, p. 60). The point could perhaps be put more positively! Religious and non-religious people can properly regard one another's beliefs as *false but not irrational*. They *may* be irrational, of course. Undoubtedly some beliefs held by some religious believers are irrational, as are some of the beliefs held about religion by some of the non-religious. But they may not be. We shall put the point by saying that it is possible to reject one another's beliefs but still regard them as having *epistemic status*. That is to say, non-believers can recognise religious claims as having rational grounds, as being one way of making sense of important areas of shared human experience, while also maintaining that those rational grounds do not oblige someone to accept them as true. Likewise, religious believers can accept that atheists have good reasons for doubting religious beliefs, but consider that these are not compelling reasons for rejection of those beliefs. And this returns us to the question: how is it that rational people can differ so radically about the strength of these rational grounds?

There are important issues about language and meaning here, and they are addressed by some of the contributors to this collection. Nick Spencer (Chapter 2) draws attention to the centrality of metaphor in religious language. He rightly says that atheists should not therefore infer that such language is meaningless, since so much of language generally, including the language of science and the language of the emotions, is inescapably metaphorical. One reason, then, why exchanges between believers and non-believers may struggle to make progress is that it's often not clear *how much* of religious language is metaphor. The sceptic may say of a particular religious belief 'That can't possibly be right', the believer may reply 'You misunderstand, it's a metaphor', and they may then quickly find themselves at an impasse. Though Spencer is right about the pervasiveness of metaphor in general, not *all* language is metaphorical. 'When I'm angry I become a tiger' is intelligible as a metaphor only because we know that, non-metaphorically, tigers are fierce animals. What then is the role of metaphor in religious language? When Christians speak of God as 'Father', they are undeniably employing a metaphor. The language of human parent–child relations illuminates the understanding of God as loving and caring. Are 'loving' and 'caring' themselves metaphors? There is an important theological tradition, often referred to as 'apophatic theology', which maintains that God can never be truly and fully described in literal language. Not all religious believers would subscribe to that position, but it does raise questions about how metaphor and analogy function in religious language, and how metaphors and analogies can refer to God. We think that further exploration of such questions can help to throw light on the disagreements between believers and non-believers, help them to understand one another's perspectives, and help to explain why the disagreements are so persistent.

Again, Robin Gill (Chapter 10) points out, as many other writers have done, the importance of the mythic level in human culture – the human need for stories, including shared collective myths, which play a role different from that of reflective theoretical understanding. Undoubtedly much religious language functions at the mythic level, but again we should ask: how much? The myths of ancient Greece and Rome continue to convey profound insights into the human condition. The stories of Aphrodite and Ares and Bacchus are powerful expressions of the sometimes irresistible forces of love and jealousy, violence and intoxication in human life. More generally, our inherited culture is replete with stories of all kinds, from great novels to TV soaps, which illuminate our lives. It is unsurprising, then, that the great stories of the Judaeo-Christian-Islamic tradition can also resonate with everyone. The story of the Garden of Eden is a rich source of reflection on the complex relationships between human self-consciousness, shame, sexuality and our relation to the natural world. The story of Cain and Abel is the archetypal story of sibling rivalry and its social analogues. The story of Noah and the flood continues to remind us of the links between overweening human arrogance and environmental catastrophe. But for most religious believers the stories are more than that. Julian Baggini (Chapter 3) rightly says that most religious believers would resist the reduction of talk of 'the divine' to merely a way of talking about the human condition. For many, probably for most, talk of 'the divine' is inseparable from talk of something 'supernatural'. But what does 'supernatural' mean?

Metaphysics – naturalism and supernaturalism

This is where questions about the meaning of religious language lead into questions of metaphysics. What *kind* of being are believers talking about when they talk about God? Does such talk presuppose a level of reality distinct from the world of our everyday experience and of scientific knowledge? If so, does that spell trouble for the believer, or does it point to the need for non-believers to enlarge their framework of understanding?

Rowan Williams, in his conversation with Raymond Tallis, repudiates 'the idea that God is another thing in a list, another agent among agents, and can be drawn on as a sort of rabbit out of a hat to solve problems'. It is, he says, an idea of God which 'a great deal of traditional philosophy and theology tries to keep out' (Chapter 1, pp. 3–4). He clearly shares their rejection of that idea of God, but it is an idea of God which a great many believers, throughout the ages, have wanted to keep in. It's what many mean by 'supernatural'. It's the idea of God which most atheists typically have in mind when they reject religious belief as metaphysically incoherent – God as a being outside the world who somehow intervenes in the world from time to time, when he responds to prayer or loses patience with or takes pity on mankind, or when there's a big job to be done such as creating life. It's a God who interrupts the natural order by 'fiddl[ing] with the screws and the levers', as Williams again puts it (p. 16).

If that idea of God requires an unsustainable metaphysics, if it cannot be squared with a view of the world informed by scientific understanding, what can be said instead? Religious believers searching for a better way of thinking sometimes say that God is not 'a being' but 'Being'. This suggests what Fiona Ellis refers to as 'a God-involving conception of reality' (Chapter 6, p. 77), an idea of God as an indwelling agency, an intelligence at work *within* the world (though bearing in mind Williams' caution about the word 'intelligence' (Chapter 1, p. 16)). We find Ellis's label 'expansive naturalism' useful. As she says, it points to a metaphysical framework within which theists and atheists can profitably engage, 'the central issue here being whether there is a conception of God which improves upon the crude supernaturalist model' and can be accommodated within the framework of an expansive naturalism (Chapter 6, p. 78).

An immediate question, she acknowledges, is whether 'the theism at issue here is indiscernible from atheism' and is 'unworthy of the name' (p. 78). Raymond Tallis, in the conversation with Williams, asks pointedly whether the idea of a 'stripped-down, non-interventionist God – the apophatic God of certain theologies' is 'modest almost to the point of extinction' (Chapter 1, p. 17). It appears, he says, 'to drain God of quite a lot of job description' (p. 4).

That may not matter. Ankur Barua reminds us of a rich alternative religious tradition, for which the question of whether there is a God is secondary at best. For Eastern religions the important debates are about 'what are the ultimate threads that constitute the fabric of the universe' (Chapter 16, p. 197). The characteristic religious beliefs are beliefs about permanence and impermanence, about the ultimate unreality of what is impermanent, and about the sources of suffering and the sources of genuine satisfaction. They may offer an alternative both to classical theism and to an atheistic naturalism, and to some people it is an attractive alternative. But as Barua says, it is not the religion of the monotheistic faiths, of Judaism, Christianity and Islam. The adherents of those faiths, if they want to talk of God as 'Being' rather than 'a being', and if they want their faith to be something other than a disguised atheism, need to beef up the job description. What does an 'indwelling' God *do*?

If talk of 'a God-involving conception of reality' in which God is 'actively present in all things' (Fiona Ellis, Chapter 6, p. 77) is to be more than just a way of talking about natural processes of a familiar kind, it has to find some way of marking the *difference* between God and the world. The description of God as 'transcendent' is one word which has traditionally been employed to mark this, but it raises the same question about what that means. To quote Ellis again, 'the theist is no pantheist'. God 'is not reducible to the world in which He is present, for He is its source and sustainer, and, as such, to be distinguished from anything within it' (p. 75). One of us has used the term 'panentheism' to make the contrast with 'pantheism', and to refer to a 'conception of God in which God is viewed as in all things and also as transcendent of all things' (Anthony Carroll, Chapter 8, p. 99). This is where exchanges between the two of us get to the heart of the disagreement between us. If God is not reducible to the world in which he is present, if he is not simply to be conceived of as the sum of natural processes but as an independent source of agency, are we back with the idea of God as 'a being'? How can purposive agency and intelligence be ascribed to such a God? If a purposive intelligence is thought to be at work in natural processes themselves – the cycle of the seasons, the growth of living things, the evolutionary process of natural selection – are we back with pantheism? Are we deifying the natural world? How, as panentheists claim, can God be both immanent and transcendent at the same time?

If these are tough questions for the theist, there are equally tough questions lurking here for the atheist. If it is unclear where and how 'the divine' can be fitted into an expansive naturalism, there is also the familiar problem of where 'the human' fits in. Tallis and Williams readily agree in disparaging what they refer to as 'reductionism' and 'physicalist determinism', not least because such metaphysical positions seem to leave no room for *us* – for the self and for human agency. As Tallis puts it, 'you've got to have an awful lot of free will in order to deny that you are free … [and] you have to have quite a lot of self to deny that you are a self' (Chapter 1, p. 12). What, then, would a satisfactory non-reductionist view of the world have to be like? Would it be something like Ellis's 'expansive naturalism'? Her argument is that the rejection of reductionist and scientistic naturalism is needed in order to account for *values*, and for the kinds of human encounter which reveal value in the world. It is, she acknowledges, still a big step from an expansive naturalism which has room for values to one which makes space for God. Nevertheless the questions for atheists are as unavoidable as those for theists. Many non-religious people describe themselves as humanists. But any version of humanism which is to be worthy of the name needs to work with a rich understanding of human experience and of what it is to be human. What, then, must the world be like in order to encompass that understanding?

These are philosophical debates of *very* long standing – about consciousness and physicalism, about free will and determinism. Nothing in any of the essays in this collection is going to unlock those debates or uncover a new solution. What they may do is bring out what is at stake. Tallis and Williams are pretty scathing about those debates – they agree in seeing them as 'an absolute quagmire of nonsense' (p. 12). Certainly the philosophical literature has become very technical. Perhaps dialogue between religious believers and humanists can help to identify what it is that is irreducibly human – what the essential features of human experience are, to which any theory has to do justice.

That leads us to our next theme – to the existential dimension of belief and non-belief, to competing religious and non-religious understandings of how we live in the world, how we make sense of our lives, and what we can learn from one another about this.

Beliefs and the existential dimension

The aspiration to live a good life is one which is common to both the religious and the non-religious alike. A number of contributions recognise this shared aspiration to foster a common life that is ethically governed. Simon Glendinning (Chapter 17) explores this issue with respect to how we make judgments about what makes a life worth living and how understandings of human emancipation and progress can be traced to a common Christian and Marxist heritage in Europe. Richard Norman (Chapter 9) emphasises our shared human nature as the best place to look for this common ground. Drawing on an Aristotelian conception of human flourishing, he argues that both religious and non-religious people can unite around the shared values that animate living a fully human life. Michael McGhee (Chapter 13) traces secular and religious continuities at the political and moral level. Drawing on William Blake, he suggests that it is in promoting a moral vision of the 'other' that one can detect a conception of the good that can be shared by religious and secular people. And Andrew Copson suggests in his contribution (Chapter 18) that this practical dimension can even form alliances between religious and non-religious groups that are stronger on particular issues than those within the same groups.

Unsurprisingly, this practical dimension of life based on our common humanity seems more suitable to building bridges than do our diverse beliefs. Yet, too neat a separation of beliefs and practices fails to capture the ways in which these overlap in the existential life projects of the religious and the non-religious. Adopting a religious or a non-religious position is ultimately fleshed out in a way of life. It determines how one approaches and understands life's rites of passage as discussed by Anna Strhan in her contribution (Chapter 12) and even our place in the universe as John Cottingham points out (Chapter 11).

This embodiment of our beliefs in our practices is of course not a one-way process. Our practices can sometimes modify our beliefs when experience informs us that such and such a way of thinking is unrealistic or for that matter insufficiently adventurous. Experience may demonstrate to us that we can achieve more than we might initially have thought as much as that we have been overly optimistic in our goals. The relation between beliefs and practices is therefore one of mutual influence rather than simply a single causal process in one direction. And, in the relation between religious and non-religious people, this is of particular significance. Deciding that God does or does not exist is thus not simply a matter of affirming or denying a fact. It is rather an 'existential' issue. It involves what one does, the symbols that one relates to as meaningful, the rituals that one engages in, and the whole understanding of oneself.

Furthermore, this determines the experiences to which we are open. Not taking part in religious liturgies or praying, for example, evidently precludes sharing in the experiential dimensions of these religious practices.

Understood in this way, the 'existential' dimension of religious belief and religious non-belief also demarcates a whole range of experiences that these groups encounter, some of which are not shared. And this has implications for the issues of language and meaning that we have spoken about above. Communication naturally struggles when people are in dialogue about different things and this is further accentuated when the existential dimensions of religious belief and non-belief are not taken into account. Not believing in God, for a non-believer, is therefore not only a cognitive denial, it also corresponds to an experience of life, as does believing for a religious person. As a result, when these experiences differ, in order for the dialogue to remain open both sides need to safeguard against inappropriately extrapolating from their own personal experiences to concluding that the experience of others is the same. It may well not be.

A further complication arises here when one views language not simply as a descriptive tool of experiences but also as something which *discloses* experiences. Expressing particular beliefs embodies these in ways which open up experiences. This 'existential' dimension of language is most powerfully expressed in the use of symbolic language. Words freighted with layers of meaning can literally reveal a world of experience for someone in ways which are inaccessible to those for whom these symbols are 'dead metaphors'. Simply uttering the date '1966' for an England football fan, for example, can conjure up a joy that completely passes the non-football fan by! Experiences are thus also *initiated* by language and when this language has many layers to it, as in the case of symbolic language, these experiences can be quite unique.

A challenge for the non-religious is therefore to forge a language distinct from traditional religious vocabulary which can open up a comparable richness of experience. Many non-religious people struggle with the question of whether to employ words such as 'spiritual' or 'sacred' or 'transcendent'. There is an element of linguistic tribalism at work here (those are not 'our' words) but also a recognition that different vocabularies are constitutive of different experiences. John Cottingham, in his chapter, argues that what may appear to be similar 'numinous' experiences will have a different meaning for the religious and the non-religious, and that 'this should raise serious doubts about the claim that there is one single phenomenon ... that is common currency' (Chapter 11, p. 136). Many atheists would agree. The writer André Comte-Sponville, for instance, has employed the word 'immanensity', in preference to 'transcendence', to describe experiences, such as being awed by the night sky, which combine immanence and immensity, a sense of being part of something which at the same time 'surpasses us ... in every direction'.[1] The different language ascribes a different human significance to what at one level may be a similar experience.

Again, there has been in recent years a rich flourishing of writing about landscape and the natural world, writing which goes beyond the narrowly 'aesthetic' to find new ways of talking about the human meanings embedded in the landscape. This secular literature of 'landscape and the human heart' articulates a different vision of the natural from the religious understanding of which Cottingham speaks, of nature 'charged with the grandeur of God' (Chapter 11, p. 137). It may speak of landscapes which link us to the recent and the remote human past, of secular 'pilgrimage', of 'the ghosts and voices that haunt ancient paths, of the tales that tracks keep and tell', or of the scars marked on the landscape by human suffering and struggle.[2] These then are just two examples of attempts to create a secular language to describe deep human experiences, elements of that 'fullness' which Ruth Abbey (Chapter 19), following Charles Taylor, identifies as a framework shared by the religious and the non-religious but articulated in different ways.

Nor is this just a matter of language, but of other complex systems of symbols in which particular commitments to beliefs and practices are encoded. Transposing one set of symbols to another domain seldom works well and, as a consequence of this, searching for new ritual forms to express and disclose the range of complex meanings associated with a non-religious view of life requires considerable creativity. It is not simply the case that one borrows from the religious set of metaphors and secularises these. Specific rituals and symbol systems which both enact and disclose these deeper dimensions of life need to be developed that articulate and express a non-religious worldview and set of beliefs. In seeking to develop this aspect of life for non-religious people the current experiments spoken of by Anna Strhan are of considerable interest and importance (Chapter 12, pp. 143–9). We can think also of the alternative, secular ceremonies developed by humanists for baby-namings, weddings and funerals. These are not simply ceremonies to mark particular events in individual lives. They are occasions for all who take part to reflect together on their own lives, their own hopes and disappointments, their own ties and relationships, and their own mortality. Once again there are both parallels and differences between the meanings embedded in religious and non-religious ceremonies and rituals.

But if religious and non-religious people are to truly enter into a wide variety of learning processes that we are proposing here, it is important to be clear about the place and function of dialogue in these exchanges. It is to this final and foundational matter that we now turn.

The purpose of dialogue and critique

What is the purpose of dialogue between religious believers and non-believers? Obviously, there are many possible objectives for such dialogues. While acknowledging this, two contrasting approaches can serve as representative positions for a range of answers to this fundamental question.

Firstly, some are interested to convince others that their position is right and that the other is wrong. This may lead a person to attempt to convert the other or at least to reveal their errors so that they may come around to one's own position in due time. Secondly, others may primarily wish to find out what another person believes and why it is that they see things in this way. When this approach is taken, the first step on the way of the dialogue is to try to understand what the other is saying; to enter into their view of things, and to come to see how this makes sense and functions for that person or community. Not that critical engagement need be suspended in this approach. Rather, this critical distance is still possible but it is viewed to be primarily situated within a context of understanding. Consequently, seeking to first understand a position does not commit one to agreeing with it. In fact, disagreement requires understanding if it is to be a genuine disagreement and not simply a misunderstanding.

Whatever the purpose for which one enters into such a dialogue, this will inevitably shape the way in which one goes about it. If one has the first purpose, then this may lead to viewing a different position as first and foremost in need of correction. If one has the second, then the approach is more that of a learning process, gradually coming to understand what the view is about, how it is held, and why it is held. One may also come to see the salience of the position of others for one's own convictions. But without this attitude of seeking to understand the other, the desire to convert the other may end up limiting the dialogue to a rather polemical sparring with opposing ideas. And, as Anthony Carroll notes in his contribution (Chapter 8, pp. 101–2), one should recognise that in a dialogue between people of religious belief and those of none, this purely oppositional sparring has been encouraged historically by the 'theist–atheist' background to these exchanges which have been so prevalent since the early modern period.

One of the aims of this book is to try to move the dialogue beyond simply the sparring of ideas of the first approach towards an enabling of learning processes between religious believers and non-believers adopted in the second approach. Within individual contributions this is not straightforward. As only one party is presenting their point of view it is difficult to obtain this dialogical engagement with other points of view. However, we have attempted to foster this approach in the contributions in this book and in the guidelines that we have shared with our contributors. But in this conclusion, we want to open up the possibility that if such dialogues are attempting to find what is really the case, then both parties need to recognise that their own views may obscure rather than illuminate. When these dialogues are about seeking truth, then neither side should be complacent. Rather, attentiveness to insights and limitations is necessary if new ground is to be uncovered, and indeed if clarity is to be achieved concerning specific points of disagreement. Misunderstandings can cause blockages in these dialogues and it takes time to come to clarity as to what exactly the deeper issues are. Not, of course, that one should assume that underlying the differences lies a common ground on which everyone will come to agree. This, if it exists at all, is to be discovered rather than assumed to be the case. But if the search for truth is to regulate the dialogue, then this should be seen as a horizon towards which both sides should orient themselves.

This is, of course, easier said than done. Inhabiting one's own position requires affirmation of it, and taking responsibility for the commitments and entailments to which we are duly bound as a consequence. Discovering inconsistencies and contradictions at both theoretical and practical levels of reasoning provides grounds to reconsider one's position and indeed should be welcomed by anyone committed to seriously searching for truth. And, given the nature of such an existential exploration, such dimensions need also to find an appropriate correspondence with the actual living out of our lives. That is to say, the ideas that we can envisage should find ways to orient us towards human flourishing rather than diminishment. Such a correlation between theoretical and practical rationality in matters of existential import is not a shying away from the truth. Rather, it should be seen as a testing of it in reality. One might say that understood in this way, there is a 'normativity' to the truth which should orient these dialogues.

Moreover, 'setting the bar' so high that only absolute perspicuity passes in this domain is inappropriate. In matters which involve the meshing of both cognitive and practical–existential life projects there is always a degree of 'acting as if' or even of 'muddling through' at times without knowing all the answers. But this allows possible development to happen, and insight and clarity may follow in time. Nevertheless, allowing questions to remain unanswered is often difficult, especially when one feels exposed. But not answering a question too quickly can be important as it may allow a considered answer to emerge or even to reveal an area which lacks clarity. An initial lack of clarity or even a certain ambiguity may also not necessarily be a problem. It may be that one is considering an issue about which a simple 'yes' or 'no' answer is not appropriate. Diverse interpretations in this case are not necessarily untrue, they may well bring out the richness of an issue and the many sidedness of the matter in hand. However, one should also recognise that they may reveal error, and once this is clear, responsibility requires their correction.

But what is it about the questions of atheists that religious people should welcome? One important contribution that atheist perspectives on religious belief and practice provide is an external assessment. Not situated within the interpretative framework of the religious believer, the non-believer can see aspects of religious belief that can be occluded to the one situated within a religious framework. Moreover, for the religious person situated within a certain power and authority structure the freedom to question certain presuppositions may be curtailed for a number of reasons. It could simply be too costly to question certain things. Once one is nestled in an institutional or 'epistemic' context it becomes existentially prohibitive to question one's own foundations. It may be that one sees certain things as unchangeable and therefore does not embark upon a process of critique as this will in all likelihood not lead to any change or improvement of the situation. Furthermore, a certain group loyalty might take priority over pointing out problems and issues that would put into question such loyalty. Whatever the case, as Fern Elsdon-Baker's contribution (Chapter 7) highlights for views on the compatibility of science and religion, one's social and cultural location with respect to a belief system will affect how that system is viewed and the degree to which it can be questioned.

Those on the inside of a belief system, like players in a game, cannot achieve the same perspective as a detached observer looking on from a distance. A commentator on such a game can bring an analysis to bear which a participant in the game is not able to because of their involvement in the situation. This is not to say, however, that objectivity is the sole preserve of an outsider to a belief system. Access to the belief system may itself require some degree of participation in it if the contents are to be manifest at all. And external analysis may simply be a redescribing of the belief system in question as a means to providing a different and alternative explanatory system rather than assessing its consistency. Yet, despite these limitations, one should recognise that it is possible for the observer to notice things which the participant is unable to. This is one of the ways in which the important difference between thinking that one is right and actually being right is maintained. In this way, an external perspective is a way in which a form of checking procedure functions in religious and non-religious dialogue.

Moreover, it may well be that the belief system is not held by the believer with a degree of reflexivity. That is to say, it may well have been something that a person has inherited without subjecting it to the kinds of rational questioning that one would with other aspects of one's life. (Dilwar Hussain's references to the tensions between 'belonging' and 'believing' in Chapter 15 are pertinent here.) Religious tradition, like other aspects of our inheritance, can avoid being exposed to this kind of critical enquiry due to a host of reasons. And this can function at both personal and societal levels. It may be disturbing to an idealised past and image of ourselves to question our religious heritage. We might have a nostalgic desire to hold on to a former place of security in a world of constant change and uncertainty. Then again, fear of losing meaning in our lives and a place for ourselves in the world can foster a resistance to exposing religious convictions to rational scrutiny. And one can understand these reasons as grounds to avoid exposing one's cherished beliefs to inspection. Yet, despite their attraction, reasons such as these which prevent the examination of a religious faith are in the end not helpful to faith. They ultimately prevent a person and indeed whole societies coming to maturity in their faith and may reveal that what is actually held dear is more akin to an ideology or perhaps even an idol.

And, on the other hand, what is it that non-religious people should welcome about the questions of religious believers? As with religious believers, non-religious people need to be aware that they too can get locked into a closed system. This can become ideological when all counter-arguments are dismissed simply because they are counter-arguments and admissible evidence is so restrictive that an inevitable outcome is already predetermined. Fern Elsdon-Baker's examination of the eliding of atheism with a scientific worldview illustrates this point. In her contribution, she explores how this confusion has led to a dominance in the public domain of a so-called 'clash narrative' between science and religion (Chapter 7, p. 88). This presumption of an incompatibility between science and religion seems to be out of proportion to the actual majority of views on the compatibility between science and religion. Moreover, it raises interesting questions about why such a conflictual view is so persistent and what the actual function of such a clash narrative in debates surrounding science and religion might be.

The denial of a certain image of God may also be something that some religious believers and non-believers share, as Rowan Williams indicates in his dialogue with Raymond Tallis. The 'God' of some non-believers may well be a fiction generated by a reaction against a certain form of theism. The theologian John McDade speaks of theism and atheism as sharing 'entangled root systems' and Jonathan Rée similarly comments that both sides of the exchange share a 'tangled intellectual inheritance' in the history of the West (Chapter 5, p. 69). This has undoubtedly led to a form of 'sibling rivalry' which can be anything but rational. This conflicted past casts a long shadow over dialogue between the religious and the non-religious in the West and it would be difficult to deny this polarising influence. As such, non-believers may be surprised to realise that a traditional branch of theology, known as 'negative' or 'apophatic' theology, focuses on denying certain ideas and images about God as these can have a tendency to fixate belief into a form of idolatry. In denying 'God', non-religious people may be voicing similar and perhaps overlapping concerns to those within religious traditions who conceive of religious language as operating analogically to express the almost inexpressible.

Dialogue between believers and atheists, if it is oriented towards mutual learning, should help both sides to move beyond their ideologies and idolatries. Such dialogue can enable both positions to recognise that other options are possible, as Robin Gill reminds us in his contribution (Chapter 10, p. 122). It can help to temper tendencies towards fundamentalisms of both religious and secular varieties. It can increase awareness of the complexity and diversity of religious and non-religious perspectives, and, as Lois Lee (Chapter 14) suggests, correct a misleading picture of a simple polar opposition between religion and non-religion. Dialogue between people with different beliefs, and exposure to rational investigation of those beliefs, can sometimes strengthen one's convictions and lead to a more mature appropriation of them. Dialogue between religious and scientific perspectives can even, as illustrated by Angie Hobbs' example of Plato and Newton (Chapter 20), lead to surprising breakthroughs in human thought, in unpredictable directions. If religious believers and non-believers are seeking a greater understanding of themselves, of each other, and of the world, then in the true interests of both parties such a process should be encouraged and fostered.

Notes

1 André Comte-Sponville, *The Book of Atheist Spirituality*, trans. Nancy Huston (London: Bantam Press, 2008), 145.
2 Robert Macfarlane, *The Old Ways* (London: Penguin Books, 2013), xi.

Index